Personalizing Place

View east along King Street, 1829.
Painting by James Cockburn (Private Collection).

Donald Swainson

Personalizing Place

IN DEFENCE OF LOCAL HISTORY

The Kingston Case

PREFACE BY BRIAN S. OSBORNE

EDITED BY BOB HILDERLEY
AND BRIAN S. OSBORNE

QUARRY
HERITAGE
BOOKS

Cataloguing in Publication data is available.

ISBN-10: 1-55082-344-2
ISBN-13: 978-1-55082-344-8

Designed by Peter Dorn.
Typeset in New Baskerville by Laura Brady.

Printed and bound in Canada.

Published by
Quarry Heritage Books
PO Box 1061
Kingston, Ontario K7L 4Y5
www.quarrypress.com

View west along King Street from the R.D. Cartwright house, 1834.
Painting by Mrs. Harriet Dobbs Cartwright (Agnes Etherington Art Gallery).

Contents

Commentary

Preface

PUTTING SWAINSON IN HIS PLACE

BRIAN S. OSBORNE

MY FRIEND AND COLLEAGUE, Donald Swainson, was a much re-spected professor of history at Queen's University, an innovative historiographer, and an engaged member of the Kingston commu-nity. Apart from *Kingston: Building on the Past* (1988) and the essays reprinted in this collection, Donald and I worked on several projects, including reports for Parks Canada on the locks at Sault Ste. Marie (1983, 1984) and the Rideau Canal (1985). Whenever we made joint presentations on our work, Swainson would declare, "I did the history, Osborne did the maps!" Of course, as an historical-geographer, a spe-cies at risk in the current world, I urged Donald to accept that good history is all about understanding people in the context of their lived-in worlds and socially-constructed places. That he accepted this prem-ise reflected his academic pedigree influenced by the work of Harold A. Innis, Donald Creighton, and W.L. Morton. But it also reflected his own multi-layered identification with several places.

While not a stereotypical Viking-warrior, Donald was proud of his Icelandic ancestry and roots. In fact, it was hard to take his saga-based allusions to his forefathers' pillaging of Celtic peoples along the Atlantic fringe. He was equally proud of his Prairie upbringing.

His boy-hood days in rural Manitoba grounded his appreciation of grass-root politics and society. While he did later experience urban life during educational stints in Winnipeg and Toronto, he identified himself with Kingston. His perspective was a combination of the gaze of the scholar looking out from the windows of Queen's, interacting with people in the streets, public institutions, and watering-holes of his home-cum-social laboratory, and the view of its evolving form and structure from the shores of his beloved Garden Island. Place *was* important to Donald. Consider his rich rendering of the essence of Garden Island:

> The island has changed during the past hundred years. Some things, however, do not change. Garden Island continues to charm and fascinate its visitors; and vast quantities of material have survived from lumbering days. The Island is littered with square spikes, boat parts, winches, anchors, loading equipment, mooring rings, decaying docks, wrecked boats, nineteenth-century household artifacts, and all sorts of machine parts. When the water is low, the ribs of sunken ships can be seen to the south-east. Divers retrieve incredible quantities of clay pipes, bottles, boat parts, crocks, chains, and lamps. Small boys forage around and find keys, and nineteenth-century coins among other "treasures."

Donald realized that particular locales are more than the coordinates of site and situation and also involve the subjective values and memories that constitute the ambience and sense of place.

But people are much to the fore in Donald's work and nowhere more significant than in his doctoral thesis: "The Personnel of Politics: A Study of the Ontario Members of the Second Federal Parliament" (1968). His approach was to compile a group-biography of 36 Conservatives, 46 Liberals, and six "Political Deviates"! Each of these 88 politicos was examined in terms of their personal data, education, ethnicity, religion, profession, business connections, and political career to better understand the political culture of nineteenth-century Ontario and Canada. But if I call it "group biography," Donald preferred the term, "prosopography"! Whatever that high-fallutin academic term means, it served him well in the rest of his career. Apart from developing his skills in biographical research that contributed to his excellent study of Sir John A. Macdonald and his several contributions to the *Dictionary of Canadian Biography*, there were other benefits. Whenever he was invited to comment on contemporary political events he could dip into his arsenal of 88 profiles and spin out an informed story of politicians' past achievements as well as their deficiencies and peccadilloes.

These are the skills and perspectives that Donald brought to so much of his scholarship collected in this volume. For him "local history" was privileged because of the opportunity it afforded for examining how Canadian society was expressed at the micro level. He championned the work of many amateur historians and community heritage organisations and castigated his fellow professional historians "who tend to separate themselves from their society, and are often insensitive to the kind of responsibility that should go with scholarship." For him, that meant ensuring that schools should have access to teaching materials and that history should be written in a way that would attract the attention of interested Canadians. These are motives that prompted his two engaging studies of his hero: *Sir John A.Macdonald: The Man and the Politician* (1970, 1989) and *Macdonald of Kingston: First Prime Minister* (1979). To this end, a good wordsmith himself, he also had a good ear for the witty and profound dialogue of others such as this political ditty that amused nineteenth-century Kingston voters:

"There goes St. Patrick who killed all the frogs.
And here comes Kirkpatrick who killed all the dogs."

His writings are studded with such apposite quotes and witticisms.

But while the following pages are replete with rich biographies of movers and shakers of Kingston's political, commercial, and social world, much attention is paid to two particular subjects close to Donald's heart: Sir John A. Macdonald and the Canadian political culture.

At a time when many in Kingston are striving to lionize Canada's first prime-minister for motives ranging from national unity to crass commercialism, Donald was sensitive to the way in which Sir John's memory is being represented, re-constructed, and represented. No mere exercise in rear-window hagiography, his position was that

Macdonald's heritage must be considered in the context of national identity. He argued that perhaps it is the public's criticism of, or disdain for, contemporary politicians that prompts the constant repetitive refrain based upon the "virtually unlimited supply of anecdotes" about Sir John's "humour, corruption, family turmoil, and bouts of drinking." Recognizing that these are, indeed, insights into "a fascinating and essentially attractive personality," Donald argues that they do not explain Sir John's historic role as a pragmatic politician and "the architect of his country." He makes an important point: "without Macdonald the origins of Canada become inexplicable." Furthermore, a "ravaged Macdonald is a shaky foundation upon which to build and understanding of Canada. We need a positive Macdonald in order to have a nation sanctified by legitimate origins."

This commitment to differentiating Sir John's substantive national role from comedic renderings ensured Donald's expertise in constitutional history and its profound contribution to Canadian identity. He loved Canada dearly. For him, it was a prosperous and pluralistic society underpinned by the British North America Act, the Rowell-Sirois Report, the constitutions of the Prairie provinces, and the Charter of Rights and Freedoms. This array of legislation rendered the political culture which he respected and in which he functioned as a scholar and public activist. As he put it, "Pluralism permits a wide variety of thought and opinion, and helps assure the maintenance of substantial freedom within a society that must be ordered in the interests of cohesion."

This was equally true in promoting the quality of life in our home communities. Not surprisingly, therefore, our work together over the years was concerned with protecting and nurturing Kingston's unique character. Several of Donald's essays highlight the threat posed by what he called the "development vandals." In his provocative *crie de cœur*, "Who's in charge here?" he declares that it is time that "our local politicians wake up to the fact that they preside over the finest single architectural mass in English-speaking Canada. Their job is to protect this heritage – not to aid and abet its wanton and vicious destruction." It is a message that has not lost its relevancy decades later, albeit with an increasingly broader definition of culture and heritage.

Issues such as these were not abstractions for Donald. So many of his biographies dealt with the philosophical ideals of the day as well as the mechanics and manipulations of political intrigue and chicanery, past and present. When, in 1973, he reports on the "depravity and venality" of one, Schuyler Shibley, he moves beyond the legerdemain of historiography into the verities of social order and declares that "the place of children in Ontario society merits careful study, as does the whole question of public and private morality." Two decades later, these words are brought home to him personally and at great cost in the form of a scandal "that has shaken the institution to its foundations and that will almost certainly reverberate for years to come." The institution was St. George's Cathedral, for long so close to his sense of community. Arguing that it would be "dishonest" not to do so, he brought all of scholarly skills and acumen to an exposé that cost him personally, physically, and emotionally. Pilloried by some at the time, others have since built on his services and respect his commitment to what, for him, was a principled cause. Perhaps there was a lot of that Viking blood still flowing in my good friend's veins. He certainly knew how to fight his battles! I am also sure that he would be most pleased with the aftermath of his struggle: the continued health and vitality of an institution he often referred to as the "jewel of Kingston."

Clearly, I am honoured to write this preface to this collection of my colleague and friend's work. We learned much from each other and, in many ways, his words still resonate for us today and his generous community spirit still graces the streets of Kingston. As I close this reflection on Donald's insights into the evolving Canadian historical landscape, I can't help but chuckle as I imagine how he would have responded to contemporary federal, provincial, and local politics — he would have had a field-day!

Introduction

WHY EXAMINE LOCAL HISTORY? THE CANADIAN CASE

Our heritage is fascinating and important. Local historians have an obligation to assist Canadians in their task of cultivating and understanding that heritage. This important task involves a co-operative effort.

THE QUESTION was put to me: "Why examine local history"? My instinctive response was, "Why not"? After all, what can be more natural or legitimate than a desire to understand one's locale in all of its dimensions, including the historical? It is satisfying in a superficial sort of way to know why in a city like Kingston we have streets named Sydenham, Bagot and Norman Rogers,[1] not to mention the famous five: Arch, Deacon, George, Okill, and Stuart.[2]

We live in communities and we desire to know about ourselves by examining the history of our communities. At its most complex, local historical scholarship is a sophisticated form, involving several disciplines and a whole range of relationships. Canadian historians have produced a number of important studies that illustrate this sophistication. *Kingston Before the War of 1812* by Richard A. Preston (1959), *Montreal: A Brief History* by John Irwin Cooper (1969), *History of the County of Ontario 1615-1875* by Leo A. Johnson (1973), *Winnipeg: A Social History of Urban Growth 1874-1914* by Alan Artibise (1975)

Presented to the Workshop on Projects and Research in Local History and published in *Historic Kingston*, Vol. 28 (1980). This article would prompt a decade of work defending local history, culminating in the book, *Kingston: Building on the Past*, co-authored with Brian S. Osborne, and revised by Professor Osborne as *Kingston: Building on the Past for the Future* (Quarry Heritage Books).

and *To Preserve and Defend: Essays on Kingston in the Nineteenth Century*, edited by Gerald Tulchinsky (1976) are only five titles from a long list. Work of the quality of Preston, Cooper, Johnson, Artibise, and the authors of *To Preserve and Defend* – not to mention massive quantities of material drawn from other jurisdictions – establishes beyond doubt the legitimacy of the *genre*. If we were not curious about our localities, we would be a very strange people.

I

PERHAPS WE should re-focus the question, "Why examine local history?" The question has about it a defensive tone, and this brings us to the problem that should receive our attention. Many professional scholars denigrate our local historians and our local history. There are a variety of factors that explain this, but they all seem to relate to one key point, and that is that much local history is written by amateur historians.

The question of amateur historians and their worth is complicated. Vast quantities of history have been written by amateurs; that is, by those who have not received professional training. Some of this work is of substantial value. Knowledge of Ontario has been enriched by books like *The Lives of the Judges of Upper Canada and Ontario* by D.B. Read (1888), *The Story of Old Kingston* by Agnes Maule Machar (1908), *The Pioneers of Old Ontario* by W.L. Smith (1923), and *Pioneer Crimes and Punishments* by James Edmund Jones (1924). These four authors were, respectively, a lawyer and politician, a novelist and poet, a journalist, and a police magistrate. Each made a significant contribution to scholarship; not one went to graduate school. Professional historians understand the fact that amateurs make a contribution and attract many readers. Canadian historians cannot escape these facts. How could they, given the omnipresence of writers like Pierre Berton and Farley Mowat? Nonetheless, the reservations entertained by the professionals are far from perverse.

Professional historians operate within the framework of the state-of-the art of the discipline. This involves a set of assumptions, practices, traditions, and rules that change over time. Historians engage in a dialogue about how events are best interpreted and history best written. Styles of scholarship change as new methodologies evolve and new concerns emerge. Let me give a very brief illustration. Fifty years ago, Canadians were enjoying the autonomy status that we earned during World War I. Canada was recognized as a sovereign state, and that was properly regarded as a great achievement. Like other Canadians, historians were proud of this achievement and celebrated it in their published work. The theme is summarized by the title of W.S. Wallace's little book, *The Growth of Canadian National Feeling* (1927).[3] By the 1970s Canada had changed a very great deal, and so had the concerns of historians. How would one today, for example, explain Quebec or Alberta in a book entitled *The Growth of Canadian National Feeling*? The more likely title, of course, is George Grant's *Lament for a Nation* (1965). Canadian historians are now more concerned, and appropriately so, with themes like regionalism, French-English relations, continentalism, social development, labour, and cultural identity. It is surely understandable that historians are irritated by books like Pierre Berton's *The National Dream: The Great Railway, 1871-1881* (1970) and *The Last Spike: The Great Railway, 1881-1885* (1971). These books possess a certain kind of merit, but they belong with the kind of history written a generation ago; they are part of the older nation-building school and they glorify the kind of Ontario-dominated Canada that is no longer acceptable to most scholars or Canadians, at least Canadians in the nine other provinces and the northern portion of this province. Even southern Ontarians now seem to be groping toward an understanding of the fact that Alberta oil cannot be nationalized in order to provide cheap fuel for Ontario industries and consumers.

Apart from such basic problems of interpretation, amateur historians tend to violate other aspects of the discipline. Events and personalities are often sensationalized or trivialized. Anecdotes are substituted for evidence. Lack of a comparative framework causes mundane events to be viewed as unique. Research is often spotty and not adequately documented. All too often the basic scholarly apparatus, footnotes and bibliographies, for example, is omitted. It goes without saying that these criticisms do not apply to all amateur historians, and the point should be emphasized that professional historians are hardly guiltless. They tend to separate themselves from their society, and are often insensitive to the kind of responsibility that should go with scholarship. At minimum, professional historians should have much greater contact with the public and secondary school systems, and should devote more time to the preparation of materials that can be used in the schools and that can be read by interested Canadians.

II

RECENT SURVEYS underscore many of these concerns. In 1968 *What Culture? What Heritage?*, edited by A.B. Hodgetts, was published.[4] In many ways this is a devastating document. I will quote only one passage, which is based on a questionnaire administered to a representative sample of Grade 12 students: "Two questions – one asking for 'five well-known or important Canadians of the past 100 years or so', and the other dealing with poets, artists and writers – were put on the Questionnaire not to test factual recall but to see what kinds of people would be named by students in different parts of Canada . . . . It is relevant to note that in the question asking for five well-known Canadians of the past, 81 percent of all respondents (with the French Canadians . . . being somewhat better informed) failed to name a single cultural leader. The answer to the question dealing with artists, poets, and writers, in which the respondents were asked to name three Canadians in each category, are equally illuminating. Remembering that our sample was 4,000 Grade 12 students from across Canada . . . it is significant that we found 88 percent who were unable to name three Canadian artists, 78 percent who were equally unsuccessful with poets, and 81 percent with the prose writers."[5] How many of us can supplement this with evidence brought home by our own children? A few years ago my children returned from a local public school and told me how the pilgrim fathers had founded our country and started Thanksgiving. One would assume that in a community like Kingston the Loyalists and John A. Macdonald might receive some of the credit – for founding the country, if not for Thanksgiving.

The Symons Report appeared in 1975.[6] This report has a substantial concern with universities. Consider the implications of this comment: "Many Canadian scholars have adopted, or accepted, the attitude that Canada is not a sufficiently interesting subject for study and research. Going further than this, many obviously feel that Canadian problems, events and circumstances are almost by definition of only second-rate academic importance."[7]

A very recent survey of 840 Ontario university students was undertaken by the popular magazine, *Saturday Night*.[8] The results indicate that Canada is still unknown and disrespected by Canadians, and that the relationship between the people and the state is not at all well understood. According to this survey, "Ninety-four percent believe that 'Our country's problems are mainly the result of its leaders and not of its people.'"[9] The implications of this kind of view are simply staggering. Does this segment of our population really believe that our leaders created the energy crisis, which is a direct result of events in the Middle East over which Canada had no influence whatever? Do university students believe that our leaders control the crisis unfolding in Quebec, or can convince Alberta that its resources belong to Ontario? Perhaps even more graphically disturbing about this survey is the portion concerned with heroes. The respondents were asked to rank those persons "they admire".[10] Thirty-three names are listed. Senator Edward Kennedy is number 1; Ronald Reagan is number 33. The top four, all of whom rate in a ninety percent or better level of support are Kennedy, Jane Fonda, Walter Cronkite, and Linda Ronstadt; Kennedy and Fonda are tied at ninety-two percent. The first Canadian to rank is Anne Murray at number 10. Pierre Elliott Trudeau ranks 18, one point above Gordon Sinclair. Harvey Kirck outranks Premier William Davis. Knowlton Nash makes the list as number 31. The rationale of this list of preferences seems clear. Ontarians admire prominent Americans who obtain huge amounts of media attention, or who are media personalities in their own right. The presence on the list of Harvey Kirck and Knowlton Nash is of considerable interest. These men are, no doubt, commendable in their capacity as news readers. How much more did the respondents know about them? The implication seems to be that they are listed simply because of their high visibility. Perhaps a similarly high visibility in schools for Canadian historical figures would assist students to learn something about Canadians who have made valuable contributions to our national life.

It might be that prominent Canadians merit no place at the top of the survey list. One only wishes, however, that one could be assured that the respondents knew enough Canadian names to exercise informed discrimination.

The situation revealed by these and other studies is truly appalling, and is evidence of a major Canadian failure. Presumably a healthy nation includes citizens who are aware of the society and understand something about its traditions. If our historians, amateurs and professionals, have any research mission, that mission must be to foster and disseminate the history of Canada. Nobody else will do it for us. If we do not study our institutions, governments, culture, ideas, personalities, cities, towns, minorities, protests, and so on, our national culture will be substantially weakened. It would be wrong to concentrate excessively on Canada, because we cannot understand Canada in isolation from world history and culture; nor, of course, do we want narrow and chauvinistic citizens. But we must never lose sight of the central fact that Canadians are entitled to the opportunity to learn about themselves. The *Saturday Night* survey of university students, which was completed this year, confirms the conclusions of earlier studies that we have failed in this area. This massive failure cannot be laid at a single door. It must be shared by the historical profession, universities, public and secondary school systems, granting agencies, publishers, book distributors, and the popular media. All should expend more of their resources to foster an awareness of Canada.

This is where the amateur historian, and especially the amateur local historian, should play a significant role. Professional criticisms of amateurs have been listed. Let us now look at the positive side.

III

PERHAPS MOST important is the fact that many of our communities now include sizeable groups of enthusiastic local historians. These people are working in the community, and often on community projects that are of interest to many citizens. An example of this kind of activity is the *History of Frontenac County Project*, centred here in Kingston. A substantial number of local historians are busily engaged on this project, which promises to gather and publish large amounts of data that relate to all phases of county history. This should result in a fairly large scale involvement in historical research, and assist many to arrive at an appreciation of the history of their community. A word of caution should, however, be inserted at this point. A good county history is as difficult to write as it is rare. While large scale co-operative efforts of this sort should be encouraged, they should involve at least some co-operation with professional historians. Any county history will be enriched if it is informed by contributions from historians who are well read in local history generally, and who have a thorough grasp of the techniques of social history.

Local historians also perform an invaluable function, and further their own work through local historical societies. The Canadian experience with such societies has been mixed, but the potential is enormous. Any kind of historical research tends to be isolated and lonely work. An historical society provides an opportunity to mitigate those disadvantages. Exchanges of views can take place; when difficult research problems arise, help can be obtained from other researchers. Papers can be read and discussed, and, if the society is able, the papers can be published. This latter point is very important. People who devote huge amounts of time to research usually want to see the results in print. This is the way the local record is made permanent and useable by other researchers.

The local societies can and should perform other functions. It is notoriously difficult to maintain an appropriate membership mix in these societies. It should, nonetheless, be attempted. Ideally, a local society should involve the active local researchers (both amateur and professional), those who teach history and related fields that touch on local history, journalists with an interest in their locale, and citizens who want to learn local history. Societies should have a representative age distribution and involve themselves in relevant public debates. At the present time, a major such issue is preservation. Development, as it is called, poses a constant threat to our visible heritage. Hardly a week goes by without a note in the newspaper about the impending demolition of some historic building in one of our communities. Local historical societies should involve themselves in these debates and develop policies from the historic perspective that relate to preservation and town planning. If this kind of issue is not faced directly and stubbornly, the development vandals will destroy our nineteenth-century heritage. Once it is gone, it is gone forever.

The question of "mix" in local historical societies is crucial. It is very easy for a society to become a small coterie of like-minded friends. That is fatal because under such circumstances the society almost inevitably concentrates on only a very narrow task: it might be historical preservation genealogical research, museum maintenance, traditional research, the collecting of primary sources or perhaps just regular discussion sessions. A society with a mixture of types of members is better able to stimulate an interest in numerous kinds of students, provide research advice and assistance to inexperienced researchers, and bring amateurs, professionals, and teachers into sustained contact. The spinoffs can be significant. Amateur and professional local historians can benefit each other. The professional historian can be encouraged to make a greater contribution to community affairs; the amateur can maintain a contact with the discipline through professionally trained colleagues. Teachers at all levels can benefit – as can their students – throughout the societies. Local history projects, whether undertaken at the primary school level or the graduate school level, can benefit enormously from this kind of contact. All sorts of projects can be facilitated by the expertise that can be organized by a local society.

A thriving local society with an appropriate membership mix can, in short, facilitate an understanding of our traditions and an awareness of our culture. How many of us were brought up in communities in which there was any sense of history or tradition? For most of us history "happened" in "the fertile crescent," Greece, Rome, Europe, and the United States. On rare occasions, something of note occurred in Ottawa, Quebec City, Montreal, or Toronto – but rarely if ever in our own communities. Local historians and others interested in local history can do much to foster an environment in which our history and traditions – appropriately called our heritage – become part of the intellectual and cultural atmosphere. These things should be built into our assumptions and form a portion of our intellectual baggage.

It would make little sense to examine the question of Canadian local history without some reference to our education system. Various surveys indicate that younger Canadians have a deplorably meager knowledge of the Canadian past (and of the Canadian present as well). Our educational institutions at all levels must share at least some of the blame for this situation. First, it should be acknowledged that much very fine work is now being pursued. Schools at all levels teach a great deal of Canadian material; several universities generate massive amounts of Canadian research, in a variety of disciplines. But second, it should equally be acknowledged that not enough is being done.

Local history can play a major role in any program designed to increase knowledge and awareness of Canada and of the discipline of history. This latter point should be emphasized, because instruction in local history at any level should involve the discipline and its norms.

A variety of approaches is attractive. There should be available, for example, well-designed courses on Canadian provincial, regional, and local history. Students should know much more about how Canada functions. They very well might be encouraged through local projects that involve real, if carefully supervised, research. Historical societies and practicing local historians can provide much useful assistance in such projects – as can libraries, newspapers, museums, and archives. Students should be encouraged to collect data on a wide range of local historical themes – leadership, urban growth, basic industries, transportation, architecture, education, police departments, markets, poets and novelists, place names, hospitals, prisons, minority groups, settlements, churches, changes in the urban landscape, preservation, leisure, sports, and basic utilities. The list could go on and on. Data can be collected from traditional sources in libraries. In addition, however, these projects should involve the community. Older citizens should be interviewed, local historians consulted, photographs sought out, privately held sources exploited, and sites visited and examined.

Data collection is only the first step. Equally or more important is the presentation of the data and the results. The basis of the project should be a research question or problem. This can be simple or complex, depending on the stage of the student. What did old railway trains look like? Why does downtown Kingston consist of stone buildings? Who were the Loyalists who settled in Brockville? The number of questions is infinite, but questions there must be or the student's concern is data collection, and not local or any other kind of history. The results of such research can be presented as displays, models, essays, slide shows, and historical plays. These and other forms can be combined by imaginative students.

Our society is now in a period of economic, social, and political peril. We require all the cohesion that we can muster. We are not going to save and reform a country that we neither care about nor study. Perhaps this concern must antedate the kind of activity that I have discussed. But surely we can do far more than has yet been done. Let me illustrate.

Hundreds of Canadian communities host science fairs every year. Thousands of students at many levels of skill and achievement work diligently to define, solve, and illustrate scientific problems. These fairs have often been extremely successful, involving students, teachers, the general public, and scientific judges. The results are commendable, and those involved are to be congratulated. My question is, why do we not see Canadian heritage fairs? These fairs could focus on local history and could involve, in addition to the students and teachers, local historians, historical societies, professionally trained historians, libraries, numerous citizens with a knowledge of the community, and a wide variety of local institutions. Surely newspapers would give generous coverage to such events, and publish the results of the more successful projects. Perhaps such fairs could be jointly managed by schools and historical societies. Such co-operation might lead to the involvement of many members of the general public. It is this kind of public and concentrated effort that would recognize the high priority that we should grant to the basic need to understand and come to terms with our own society. Local history can and should play a leading role in such programs.

In closing, let me emphasize again the importance of the study of local history. We are a nation with very substantial current problems in the economic, social, and political sectors. Perhaps there is nothing unusual about that; what nation does not have serious problems in this decade? However, how many are troubled by the question of who and what they are? Cannot we pull ourselves together at what we all know is a grave and decisive juncture? Surely we must be able to assure our French Canadian future – dubious as that future might be – that we are learning to understand what Canada is about and that as a consequence we welcome partnership with an articulate and self-conscious community.

Our heritage is fascinating and important. Local historians have an obligation to assist Canadians in their task of cultivating and understanding that heritage. This important task involves a co-operative effort. Amateur and professional historians must learn to work together in ways that are mutually enriching. Local historical societies should be recognized as major public resources that can facilitate co-operation among all the principal actors. In this way we can, I have no doubt, combine a number of themes. We can pursue our interest in local history; we can involve an increasing number of Canadians in that interest; and, perhaps most important of all, we can help our fellow citizens to come to some better understanding of what Canada is all about.

Place

*Bird's eye view of Kingston in 1875 showing Rockwood Asylum inset lower left,
the Shoal Martello Tower centre, and Kingston Penitentiary lower right.
Drawing by H. Brosius (Queen's University Archives).*

Chronicling Kingston

AN INTERPRETATION

*What was fortuitous and ephemeral seems natural and logical.
Kingston never really had the seat of government. It was merely the
scene of a passing political compromise.*

KINGSTON IS one of the oldest towns in Ontario. Its history, from
the French period to the present, is rich in sources and illustrates
a variety of themes of interest to urban historians, local historians, and
those interested in the great traditional themes of Canadian history:
the Laurentian economy, politics, biography, immigration, institutions, the military, intellectual development, and religion. Historians,
both amateurs and professionals, have devoted impressive amounts
of time and energy to Kingston's past. The result is a historiography
that is extensive and rich. This paper was written with four objectives
in mind. First, an attempt has been made to provide an overview of
the town's history. Second, the nature of the historical literature is
analysed with a view to explaining its particular and skewed nature.
The analysis is concerned with ways in which the perspective of the
historian can shape and distort our understanding of the process of
urban growth (or lack thereof). Third, the historiography is criticized
and suggestions are made concerning future scholarship in this ad-
mittedly limited field. Fourth, and finally, the footnotes are designed

In this essay first published in *Ontario History*, Vol. 74, No. 4 (December 1982),
Professor Swainson announces his Kingston themes in full academic dress,
with 50 footnotes –which befits the style of the prestigious journal, *Ontario
History*. He would in that same year publish a popular version of this article in
the Kingston *Whig-Standard Magazine*, 17 July 1982. Roger Bainbridge, editor
of this omnibus magazine, gave Professor swainson direct access to the public.

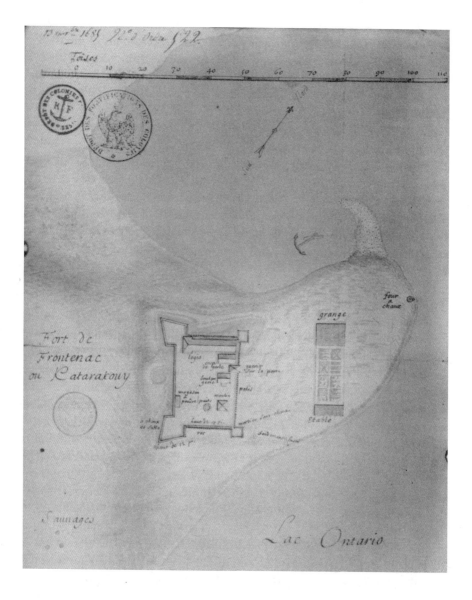

Map of Fort Frontenac showing the strategic site of the fortifications at the confluence of the Great Cataraqui River and the St. Lawrence River (Queen's University Archives).

to provide an illustrative guide to the historical literature relevant to
the King's Town.

I

FORT FRONTENAC was built under dramatic and well known circumstances in July 1673. It fell to the English in the summer of 1758.
During its 85 years of existence, its fortunes were mixed. It was abandoned for a few years late in the seventeenth century; it was often in
disrepair and very lightly garrisoned. For much of the time its prime
function was as a trading centre, not as a fortress. It never generated
permanent agricultural settlement. Leading officials in Quebec and
Paris had mixed views concerning the utility of the fort. Nonetheless,
for almost a century it remained an important and exciting place.
Great men like Frontenac, La Salle, and Montcalm were associated
with Fort Frontenac. It remained at the centre of the fur trade, the
westward communications system of French Canada, the continental
designs of French imperialism, missionary activity, defence against the
Iroquois, and the protracted debate over French policy in the North
American interior. There is a heroic tone about the history of Royal
Fort Frontenac that finds an appropriate echo in a remark of LaSalle:
"The more perilous and toilsome, the more worthy of Honour are
those enterprises."[1]

The British were in effective possession of the north side of Lake
Ontario and the St. Lawrence after 1760, but there is a period of
discontinuity in the history of Kingston between the fall of Fort Frontenac in 1758 and the establishment of a Loyalist settlement in the
early 1780s.[2] The area resumed its strategic importance during the
revolutionary war, but British activity was concentrated on Carleton
Island, not at the site of the old French fort. Again transshipment was
a key activity, and much military material was transshipped at Carleton Island during the late 1770s and early 1780s.

The little island, some 10 miles south and east of Kingston (on
the American side of Wolfe Island), was not suitable to British needs
in the post-war era. It was too small to sustain much in the way of a
settlement, and settlements for Loyalist émigrés were needed. In any
event, the island was probably going to be passed to the Americans
under the peace settlement.

Attention shifted back to the neighbourhood of Royal Fort Frontenac. Preparations were made in 1783-84, and, as R.A. Preston reports,
in 1784 "the great migration up the St. Lawrence River" took place.[3]
The history of the modern town had begun, and certain characteristics of Kingston familiar to us all were quickly manifest. Kingston
was conservative, loyalist, and dedicated to the interests of the mother
country. Anti-Americanism was a recurring theme; the military presence was apparent and popular. The town was tightly controlled by
the upper class, which tended to be dominated by Anglicans, Tories,
officials, officers, and wealthy businessmen. The attractiveness of the
town was much enhanced by the magnificence of its site.

Kingston became the pre-eminent town in Upper Canada, although
it must be remembered that until well into the nineteenth century
it was really just a large village. The economic base of the town was
transshipment. By the late 1780s, the military had shifted its transshipment business to Kingston. As the economy of the colony developed, increasing quantities of transportation modes on river and lake
remained discrete until well into the nineteenth century. Fur and
potash were the key goods during the very early years of British settlement. They gave way to wheat, flour, peas, salt pork, and consumer
goods. Men like Richard Cartwright, John Forsyth, Robert Macaulay,
John Kirby, and Thomas Markland dominated the lucrative trade.
The port was the centre of Kingston's economy. Shipbuilding joined
transshipment as a major activity. Naval construction and the garrison
supplemented the civilian economy.

The importance of Kingston in early provincial life could not be
gainsaid. John Graves Simcoe, Upper Canada's first lieutenant-governor, was no friend of Kingston and was determined that the town
would not become the colony's capital. But even Simcoe had little
choice about some things. In 1792, he proclaimed the new constitutional order from the little church that became St. George's Cathedral, and he met his executive council several times in Kingston.
Simcoe took the province's administrative centre west, but for a generation Kingston held its place as Upper Canada's largest and most
important town.

In some respects, the impact of the War of 1812 upon Kingston
remains obscure. But some things are known. Strategically Kingston was the centre of Upper Canada, a point well made by the great

American military analyst, Rear Admiral Alfred Thayer Mahan: "No other harbour was tenable as a naval station; with its fall and the destruction of shipping and forts, would go the control of the lake, even if the place were not permanently held. Deprived thus of the water communications, the enemy [i.e. British] could retain no position to the westward, because neither reinforcements nor supplies could reach them."[4] The British recognized the centrality of the town, which bustled with military activity and construction during the hostilities. The garrison became dramatically larger, as did the town itself. In 1812 Kingston consisted of some 1,000 persons and 150 houses. Another hundred houses went up during the war and 150 were built right after. In fact it would seem that the war saw Kingston change from village to town, a point underscored by James Strachan, a brother to the future Bishop of Toronto, in 1819: "Kingston looks well as you approach it from the water. The war was of much use to it, not only more than doubling the population, but likewise distributing among its inhabitants large sums of money. The number of houses built, and well built since the war, is very honourable to the taste and enterprise of the people."[5] Trade flourished during the war; shipbuilding was given considerable stimulation. The quasi-demilitarization of the lakes after the war caused the British to look again at defence policy.[6] Amongst the permanent results of the re-examination are the Rideau Canal, which was completed 150 years ago, and Fort Henry, built 1832-36. Kingston emerged from the war with its loyalism, conservatism, and anti-Americanism strengthened. Not incidentally, the War of 1812 made Tory Christopher Alexander Hagerman a man of wealth and power, and he became one of the defining influences in Kingston's political tradition.

A post-war recession notwithstanding, Kingston continued to thrive and consolidate its position as Upper Canada's leading commercial centre. Joseph Bouchette made this point in 1831: "The town has obtained considerable mercantile importance within the last twenty years: wharfs have been constructed, and many spacious warehouses erected, that are usually filled with merchandise: in fact, it is now become the main entrepot between Montreal and all the settlements along the lakes to the westward...[V]essels of from eighty to nearly two hundred tons, employed in navigating the lakes, are continually receiving and discharging their cargoes, as well as the bateaux used in the river."[7] Comparative population figures confirm Bouchette's happy view. In 1830 Kingston's population was 3,587 compared with 2,800 for Toronto, 2,416 for London, and 2,013 for Hamilton. Twenty years later the situation was radically different. Toronto had become the largest Upper Canadian centre with 30,775; Kingston with only 11,697 ranked third behind Hamilton with 14,112.

Kingston was not destined to head Ontario's urban hierarchy for long, but it held that place during the 1830s and enjoyed considerable glory as first capital of the Province of Canada, 1841-44. These were exciting years. Kingston was the centre of a vast province that extended from Gaspé to Thunder Bay. Major public figures like Sydenham, Bagot, Metcalfe, Draper, Baldwin, Hincks, and La Fontaine conducted their business in the little city. One of the government officials who moved to Kingston was the architect George Browne, who built a number of structures that still define the Kingston streetscape. Browne was responsible for Wilson's Building (now a beautifully restored office for the Victoria and Grey Trust Company), the Commercial Mart (now the cluttered S & R Department Store), the manse at St. Andrew's Presbyterian Church, Rockwood Villa and, most important of all, City Hall.

Possession of the capital was very gratifying to Kingstonians, who had always felt that they should possess the seat of government. The economy, fueled by some irresponsible speculations, underwent rapid expansion. Printers flourished by acquiring extensive contracts for government printing; many houses were constructed and the population increased markedly. Transshipment, much abetted by a Laurentian trade that was fostered and protected by the umbrella of British mercantilism, continued to bring wealth to the town and its merchants.

The decision to remove the capital from Kingston to Montreal overwhelmed leaders and common citizens alike. They were desperate to save their town's greatness. The city fathers pleaded with the government and offered to give the province the new city hall, free of charge, for whatever period was necessary. City Hall, ostensibly a municipal building, had been designed in such a way that it could easily serve as a meeting place for a bicameral parliament. It was all to no avail. Reform politicians were in charge – and they had no use for Kingston. Robert Baldwin dismissed Kingston as an "Orange Hole."[8]

Kingstonians were embittered by the withdrawal of the seat of government. James Hopkirk, commenting on the departure of some 1,700 people, suggested that "[t]wo thirds of [the people of Kingston] will be ruined."[9] For the *Chronicle and Gazette* it was an awesome calamity. "The dread news has fallen upon the good people of Kingston like one of those sudden convulsions of nature, which all regard as possible, yet few look for as probable. Had an earthquake laid down the fairest portion of Kingston, the population being preserved from destruction, we do not believe that the injury would be less to the sufferers, while they would have the consoling satisfaction of public sympathy, if not pecuniary relief. Kingston must descend from metropolitan rank to the condition of a second rate provincial town."[10]

The depths of the feelings of Kingstonians were revealed when Governor General Metcalfe made his exit from the town. It was clear that the loyalty of the citizenry had been strained to the limit. "The inhabitants did not muster strongly," reported the *British Whig*, "and of those present a general air of gloom and discontent was on each countenance. Shortly after twelve o'clock a salute of nineteen guns commenced firing, and His Excellency moved towards the steamer, accompanied by his guests. During his progress to the Ottawa and Rideau Wharf, no cheer greeted his ear, no single hat was lifted to do him reverence – he passed to his boat amid the most profound and ominous silence...Thus did the Governor General leave Kingston, the chosen capital of Canada, 'after mature deliberation', and with him departed the pledged faith of the Imperial Government."[11] Alexander Scougall set to verse the prevailing gloom and depression:

> *Thus now I wander on Ontario's shore,*
> *Where Kingston, sheltered from tempest's roar,*
> *Spreads its fair front expansive to the view,*
> *With cots and villas where the pine wood grew,*
> *With wharfs and mansions springing up anon,*
> *'Midst varied comforts for the busy throng;*
> *And see! The spacious pile no rival knows.*
> *This vast stone-mart, which amply, nobly shows,*
> *A spirit and an enterprise, unspared*
> *Since Kingston the Capital was declared,*
> *Since Sydenham's promise and Stanley's pen*
> *Proclaimed it so to every citizen,*

and caused them with an outlay large and free,
Extend its bounds with rich rapidity.[12]

Some Kingstonians avoided reality, but the capital question was dead after 1844. In 1856, John A. Macdonald, then Attorney-General for Canada West, admitted as much to his mother. "We are now discussing the question of the seat of Government," he wrote. "I am afraid that we have no chance for Kingston. We will however make a fight for it."[13]

The loss of the capital function was a major blow to Kingston. Perhaps most important was the psychological damage done to the city's elite. Kingston's leaders were convinced, and perhaps correctly, that the damage occasioned by the loss of the capital was irreparable. It has been suggested that the reality was probably less grim. Max Magill explained: "When the capital was transferred to Montreal in 1844, Kingston businessmen realized that the future of the city depended on its success in meeting the competition of Toronto for the commercial leadership of Canada West. In spite of some disadvantages, it must have seemed that its chances in this competition were good. It was still an important lake port, with a flourishing local trade and growing industries and, above all, as the headquarters of the Commercial Bank it was the financial centre of a region extending eastward from the vicinity of Port Hope to the old boundary with Lower Canada."[14]

Magill's retrospective prognostication was far too sanguine. Post-1844 Kingston was in deep, structural trouble. Greatness would not result merely because of the presence of the capital. Kingston had lost its leading place in the urban hierarchy and that loss was definitive. The prediction of the *Chronicle and Gazette* was all too apt. It seemed that Kingston was destined to sink "to the condition of a second rate provincial town."

Of course, Kingston possessed certain advantages. It still had the garrison and the port. Unfortunately, these, too, were to go. Reorganization of imperial defences led to the withdrawal of the British garrison in 1871. Major problems for the port began in the 1840s and were many. Britain's repeal of the Corn Laws and Navigation Acts meant the end of the old mercantilist empire, with a consequent weakening of Canada's Laurentian economy. That meant less transshipment. More important were major changes in maritime technology. The St. Lawrence was first canalized during the 1840s and, as the century advanced, steamboats replaced sail. Both developments hurt Kingston's port. Once the St. Lawrence canals were built, substantial amounts of freight could bypass Kingston altogether. This did not devastate the port immediately. Ships had to be constructed to fit the canals and that process was not completed for many years. Also, sailing ships tended to have problems navigating the river and, consequently, often continued to transship their cargoes at Kingston. Nonetheless, the transshipment business was doomed. The process was inexorable. John D. Wilson, a recent student of the port, notes that "the late 1880s or early 90s marked the beginning of the end for Kingston as a major port." He adds that "a violent downturn occurs" after 1890.[15] Population data confirms the existence of an economic crisis late in the nineteenth century. In 1891, Kingston's population was 19,263. Ten years later it had sunk to 17,961. The collapse of the port was decisive. To quote Wilson again: "The port had been the prime factor that gave Kingston a significant role in the economy of Ontario."[16] The ultimate impact of canalization was put nicely in a remark attributed to Clifford Curtis, an economist and mayor of Kingston during the 1950s. When asked about the potential impact of the St. Lawrence Seaway on Kingston, he replied that the Seaway would permit much larger ships to bypass the city than could currently bypass Kingston.

The civic and business leaders of the post-1844 era were appalled by their city's plight and conducted a frantic struggle to save Kingston's place in the urban hierarchy of north-eastern North America. A substitute was needed for transshipment. Two broad and often interconnecting strategies were pursued simultaneously during the second half of the nineteenth century. Both were posited on the assumption that the city had a destiny greater than that of a second-rate Ontario rivertown, and both sought to simulate the role that Kingston had enjoyed as Upper Canada's primary port of transshipment. One thrust was toward the north in an effort to find a hinterland that could be exploited. This was an admission that the old economic strategy was dead, and that all of Ontario and parts of the United States could no longer be regarded as tributary to the old Loyalist capital. The other thrust assumed a variety of forms but was directed to a more exact replacement of the transshipment-entrepôt function. It sought a new method of breaking bulk, and restoring Kingston's greatness. It was thought possible, for example, to use Kingston as the connecting point between traffic from the west and the American railroad system that connected Lake Ontario with the ice-free port at New York. According to this scheme, eastbound freight could arrive at Kingston by either rail or water. An analogous approach was the search for a direct substitute for the obsolete system. This would involve the construction of a much better harbour with first-class port facilities that could accommodate very large lakers and transship goods to rail.

These strategies, while ultimately unsuccessful, ramified in many ways during the nineteenth century and were by no means abandoned. The Rideau Canal had failed to generate an adequate hinterland, so roads were tried. Numerous feeder roads were built during the 1840s and 1850s. They brought many farmers into Kingston's economic orbit but were unable to give Kingston the kind of hinterland enjoyed by Toronto or Hamilton. Needless to say, railroads were considered. The completion of the Grand Trunk in the 1850s had harmed Kingston's transshipment function, but civic leaders were convinced that a line to the north could bring on the needed hinterland. Railway mania swept the town. As the *Chronicle and Gazette* put it, "Let every one think of the Railroad, speak of the Railroad, and all who can, write of the Railroad. Agitate! Agitate! Agitate!"[17] Several schemes failed, but the northern line finally materialized. The Kingston & Pembroke Railway, the Kick and Push as it was called locally, was built to Renfrew between 1872-76. Like the road projects, the K and P had its utility but it could not create the necessary hinterland because the lands between Kingston and the Ottawa River were not productive enough to generate the necessary trade. Robert Gourlay had been correct in 1822 when he noted: "Kingston is subject to one local disadvantage, the want of a populous back country."[18]

The Kingston & Pembroke Railway was the most substantial transportation enterprise to originate in Kingston, but it was by no means the grandest in conception. The plan to make Kingston a hub in a network that included both the Canadian and American rail systems was much grander, but came to little. True, the Wolfe Island, Kingston and Toronto Railway was promoted, but construction never commenced. A canal across Wolfe Island was built in the 1850s but it too failed. Its remains, filled with silt and debris, can still be inspected.

Dreams of greatness die hard. During the Laurier period, several schemes evolved to make Kingston the transshipment point for western wheat. These made little economic sense. As late as 1919, the city hired C.D. Howe to report on harbour improvements. His report, completed in 1920, was a bold and able document designed to secure for Kingston the large wheat terminal that the federal government finally built at Prescott. But it was all to no avail. Even before World War I, much western grain was already transshipped from lakers to freight cars at Lake Huron ports. Only about a tenth of prairie wheat moved along the old Great Lakes–St. Lawrence route; Kingston profited from a mere share of that small residue.

The grand economic strategies failed in the final half of the nineteenth century, but Kingstonians managed to subsist. They sought industries and met with some, if not much, success. Shipbuilding was an important enterprise after the War of 1812. Construction, and especially stone masonry, throve during the 1840s, as did printing and publishing. Cabinet making was a vibrant and important enterprise until the middle of the nineteenth century. Men like James Morton contributed substantial amounts of entrepreneurial skill to the community. From the 1830s, he was active in brewing, distilling, docking, lake shipping, locomotive engine construction, and railway contracting. D.D. Calvin and his son operated a huge rafting, shipbuilding, shipping, wrecking, and tugging operation from Garden Island, 1836-1914. A number of small manufacturing plants located in Kingston, but the most important single nineteenth century industrial enterprise was the Canadian Locomotive Company. It emerged out of Morton's engine building firm and employed substantial numbers of men until the 1950s. Nonetheless, Kingston did not develop into a major or even important industrial centre. It had too small a local market, an inadequate labour pool, and was too far from major markets.

While the commercial and industrial destiny of Kingston was unfolding, another development was taking place. This development is the key to Kingston's uniqueness. The city acquired the role of what Arthur Lower terms a "sub-capital."[19] It acquired this status in a surprising variety of spheres.

Perhaps Kingston's best known sub-capital function is as a major prison centre: for generations of Toronto hoods, going "down east" has been synonymous with incarceration in Kingston Penitentiary or one of the other penal institutions that came to dot the area in the twentieth century. [20] The founder of "KP" was Hugh Christopher Thomson, a member of the Tory elite, and a product of the family that later produced Lord Thomson of Fleet. KP was opened for business in 1835. Closely associated with the nineteenth-century prison was Rockwood Asylum, an institution for the insane. It became a provincial asylum in 1856 and evolved into the massive Kingston Psychiatric Hospital. Queen's University was established by Kingston's burgeoning community of Scots Presbyterians during the 1840s. Classes opened with fifteen students, a principal, and one professor on 7 March 1842. Bishop Alexander Macdonell obtained incorporation for a Roman Catholic seminary called the College of Regiopolis in 1836. It was never a strong institution, but Regiopolis did function as an arts college and seminary until 1869. It is now a co-educational high school that uses the name "Regiopolis Notre Dame." It continues to be Kingston's most important private school and a vital cultural centre for the Roman Catholic community of eastern Ontario. Regiopolis failed as an institution of post-secondary education. Nonetheless, Kingston did acquire a second university. It was a product of one of the main continuities in the city's history: the military. Royal Military College, a pet project of the late nineteenth-century Liberal Party, was founded in 1874. RMC's first class, the "Old Eighteen," reported to the college on 1 June1876. The institution has been an integral part of Kingston's social fabric ever since.

Kingston also became a sub-capital for three of the major religious denominations of Ontario: Presbyterianism, Catholicism, and Anglicanism. Queen's University and its leadership provided a centre for "old kirk" Presbyterians. Catholicism and Anglicanism evolved differently, in part, because those faiths are episcopal in organization. Kingston has long possessed an important Roman Catholic community. This was recognized in 1826 when Reverend Alexander Macdonell, a powerful leader and pillar of the Family Compact, was made a bishop in ordinary with the title Bishop of Regiopolis. He established himself in Kingston, which has remained a diocesan or archdiocesan seat ever since. The Roman Catholic cathedral, St. Mary's, was built during the 1840s. Anglicanism is the premier religion of Kingston. John Stuart, the founding rector, was the town's first clergyman. However, Kingston did not become an Anglican diocesan centre until 1852 when

John Travers Lewis was consecrated Bishop of Ontario. St. George's church, one of the finest church structures in Canada, then became a cathedral.

By the 1920s Kingston clearly had lost the economic race. It was a small centre located in a beautiful setting. The town was dominated by prisons, asylums, universities, hospitals, the military, and great cathedrals. The Second World War was greeted with the kind of patriotic fervor that distinguished Kingston's response to the Rebellion of 1837, the Riel Rebellions, the Boer War, and the Great War of 1914-18. The Second World War had a greater impact than some earlier conflicts. It led to some substantial industrialization that proved long-term, but the character of the town was not really changed. It continued to be defined by its sub-capital functions and nineteenth-century heritage. If anything, these characteristics are now stronger than ever before. Queen's and RMC have undergone massive expansion in recent years, and have been joined by a community college and military staff college. The military is very much in presence, as are a variety of well established churches. Federally and provincially funded institutions are omnipresent. Kingston is the centre of a maze of hospitals, prisons, government offices, and research units. The town has been so enormously successful in attracting government facilities that its politicians occasionally complain about the extent of tax exempt property in the community. Presumably the objective is to tax the public largesse that provides the city's economic base.

In recent years, Kingstonians have become very concerned about preserving the nineteenth-century heritage. Much has been destroyed, but much has been saved and restored. The streetscape of modern Kingston is thoroughly consistent with its nature and especially with its abundance of sub-capitals.

Even the most cursory glance at the history of Kingston would be incomplete without mention of the town's political tradition. Kingston has existed as a separate constituency since 1820, but its political history dates from the eighteenth century. The town has always been both politically active and much more influential than its size and wealth would suggest. For the pre-Confederation period, a simple list of Kingston's key politicians illustrates the power of the town: the Honourable Richard Cartwright (Legislative Councillor, 1792-1815); George Herkimer Markland (Legislative Councillor, 1820-38); Bishop

Alexander Macdonell (Legislative Councillor, 1831-40); John Macaulay (Legislative Councillor, 1836-57); Christopher Alexander Hagerman (MLA, 1820-24 and 1830-41); S.B. Harrison (MPP, 1841-44); and, John Alexander Macdonald (MPP, 1844-67). After Confederation, Kingston possessed both federal and provincial representation. Federally, Sir John A. Macdonald and Senator Sir Alexander Campbell were dominant influences during the late nineteenth century. Sir Richard Cartwright, although he never represented his own town, was a senior Liberal politician from 1873 until the fall of Laurier in 1911. Provincially, Kingston did not amount to much in the nineteenth century. Liberals ruled in Toronto, 1871-1905, and Kingston was usually Conservative, although William Harty did serve as a Liberal minister. The Conservative pattern has persisted at the provincial level, but in the twentieth century Conservatives have normally been in power. The result has been a succession of Kingston cabinet ministers at Queen's Park, including Arthur Ross, William Nickle (whose election slogan was "Put Another Nickle In"), Syl Apps, and Keith Norton. Federally, Kingston became a highly competitive seat in the twentieth century. Both Liberals and Conservatives have held important federal portfolios: Sir Henry Drayton (Conservative); Norman Rogers (Liberal); Angus L. Macdonald (Liberal); E.J. Benson (Liberal); and Flora MacDonald (Conservative). Whether Liberal or Conservative, these politicians have all been pretty much on the small "c" conservative side of the political spectrum.

In 1855, John A. Macdonald wrote to his close Kingston colleague, Henry Smith. He was concerned about some local patronage and noted, "As soon as the Court House is finished we will build a Custom House & Post Office, thus getting up three fine public buildings in old Kingston ... It would be a splendid thing to see the 3 buildings abuilding at one time."[21] Kingston politicians have been "abuilding" ever since: the Macdonald-Cartier Building, which houses Ontario Health Insurance Plan and other provincial offices, is the most recent contribution. Kingston has been made one of Canada's model public-sector towns. Is it not ironic that that is the accomplishment of a profoundly conservative political tradition that claims loyalty to free enterprise, individual initiative, and limited government?

II

A LL OF THIS IS reasonably straightforward, and the history of Kingston has received a massive amount of attention from both gifted amateurs and professional scholars. Several disciplinary approaches have been applied to the study of the town. Of particular interest are those of geographers, economists, historians, and art historians.

Much of this material is extremely good. To suggest that our understanding of Kingston's past is distorted by a number of fine studies is not to denigrate the work of other writers. Rather it is to suggest that the focus of some old questions about Kingston's history be changed and that some new questions be posed.

At the heart of the problem seems to be an idea or doctrine that originated in the late seventeenth century and came to mesmerize generations of scholars, thinkers, and writers. For many it became (and remains) a basic assumption acquired from the intellectual milieu and not from conscious consideration. In short, it is part of the intellectual baggage of the nineteenth and twentieth centuries.

The idea is "the idea of progress," which received brilliant analysis from the British historian, J.B. Bury. He gave the concept succinct definition: "This idea means that civilization has moved, is moving, and will move in a desirable direction ... The idea of human progress then is a theory which involves a synthesis of the past and a prophecy of the future. It is based on an interpretation of history which regards men as slowly advancing ... in a definite direction and infers that this progress will continue indefinitely."[22] In Anglophone historical scholarship this fallacy is usually known as "the whig interpretation of history." As Herbert Butterfield, its most celebrated proponent, notes, the whig interpretation "organizes the whole course of centuries upon what is really a directing principle of progress."[23]

Now we know that Kingston did not rise from her humble beginnings to the status of metropolitan greatness. The history of Kingston cannot be written around the theme of a phased growth to metropolitan triumph. The pervasiveness of the idea of progress is revealed by what seems to have happened at the assumptive level. A model of what should have happened has evolved. The thriving little community at the junction of lake and river should have built up enough growth momentum from the garrison and the port to "take off" and retain her place as the leading – or at least a leading – unit in Ontario's urban hierarchy. A substitute for the initial transshipment function should have been found. Political weight should have led to the retention of the seat of government. The town's economy should have been strengthened and diversified by the location in Kingston of a variety of industrial concerns. Kingston should have emerged as "Canada's Buffalo," to use the phrase of the boosters of the 1880s.

Had all of these things happened, the "progress" model could be applied with ease and confidence. This is where a peculiar variant of the progress model enters. Many students have been less concerned with what Kingston became than with the city that did not happen. That is, the progress model is *assumed* to apply. Because it obviously does not, the question becomes why not. Attention is focused on explaining the *absence* of metropolitan success. This has led to the "decline" school of Kingston historians.

An eminent economic historian puts it thus: the "leading concern in the latter nineteenth century has to be [Kingston's] slow development relative to other urban centres in Canada."[24] This kind of view follows logically from a historical perspective that emphasizes economic development in particular and growth in general. But this emphasis on decline or relative decline distorts our focus. Our concern becomes the failed city rather than the uniqueness of the city that did evolve from its nineteenth-century origins. The Kingston that emerged in the early twentieth century was not simply a second- or third-rate centre. It developed unique characteristics that make it distinct from other Ontario and Canadian towns. These aspects of Kingston's development occurred simultaneously with the town's rise to economic primacy and decline to minor status. In fact, these developments are almost certainly both more important and interesting than economic development. After all, if Kingston's trading or industrial strategies had met with success, the town would have become a typical North American commercial/business centre. With truly phenomenal bad luck Kingston might indeed have become "Canada's Buffalo." That did not happen and Kingston became a unique community. Twentieth-century Kingston is a legacy of the second half of the nineteenth century, which might well be regarded as the town's age of definition.

The distortions in Kingston's history are really matters of emphasis.

The economic mainstay was the port and its transshipment function, aided by the profits derived from the garrison. We have numerous studies of the port, transshipment, and soldiers. [25-26] Early Kingston, say prior to 1830, was the germ of a potential metropolis so we have a historiographical focus on the years 1783-1830, the character of the early town and the key personalities. [27-28] We even have some work on the intellectual history of Village Kingston.[29] Possession of the capital was crucial and should have aided the development of the all important urban momentum that helps great cities. This is another area that has received exhaustive coverage.[30] The crisis of mid-century and the town's response are crucial to the decline historians, and consequently have received massive attention.[31] Key public sector institutions are by no means ignored, but books and articles in this area tend to treat Queen's, RMC, Kingston Penitentiary, the hospitals, and the Roman Catholic and Anglican dioceses as discrete entities – in but not of the town and certainly not integral to the very social fabric of the city.[32]

III

TWO FURTHER areas merit attention. First, the weaknesses and distortions of the decline variant of the growth-progress model should be illustrated. Second, some suggestions for corrective research are in order.

Weaknesses and distortions can be illustrated by examining three questions: Did Kingston ever have the potential for major and sustained urban growth? What were the implications of *site* for Kingston's transshipment and military functions? Was it ever likely that Kingston could retain the seat of government – even in the short run?

Testing the growth potential of a village, town, or city is difficult. There is no test that can be regarded as scientific or absolute. However, it is possible to use a test that is at least suggestive. One of our most famous urban biographies is D.C. Masters' study of Toronto during the latter part of the nineteenth century.[33] Masters' concern is very much with the rise of Toronto to metropolitan status. He concludes that such status is posited on conditions that are as certain as they are clear. First, the city must create for itself and its hinterland a well-organized marketing system, including wholesale, storage, and exchange facilities. Second, the centre must control a manufacturing complex. Third, the metropolis must build a transportation system sufficiently sophisticated to make possible a free movement of goods. Fourth, the city needs a mature financial system to meet some of the capital and investment requirements of its hinterland. One can quibble about some of the details of Masters' points, but his basic definitions make sense.

When applied to Kingston, they produce interesting results. It is clear that Kingston was never even remotely close to meeting those standards. It might be argued that the first test was passed. But was it? Kingston never really created any complex marketing system. It subsisted on the break-in-bulk function, and for a time developed that service effectively. But it never produced a multi-layered marketing system that effectively tied Kingston to any hinterland of major consequence. Ontario's wheatlands never became a useable hinterland for the city. The second test was failed: Kingston never controlled a manufacturing complex of any importance. Ditto for the third test. Kingston never controlled the lakes-river transportation system upon which it subsisted. Its major effort was the Kingston & Pembroke Railway, which, after all, was a minor affair. Finally, the embryonic banking system that dates from the early period was less than successful and never met the needs of Kingston, let alone its meager hinterland.

In short, Kingston never developed anything like the facilities and infrastructure necessary for real urban growth. When tested along the lines of Professor Masters' model, the question that emerges is not: Why did Kingston fail to emerge as a major centre? The real question is: How do we explain the city's brief periods of private sector success, periods which are really aberrant rather than normal within the pattern of development suggested by the evidence?

The question of site is very important. W.L. Morton notes: "By site is meant a position of comparative advantage for production, exchange, or transfer. It is at once apparent that site, so defined, is not mere position, but a function, more or less complex, of position, environment, and technology. The significance of site, that is, varies with the nature of the environment and the state of technology."[34] Morton's comment is as realistic as it is succinct, and it lays bare the long-term weaknesses of Kingston's situation.

The essence of the history of Kingston is far from complicated. Site explains much about the town. Militarily, Kingston was superbly located, resting as it does at the foot of the Great Lakes system. After the quasi-demilitarization of the Lakes, it became central to the defence of the Rideau system. But in 1871, with the signing of the Treaty of Washington, came Anglo-American détente. That destroyed the strategic role of Kingston. The town could have a military base and a college to train officers, but it ceased to be a centre of any strategic importance.

The site implications for the port are equally dramatic. Early economic success came because of Kingston's ability to dominate the wheat trade. That function could last only as long as the need for transshipment from lake to river craft remained. Urban momentum could not develop because Kingston had no way of controlling the wheat hinterland to the west (hemmed in by the Canadian Shield) and could not develop her own hinterland to the north. The area between Kingston and Ottawa was not suited to the kinds of prosperous and extensive settlements that grew up around Toronto. Without a large and wealthy population in its hinterland, Kingston could not draw upon a diversified and educated labour pool. It had no large local market. An industrial base in competition with larger centres was never really possible. When technology – steamboats, canals, railroads – overtook the port, there was no recourse. What is of interest is Kingston's good fortune in enjoying some temporary private sector success. Only massive political and uneconomic pressure could ever have shored up the port.

IV

KINGSTON HAS enjoyed a brilliant political tradition, but it never possessed anything remotely close to the political authority that would have been necessary to counter the site disadvantages that were clearly evident by the middle of the nineteenth century. Rehabilitating the private sector economy in the late nineteenth century was simply a pipedream.

The capital question is extremely interesting. Kingstonians had always wanted the seat of government and felt aggrieved because of its absence. The decision in February 1841 to locate the capital in Kingston seemed logical enough to the local people. It was almost as though a rightful possession had been restored to the town. Kingston's growth and progress was thus illustrated. Historians have tended to think along similar lines, and the brief capital period has received a substantial amount of attention.

This is logical enough. The capital period was glittering and glamorous. Kingston was briefly the centre of a huge province. Fascinating personalities lived in the town, and a major result of the presence of the capital is a magnificent architectural legacy.

What is not noted is the extremely tenuous hold that Kingston had on the capital function. Margaret Angus, an excellent historian, has described the famous civic offer concerning the City Hall as follows: "Frantically the town fathers attempted to end such talk [of moving the capital out of Kingston] by offering *the free use of the City Buildings and Market House now in the course of erection for the meeting of the Legislature for any period that they may be required.*"[35] The points of interest here are the date of the offer, October 1843, and the phrase "such talk." It was not of course "talk" at all. The policy of the assembly to move the seat of government to Montreal had been public knowledge for months. What is surprising is not that the capital left Kingston in 1844, but that it arrived in the first place and then remained for several years. The location of the capital of the Province of Canada in Kingston feeds the view that Kingston was on the march and about to "take off." In reality, the famous decision of Lord Sydenham was largely fortuitous and did not represent any long-term commitment at all. In a very real sense Kingston never possessed the capital of Canada.

Kingston became the capital for ephemeral, if pressing, reasons. After the rebellions of 1837-38, Lower Canada had its constitution suspended. The French province was easy to manipulate: its special Council would do the bidding of any governor general. Upper Canada suffered no such loss. Its constitution easily survived the Rebellion, and the Family Compact emerged from 1837 firmly in control. The Compact-controlled Assembly could not be easily manipulated; it possessed real power. Upper Canada's Tories did not want union with the lower province. To secure union, Sydenham had to bargain with the Compact leaders. Concessions were made, one of which was a promise to locate the seat of government in Upper Canada. Once the struggle for the capital was limited to Upper Canada, Kingston won by process of elimination. The province after all was only a generation and a half removed from the wilderness. It did not have many towns, and those that did exist were hardly appropriate as the capital of a province that had as its largest unit a section that was preponderately French and Catholic. Hamilton was too far west, as was Toronto, which also suffered from political problems that, in the words of Governor General Sydenham, "would make this city an extremely unfit place for the seat of Government."[36] Bytown was perfectly located, but was "too cold and too far.[37] That left the towns of St. Lawrence valley: Cornwall, Prescott, Brockville, Kingston. Of these Kingston, with its convertible buildings and ample crown property, was the easy winner.

Unfortunately, Kingston was not up to its status as capital. It was too small and primitive to provide the amenities demanded by the politicians, who were in some cases sophisticated and travelled. Kingston was too British for the French Canadians and too conservative for Reformers of either race. Lord Sydenham made Kingston the capital, and defended his choice. But he found the town trying. In June 1841, he complained to Lord Russell, "I am ready to hang myself half a dozen times a day ... I long for September, beyond which I will not stay if they were to make me Duke of Canada and Prince of Regiopolis, as this place is called."[38] Sir Charles Bagot, who succeeded Sydenham as Governor General, rendered judgment exactly one week after arriving in Kingston. The town, he reported to Colonial Secretary Stanley, is "small and poor, and the Country around it unproductive." It lacks "accommodation for the members of the Legislature when the Session is in progress." Bagot's ultimate argument was political. Kingston, reported the Governor, was "unacceptable to the great body of the people."[39]

It was unavoidable then that the issue would quickly be reopened. More correctly, it might be said, the seat of government issue was never closed. Assaults on Sydenham's decision were immediate. French Canada was appalled by the choice, as was Toronto. Official views were ominous. As early as June 1841, Sydenham replied to an address from a group of Kingstonians with a statement that included the phrase, "*Should* Kingston become the permanent Seat of Government."[40] The single word "*Should*" was fateful. An assembly committee considered the matter during the first session of the first Parliament. It reported on 1 September 1841, and endorsed the relocation of the capital to Quebec and Toronto on an alternating system. On 16 September 1841, the essence of the committee report was supported by the assembly as an address to Queen Victoria. The address concluded, "wherefore we most earnestly entreat that Your Majesty, in the exercise of Your Royal prerogative, will be pleased to order that the Parliament of Canada, hereafter, assemble alternately at *Quebec* and *Toronto*."[41] The MPP for Kingston was hardly pleased, but he was virtually isolated.

Opponents of Kingston were not united on the choice of an alternate capital. That worked to Kingston's advantage, but from 1841 it was public knowledge that the Parliament wanted to move the seat of government out of the city. There was never a single parliamentary endorsement of Kingston as the capital. No city father who was even vaguely responsible or peripherally aware could have misunderstood the importance of these Assembly resolutions.

It was within this political context that City Hall was conceived and built. The city fathers knew that they were in profound trouble but proceeded anyway, and then tried to use the building as a bribe. This context changes the whole nature of the debate over the origins and nature of City Hall.[42] The motives and decisions of the city fathers can be explained in one of two ways: either they were irresponsible, or they combined stupidity with dishonesty.

There has been disagreement about the conception of City Hall. Was it built as a bribe or was it a coincidence that such a building was under construction in 1843-44? Donald Creighton argues that the city fathers "had realized for some time that their rapidly growing capital was badly in need of a new town hall and new market buildings; and they were aware also – and the thought hovered always at the back of their speculations – that the provincial legislature, completely ignoring the need of permanent provision, still occupied its avowedly temporary quarters, the four-storey limestone building which had been erected as a hospital. Contemplating these two necessities, the town council reached an audacious and grandiose decision. It would build an elegant, spacious, and splendid town hall, a town hall amply sufficient to accommodate not merely the offices and council rooms which a rising town like Kingston was certain to require, but also still larger chambers, fit, perhaps, for the deliberations of still greater and more august assemblies."[43] Historians of City Hall take grave exception to this interpretation. J.D. Stewart, for example, comments: "Perhaps the most persistent myth of all is that the Kingston City Hall was originally designed as the Parliament Buildings for the province of Canada. Local tradition clings firmly to this idea."[44] According to this latter view, the genesis of the City Hall can be traced to the great fire that devastated the downtown-waterfront section, including the market area, in the early hours of Saturday, April 18, 1840. (For a superb account of the fire and its influence on the development of Kingston, see John W. Spurr, "The Night of the Fire, *Historic Kingston*, No. 18, 1970, 57-65. Spurr argues, persuasively, that the fire "explains why and how Kingston became 'the limestone city.'"[45]) The devastation of that Easter weekend wrecked the market, which was of substantial economic importance to Kingston. It is not surprising that civic boosters like John Counter, who became mayor in April 1841, had called for a new market house immediately after the fire of 1840. It would have been surprising had such demands not been made. That does not of course lead in any logical manner to the magnificent building that ultimately was constructed, a building so large that it "is doubtful in fact that any building in British North America even rivaled it in size."[46]

Resolving this conflict of interpretation is difficult. Mayor Counter and other city fathers were hardly likely to give public (or possibly even private) utterance to a resolve to undertake an inordinately expensive municipal work for purposes of a bribe that had virtually no chance of being effective. The evidence does suggest that the genesis of the City Hall was murky at best.

Our conceptual framework concerning the evolution of Kingston has distorted our view of the capital period. What was fortuitous and ephemeral seems natural and logical. Kingston never really had the seat of government. It was merely the scene of a passing political compromise.

V

THE HISTORIOGRAPHY of Kingston has evolved and passed through various stages, as has the city itself. This is a large and rich historiography. It has focused on certain aspects of Kingston's development, and because of widely held assumptions by historians, has presented us with a view of the past that distorts the nature of the historical process. Surely it is time to ask some different questions and examine problems that have been neglected. Twentieth-century Kingston has been largely ignored and cries out for attention. Of particular importance is the Second World War and the industrialization that occurred in the 1950s and 1960s,[47] the rapid expansion of education institutions in the 1960s and 1970s, changes in waterfront development, and the rise of the heritage movement.[48] Key institutions in the town should be analysed within the local social context. We should try to understand more about how prisons, universities, dioceses, hospitals, and government agencies became integrated into the town's social structure and how they have influenced the nature of twentieth-century Kingston.[49] And of course we should learn much more about Kingston as a public sector town. We should certainly try to determine the extent to which the public sector is dominant.

Research might well reveal that even some of our industries are less entrepreneurial than has been realized. For example, during the Laurier period, the Locomotive Works, which were headed by an important Liberal politician, received a substantial amount of business that was really federal patronage. Perhaps the most intriguing question of all relates to Kingston's political tradition. Who has really controlled the town? How important has been the role of civic leadership? Why and how did Kingston's clever Tory elite found and sustain a public sector community that is unique amongst the cities of Ontario and Canada?

View of Kingston from Brock Street at Montreal Street. Painting by James Cockburn, 1829 (Library and Archives Canada).

The Kingston Community

It is not often that failure should be saluted, but that is what should be done by those who hold Kingston in affection and respect.

I WAS ASKED TO address a number of points: "the evolution of Kingston; key characteristics; institutional development; social, economic, and political influences." This is a formidable assignment. For example, the first component is "the evolution of Kingston." If we ignore the French period, which is reasonable enough, because there is no continuity between the Francophone and Anglophone period (except evidence relating to toponomy), we have some 275 years of history. I was asked to speak for about 35 minutes. That allows for .17 of a minute per year, or 1.7 minutes per decade. And "the evolution of Kingston" is only one part of the assignment.

Clearly, I must be highly selective and will make no attempt at a comprehensive survey of the history of Kingston. Rather, I will attempt to explain those developments and circumstances that have made Kingston a unique community. I will also try to explain why – in my view – that uniqueness has not been destroyed by the course of development and growth.

This is the text of the first of five addresses that constituted the Queen's University Town Hall Series, a component of the University's sesquicentennial celebrations. The address was delivered on 7 November 1991, written specifically for this audience. By now, *Kingston: Building on the Past* had been in print for three years, where Professor Swainson had his word on civic evolution and heritage-wise development.

*View of Front (Ontario) Street at Fort Frontenac. Painting by James Cockburn, 1829
(Library and Archives Canada).*

I

ONE OF THE most notable aspects of Kingston is its site. The town is located in a magnificent situation. If you stand at the right place on the waterfront you can see the source of the St. Lawrence River, the entrance way to the Rideau Canal, an open expanse of Lake Ontario, and several of the beautiful Thousand Islands. There is a very good reason for the selection of this particular site. During the American revolutionary war, the British military headquarters for this sector was Carleton Island, a little piece of territory south of Wolfe Island and about 10 miles south east of present day Kingston. Attracted by the military presence were a number of merchants who provisioned the British. Also, a number of Mohawk loyalists gravitated to Carleton Island. When the revolutionary war ended, it transpired that Carleton Island was part of the United States and the British had to relocate. The British also had to find a settlement area for a number of Loyalist refugees, including some Mohawk leaders like Molly Brant. The site of present day Kingston was selected. It was well known to the British military as the location of Fort Frontenac. The Loyalists were more than happy with the place. For the merchants, it was almost a perfect spot for their activities because it was situated at precisely the point where Lake Ontario was transformed into the St. Lawrence River. Different modes of transport were used on lake and river. That meant that both eastbound and westbound traffic required transshipment, and Kingston was the obvious place for that activity, even if its harbour is not nearly as good as many may assume.

The nature of the founding of the town is important. Early Loyalists and merchants were often inter-changeable. The military elite was both powerful and very close to the Loyalist establishment. These people shared many attitudes. Socially, they were very conservative with a strong orientation toward deference. They were purely voluntary members of the British Empire and very loyal to their King, after whom they named their town. Their heavy personal and military involvement in the American revolutionary war – and many Loyalists lost homes, family, and capital – made them powerfully anti-American. In fact, Ontario in general and places like Kingston in particular possess what is arguably the oldest continuous anti-American tradition in the world. They believed that the United States was a "mobocracy," a state governed according to the rule of democracy and anarchism. Hence, the Loyalist tradition has a powerful anti-democratic component. Loyalists were also very close to the state and very supportive of the state. After all, they were monarchists who had suffered much in the service of the state. They were rewarded for that service with lands and subsidies. One of the many historians of the Loyalists, Bruce Wilson, has commented on this close association between Loyalist and state. "Historians," he notes, "have calculated Great Britain had spent £1 million in start up costs in Upper Canada by 1787, not including the disbursement of free lands and that the grand total for all expenditures on Loyalists, including compensation, was a phenomenal £30 million! Many people have benefited from the spoils after winning a war, but no people in history ever did so well by losing one."

After the Loyalists founded Kingston, we had many waves of immigrants. Scots, Irish, and American groups arrived in the nineteenth century. A variety of European and third world immigrants came in the twentieth century. A number of the characteristics that marked the Loyalists became enduring characteristics of Kingston. This community still tends to be socially conservative, deferential, monarchist, and anti-American. This latter characteristic probably explains the Kingston result in the 1988 general election, when we voted against free trade. Kingstonians have also shared a close and special relationship with the state over the past couple of hundred years, a characteristic that explains much about the city. I will return to this point a little later. These Loyalist and founding characteristics were heavily reinforced by the War of 1812-1814, which was as defining for Kingston as it was for Ontario society in general.

Another absolutely crucial defining circumstance in the city's evolution was Kingston as the capital of the Province of Canada. From 1841 until 1844 Kingston was the political and administrative centre of a huge colony that extended from Gaspé in the east to Thunder Bay in the west. The decision to locate the seat of government in Kingston made a certain kind of sense. One of the reasons for the union of 1841 was the imperial decision to accept Lord Durham's recommendation that Francophone Canadians be Anglicized. That caused the first Governor General, Lord Sydenham, to reject any Lower Canadian site as capital.

Once it was agreed that the capital was to be in Upper Canada, Kingston, which was still the largest urban centre in the western province, won by process of elimination. Toronto was too far west and too much dominated by Compact Tories – a group that Sydenham detested. Other towns along the Lake Ontario and St. Lawrence front – Belleville, Brockville, Prescott, Cornwall – did not have anything like the required amenities or supports that a seat of government required. Ottawa continued to be, as Goldwin Smith described it, a "sub-arctic lumber village." Kingston was appropriate at some levels. Geographically it was reasonably central and it was in a position where it could be protected from quick American attack. It also had a lot of ordnance property that could be used for government purposes. The present magnificent park in downtown Kingston, between King Street and the Frontenac County courthouse, was part of that property and could easily have been used as the site of a parliament building. So Kingston was selected as the capital – a role that the town had thought appropriate since at least 1791.

The capital did not remain here for very long. It was removed to Montreal in 1844 for a variety of reasons, one being that the Reform politicians detested the conservatism of Kingston. Robert Baldwin, the great Reform leader, dismissed Kingston as an "Orange Hole."

However, the capital years, 1841-1844, were very important to the city. In the short-run some major ambitions were satisfied. Kingston was for this fleeting moment easily pre-eminent within Upper Canada. The city was the largest and probably the wealthiest community in Canada West, as the old province of Upper Canada was called from 1841 to 1867. Even more important from the psychological perspective, Kingston had defeated her arch rival – the hated Toronto – and attained the status of capital. All of this was very satisfying.

In some respects, the long run implications of the capital years were more important. The government of the province of Canada employed an architect named George Browne. He modified Alwington House for Governor General Sydenham and fixed up various other structures to house the bureaucracy. More importantly, Browne was also a free-lancer. He was responsible for such buildings as City Hall (which was conceived as a municipal bribe to keep the capital from being moved to Montreal), St. Andrew's manse, Wilson's Buildings (now the Victoria and Grey Trust), the Commercial Mart (now the S&R Department store), and Rockwood Villa. These magnificent creations have done much to define our impression of the physical Kingston. Of course, George Browne was not the only architect and builder at work. There were many others, and Browne's creations should be considered in conjunction with St. George's Cathedral (part of which he apparently designed), St. Mary's Cathedral, Earl Place, the Cartwright house, the Gildersleeve house, the Frontenac County Court House, the drydock, Elizabeth Cottage, Summerhill, Hales Cottages, the Custom House, Bellevue House, Roselawn, the old Post Office, the Martello towers, and Fort Henry – to name only a sample of the structures that, along with Browne's, give us the visual Kingston that is both distinctive and beautiful. Not all of these buildings were the product of the capital period, but many were, and Kingston would not be the city that it is today without the architectural initiatives of 1841-1844.

In psychological terms, the acquisition of the capital resulted in collective elation and three years of frenzied activity and growth. The loss of that status had as strong a psychological impact, but in reverse. Kingstonians were devastated, angry, and frightened for their futures. The *Chronicle and Gazette* put it nicely: "The dread news has fallen upon the good people of Kingston like one of those sudden convulsions of nature, which all regard as possible, yet few look for as probable. Had an earthquake laid down the fairest portion of Kingston, the population being preserved from destruction, we do not believe that the injury would be less to the sufferers, while they would have the consoling satisfaction of public sympathy, if not pecuniary relief. Kingston must descend from metropolitan rank to the condition of a second rate provincial town." The city's situation would quickly become even worse. Over the next generation or so the economic news was very bleak.

First, the transshipment function – central to the town's economy – was in process of being destroyed. There were a variety of reasons for this. The St. Lawrence was gradually canalized. Canals were built around the rapids: then they were improved and enlarged to permit bigger and bigger boats to use them. This meant that transshipment became ever less necessary, and that of course meant increasingly less economic opportunities for Kingston's businessmen and workers. This development, very worrisome in the nineteenth century, culminated in the 1950s when the St. Lawrence Seaway completely destroyed an economic function that had in fact been marginalized for decades. The ultimate impact of these developments was put nicely in a remark attributed to Clifford Curtis, a Queen's economist and mayor of Kingston during the 1950s. When asked about the potential impact of the St. Lawrence Seaway on Kingston, he replied that the Seaway would permit much larger ships to by-pass the city than did already.

II

WHILE POST-CAPITAL period Kingstonians watched the transshipment function fade, they also watched – with alarm and horror – the disengagement of the British military. The garrison had been a mainstay of the town since the 1780s, and any weakening of it was an economic and social blow of serious proportion. Anglo-American relations were sufficiently sensitive during the 1840s and 1860s to keep the army presence reasonably important, although the naval presence was pretty much dead. There was a very dramatic change after the American Civil War in 1865. Geopolitical factors forced the British to re-evaluate and re-formulate their basic military strategy. European concerns overwhelmingly overtook North American concerns. That led to an Anglo-American détente, which, in turn, led to the withdrawal of most British military forces from Canada. For Kingston, the end came in 1870 when the Imperial garrison left. The last noon gun to be fired by the British garrison at Fort Henry was fired in 1870, although a caretaker fired off a noon gun from time to time – to the intense nostalgic pleasure of the town.

The loss of the capital, the decline of transshipment, and the evaporation of the garrison did not take place simultaneously, but Kingstonians were worried and frightened by each step in the process. As the century progressed, Kingston lost its place in Ontario's urban hierarchy and slipped lower and lower. The gloomy prediction of the *Chronicle and Gazette* was turning out to be completely correct. Kingston was descending "from metropolitan rank to the condition of a second rate provincial town."

The urban leadership had to respond, and did. It saw salvation in the area to the north of Kingston. What was wanted was a "populous back country" – a hinterland. A well-populated and economically progressive tract of territory running from Kingston to the Ottawa River would solve many of Kingston's economic problems. Compensation would thus be found for the loss of the capital and the de-emphasis of the transshipment function. This position was well put by D.D. Calvin, who operated an extensive shipping and rafting firm on Garden Island and served as Conservative MPP for Frontenac County, 1868-1875 and 1877-1883. In 1871 he said: "I am strongly in favour of encouraging a healthy immigration of the industrial classes into our splendid province. The extensive wild lands, with their vast amounts of mineral and timber resources, require only to be developed to make the Province of Ontario one of the most desirable resorts for the redundant population of the old countries of Europe; and I do not know of any better plan to make these resources more readily available than by encouraging and aiding the construction of railways, gravel roads, and improving the inland navigation …. I am in favour of offering large facilities to intending settlers who will occupy and render productive our present fertile territory, as yet almost wholly unoccupied." Calvin might have referred to "our splendid province," but he was really talking about his own constituency, in which he had made heavy investments and which constituted a large portion of the hinterland that the Kingston elite was anxious to develop. In this, D.D. Calvin was totally representative of his business and political colleagues in Kingston and Frontenac County.

To obtain the changes that they desired, they needed to use all levels of government as well as the public sector. The Province could release crown lands for settlement, encourage settlers to go into the county and subsidize road and rail construction. The Province of Ontario could also play a significant role in encouraging the growth of mining and timbering operations. The federal government could assist as well. It could fiddle tariff schedules in order to make imported materials used in railroad construction and ore extraction and refining processes less costly. Also the federal government owned and operated the Rideau Canal. It was heavily pressed to improve and expand that system so that it would be more useful to business and industry. Municipalities had their role as well. They could bonus road and rail construction. They also supply urban land for railway stations and yards. Of course, the private sector was called upon to play a major role.

Various companies could accept the subsidy money and build the roads and railways. They could find the minerals, extract them, and build the various necessary refining facilities. Entrepreneurs were expected to obtain timber limits, cut the trees and ship the product south. The assumption was that Kingston would reap rich dividends from all of these activities. The town would sell the farmers their supplies and market their produce. The minerals and timber would be transported to market via Kingston. Some products would be turned into manufactured goods in Kingston. The town would also become a head office centre. Jobs and wealth would flow into the newly energized metropolis.

There was hinterland activity, much of it directed from Kingston. There was a fair amount of road construction during the middle years of the century and a fair number of farming settlers did in fact move into the townships north of Kingston. There were timbering operations and mica, feldspar, potash, and other minerals were pulled out of the rock and soil. Perhaps the most important northern initiation was the Kingston & Pembroke Railway (known locally as the "Kick and Push"). It was designed to be the transportation medium for the opening of the hinterland and for the transfer of the wealth of that region to Kingston and beyond. It was chartered in 1871, and construction proceeded in subsequent years. The Kick and Push did transport goods and people both north and south: it provided a useful service for a number of years, but ultimately it failed. The best study of the K and P has been written by Walter Lewis, and his conclusion is that the line was "a dismal failure." Nonetheless, the Kick and Push did become a part of the local folklore, as is indicated by the following rhyme:

> Listen to the jingle, the rumble and the roar,
> As she glides along the woodlands,
> By the lake and by the shore;
> Hear the mighty side-rods pounding,
> The lonesome whistle call:
> You're northward bound to Renfrew
> On the K. and P. Cannonball.

The Kingston & Pembroke Railway was able to do regular runs until 1957. It was then a subsidiary of the CPR and was effectively defunct. Its Kingston yards became the park in front of city hall during the 1960s and the actual rail track was removed in 1987.

The fate of the railway was the fate of Kingston's hinterland initiative: it was a total failure. Robert Gourlay observed as early as the 1820s that "Kingston is subject to one local disadvantage, the want of a populous back country." Unfortunately, that was a problem that could not be rectified. The area north of Kingston quickly becomes Canadian Shield country. There was no real potential for extensive agriculture. There were minerals, but not enough. The Richardson family was the biggest operator of mines in the area. A member of the family referred on one occasion to the "40 or so 'fun' mines we had around Kingston," indicating that these enterprises were not taken very seriously. Much timber went east to the Ottawa River and then to Montreal rather than to Kingston. The Rideau Canal could not generate enough commercial activity to be of much use to the Kingston economy.

The hinterland strategy was not the exclusive solution to Kingston's economic problems. There were two others. One was the encouragement of heavy – or any – industrial activity. The municipal politicians were willing to do anything within their power to generate industrial activity. A few industries did establish in Kingston, some with municipal assistance and some promoted by figures within the local elite. The most famous examples here were the shipbuilding dockyards and the locomotive works. These operations had their successes and were very important at various times, especially during wars. As many as 1,800 people were employed by these enterprises during the Second World War. Ultimately, however, the economics of location, workforce, and scale rendered these and other industrial activities obsolete. Another approach to the salvation of the Kingston economy related to transportation. Kingston entrepreneurs were convinced (and occasionally still are) that the city can become a transshipment centre once again. Through harbour improvements, Kingston can become the terminus of Great Lakes shipping, where wheat and other bulk products can be transshipped to rail, and sent either east or south. The Wolfe Island canal was one of the earliest of these schemes: "container" transfers is one of the latest. None of these approaches ever came to anything because they never made any locational sense.

III

WHILE ALL OF this economic floundering was going on, developments of profound importance were taking place. This process was quite unnoticed by the civic fathers, and is still not really understood by them – as far as an observer can tell.

During the course of the nineteenth century – and through the twentieth century – a series of developments transformed this community and made it unique. Kingston became an institutional town, the seat of a set of sub-capitals, the public sector town par excellence. This set of developments is largely, but not exclusively, related to the old loyalist instinct to associate closely with and use extensively the power of the state.

During the 1830s we acquired the provincial penitentiary known as Kingston penitentiary or "KP". This became the nucleus of our current massive network of prisons and related facilities. Out of KP emerged the psychiatric unit that has become a huge operation in this century. Kingston obtained a Roman Catholic archdiocese and an Anglican diocese with a cathedral that has, over the centuries, been substantially subsidized by the politicians. Queen's University was founded, with material assistance from politicians like John A. Macdonald, William Morris, and Alexander Campbell. It has expanded into a huge enterprise within a small community.

The founding of the Royal Military College in the mid-1870s was important in its own right and also symbolizes the return of the military to Kingston, a return that has blossomed into a very large operation that provides a large amount of revenue for the Kingston economy.

This "public-sectoring" of Kingston went on and on and was openly enhanced by provincial and federal politicians, who belong to a local political tradition that has consistently produced politicians able to exert much more authority in Toronto and Ottawa than the town's size and wealth would suggest. Christopher Thomson, a Tory politician who supported the Family Compact, brought Kingston Penitentiary here for reasons that primarily related to patronage, and the psychiatric hospital is a direct outgrowth of the prison. Queen's University was heavily assisted by prominent political figures. During the 1850s, John A. Macdonald was personally responsible for the construction of the old Post Office, the Custom House, and the Frontenac County Court House. He openly bragged about these coups. Macdonald's last major gift to his town was the dry dock facility, which is now the Marine Museum. RMC was a Liberal university – a pet project of Prime Minister Alexander Mackenzie. His finance minister was Sir Richard Cartwright, a Kingstonian who loathed Macdonald. He was instrumental in bringing RMC to Kingston in order to demonstrate that the town could receive patronage gifts without Macdonald. Cartwright was anxious to weaken Macdonald's political base and he was successful: Sir John lost the Kingston seat in 1878. The pattern goes on and on. The last major illustration was provided by Keith Norton when he was able to have the OHIP head office and a large number of jobs shifted to Kingston. This public sector presence is very important to Kingston.

In 1988 when Brian Osborne and I were completing our history of Kingston, we conducted a survey. We discovered that the "big four" manufacturing operations (Du Pont, Alcan, Celanese, and Northern Telecom) employed only 3,698 persons. That number is doubtless considerably less today. The major public sector operations – the military, education, hospitals, OHIP, and the prisons – employed some 20,878 persons in the Kingston region. Those figures say a very great deal about the nature of the city.

Why is this public sector presence so important? It becomes fairly evident if you subtract say three quarters of the public sector from Kingston in order to make the town comparable to many others within a similar population range. An enormous payroll would go and that of course would have a massive ripple effect throughout the community.

More important than that is the nature of this community. Kingston is a highly sophisticated community in a number of key respects, and that is largely because of the institutions. It has more big city amenities than any other comparable city in Canada – many more. Hence, we have a multitude of medical experts and several hospitals. That is one of the reasons that explain the fact that Kingston is becoming a leading retirement haven. It is obvious that our opportunities for high quality education are superior. The town's major musical traditions are rich, and in some cases brilliant. Painters and sculptors are plentiful. Live theatre is healthy and provides vast amounts of pleasure and instruction. We even have a successful commercial press, probably in major part because Kingston doubtless possesses more writers per capital than any other city in Canada.

IV

To SUMMARIZE the unique qualities of Kingston, this should be said. The city enjoys a magnificent physical site. It is located in one of Canada's most beautiful places. We continue to enjoy that beauty in spite of the ongoing decisions of the City that have wreaked terrible damage to the waterfront area. The City's locational beauty is enhanced by one of the finest and largest collections of superb nineteenth-century architecture in Canada. These structures are so commanding that they continue to give Kingston the ambience of a nineteenth-century town. Kingston is a sophisticated society, possessed of an unusually large set of big city amenities. All of these characteristics are brought together by scale. We never grew very much, so our nineteenth-century architecture was neither pulled down nor overwhelmed by huge and ugly twentieth-century buildings (with some notable and really tragic exemptions). Because we are small, everybody can have access to the waterfront with ease. We can do much of our shopping and many of our errands by foot. We do not require the frantic pace of big cities. The market can become a real community each market day.

Let me close by trying, briefly, to explain why we have this uniqueness. Our location is explained by pure luck. The merchants and military officers did not select the site for aesthetic reasons. They operated according to military, commercial, and settlement considerations. The fact that Kingston was ever capital was largely fortuitous. It explains some of our most remarkable architecture. What is relevant about much of the other nineteenth-century architecture is not why it was put up, but why it was never knocked down. That will be discussed in a moment. The institutionalization of Kingston is explained by Upper Canadian, Union, and, after 1867, provincial and federal politicians. That is a powerful, successful, and occasionally brilliant tradition that contrasts so starkly with the tradition at the municipal level. Finally, the question of scale. Here responsibility can be given to the local leadership because of the consistency of its failure. Had their bribe to the Province of Canada been accepted and the capital retained, we would almost certainly be the capital still. We would then have the Queensway and no doubt the bulk of our heritage buildings would have been demolished in order to build office towers. Military lands like the east side of the Cataraqui would almost certainly have been converted to bureaucratic use and RMC would be elsewhere. Similarly, if the nineteenth and twentieth century push for hinterland development and industrialization had been successful, we would have developed like a normal medium-sized North American city and our uniqueness would never have been able to evolve. It is not often that failure should be saluted, but that is what should be done by those who hold Kingston in affection and respect.

The Early Years of St. George's Cathedral

St. George's rectorship is the third-oldest institution in Ontario; the wardenships are the fourth. Certainly these are the oldest institutions in this community. This is indeed a first-rate reason for celebration.

L IKE KINGSTON, and the province of Ontario itself, St. George's Church is a direct product of the American Revolution. After the British conquest of Fort Frontenac in 1758, there was no permanent settlement here for a generation. During the American revolutionary wars, the British military – units of the army and the navy – and its Mohawk allies used Carleton Island as the base for this region. Carleton Island, which also attracted the merchants who provisioned the military, is a little island on the south side of Wolfe Island. When the war ended and the Treaty of Paris was signed (1783), it became necessary to delineate the border that separated the new republic and what was left of British North America: it transpired that Carleton Island was part of the United States of America. A new site was needed for the navy, the garrison, and the merchants. The site of the future city of Kingston, known because of Fort Frontenac and perfectly located, was selected.

The British authorities also had to consider the interests of the Loyalists – those Americans who remained loyal to the Crown during the revolutionary wars. It was determined to settle a substantial

First published in the 27 May 1989 issue of the Kingston *Whig-Standard Magazine*, this article was reprinted in the Quarry Press edition of *St. George's Cathedral: Two Hundred Years of Tradition* (1991)and shows Professor Swainson studying his favourite community.

*Watercolour of the first St. George's church. Unknown painter, 1792
(Queen's University Archives).*

number of them in the district of which the new settlement would be a logical capital.

I

THE MILITARY decision to move from Carleton Island to Cataraqui (as Kingston was initially called) was made in 1783. The first substantial group of Loyalists arrived in 1784. The history of Kingston, as it was called after 1788, had begun. Then as now it was heavily influenced by the military and essentially conservative in nature.

In the meantime another development – one of the many little tragedies of the war – was working itself through. One John Stuart, an American Anglican clergyman – well over six feet in height and known as "the *little* gentleman" – had a posting at Fort Hunter, New York, where he was the missionary to the Mohawks. Stuart was "a missionary of almost boundless energy." Among his many achievements, Stuart, in collaboration with the great chief Joseph Brant, translated the Gospel of St. Mark into the Mohawk dialect. The work was published in 1787.

Stuart was not particularly political, but he was an Anglican priest and, revolutionaries notwithstanding, remained loyal to the king for whom he prayed every Sunday. The revolutionaries assumed his guilt and actively tormented him. His house was looted and his property confiscated. He lost, personally, some £1,200, a not inconsiderable sum in the late eighteenth century. More important to Stuart, his church was first seized, then desecrated. Stuart described the fate of his church: "I cannot omit to mention that my church was plundered by the rebels, and the pulpit cloth taken away from the pulpit; – it was afterwards imployed [*sic*] as a Tavern, the barrel of Rum placed in the Reading Deck. – the succeeding season it was used for a stable; – and now [1781] serves as a Fort to protect a set of as great villains as ever disgraced humanity."

Ultimately, Stuart was given permission to leave New York. In October 1781, he took his wife, children, and two black slaves to Montreal.

Montreal, then as now, had its attractions, and Stuart found his time occupied. But he wanted a permanent position and he wanted land. Consequently, in December 1783, Rev. John Stuart petitioned Governor-in-Chief Sir Frederick Haldimand: "As your Memorialist has been informed that a Garrison is established and a Colony of Loyalists intended to be settled at Cataraqui; he humbly presumes that ... he will be thought a proper person to reside there as a Clergyman ... Your Memorialist therefore humbly begs ... that he may be appointed Chaplain to the Garrison of Cataraqui, with the same allowances and privileges as are enjoyed by the Chaplains of the Garrisons of Quebec and Montreal. And that your Memorialist may have his proportion of Land assigned to him contiguous to that Garrison."

Stuart received his appointment and settled permanently at Cataraqui in August 1785. He was very pleased that, as he put it, he "found everything agreeable to, and even beyond any expectation the situation pleasant, the climate wholesome, and what was still more flattering, the people expressing, unanimously, their wishes that I wou'd [sic] settle among them." In this way, John Stuart began his Kingston career as "Garrison Chaplain" and "Curate of Kingston." This was the beginning of the Anglican Church in Kingston and in Ontario. It is instructive to underscore the point that Anglicanism in Kingston had its beginnings, as did St. George's church, in a British garrison chaplaincy. The close connection between St. George's and the military is old, real, and honorable.

II

THE "LITTLE GENTLEMAN" was paid by the Crown to work as garrison chaplain, but he was also "Curate of Kingston." He ministered to the soldiers and sailors; he also had a civilian flock. His initial headquarters was the Tête-du-Pont Barracks. This is a very important institution and physical structure.

When the British army moved from Carleton Island to Kingston in 1783-1784, it built its barracks inside the ruins of Fort Frontenac – ruins that had been made by the British when they conquered the site in 1758. The name Tête-du-Pont Barracks came into use in 1787 or 1789. The name was used until the late 1930s when the older name, Fort Frontenac, was brought back. The Tête-du-Pont was the headquarters of the British garrison until the British troops left in 1870. The barracks were then used by the Canadian military until 1939. During the Second World War, Fort Frontenac was used as a depot. A Fort Frontenac publication describes its current function as "the home of the National Defence College and the Canadian Land Forces Command and Staff College."

The Tête-du-Pont Barracks was the hub of Kingston in the 1780s because the military was absolutely central to the society and the economy of the town. Stuart conducted his services within the barracks. He explained to Charles Inglis, his bishop: "I still continue to perform divine service in a Barrack Room and preach one sermon every Sunday, and administer the sacrament four times a year. I have neither surplice, clerk, pulpit nor Communions Table; neither do I see any prospect of these wants being soon supplied."

Rev. Stuart was not altogether pleased with his civilian flock, and his description of the Loyalists is hardly consistent with many of the stereotypes we are familiar with: "My Parish," he said, "consists chiefly of the New York, loyal refugees, a description of men not remarkable for either religion, Industry or Honesty; which perhaps may be, in some measure, the Consequence of the Life they led at New York during the war – The Town of Cataraqui," Stuart continued, "has upwards of 40 houses, and the township [more or less the present Kingston] is six miles in front, and nine deep; – the number of inhabitants in both, 475 – of which 19 families are professed and 7 actual members of the Church of England. – I have experienced great discouragements in the discharge of my duty; for although I can venture to assert, that not a man in the Parish has any reasonable objection to my conduct; or, if asked, wou'd [sic] wish to have another in my Room: yet, they are careless in their attendance on public worship, dissolute in their morals, and in general, not industrious in providing even for their own families. – But this censure is only to be understood of the Bulk of the inhabitants of the Township of Kingston; for there are a few worthy families in town, who attend regularly and are an ornament to their profession."

III

STUART'S EARLY years in Kingston were not totally dominated by "discouragements." He enjoyed his initial grant of land, which was bounded on the north by what became Union Street, on the west by University, on the east by Barrie and on the south by Lake Ontario. Stuart built his house on the water. To this initial 200-acre property

Stuart added lot after lot and farm after farm. By the time he died in 1811, the Stuart family owned a minimum of 7,000 acres. Much of this property was "developed" by Stuart's son, Archdeacon George Okill Stuart, Rector of St. George's, 1811-1862. Okill Stuart's subdivision, Stuartsville, was centred on what is now the eastern part of Queen's University campus. Hence five streets were named for him: Arch, Deacon, George, Okill, and Stuart.

Rev. Stuart continued his ministry to the Mohawks, many of whom had settled a little west of Kingston. He took great pleasure in this. He also, in 1786, founded a school – no doubt the first in this district. Stuart explained: "I have erected a useful seminary, where Latin, English etc. are taught, and children carefully instructed in the Principles of Religion, as contained in the Catichissm [sic], etc. etc. The master is a man of learning and experience in his profession, and is particularly under my direction in the management of the school."

Stuart also had his optimistic moments, as he should have had because in Kingston he largely recovered from the tragedy of the Revolution. To one, Dr. White, he wrote in 1785: "I have two hundred acres within half a mile of the Garrison, a beautiful situation and tolerable good land." Later in the same letter he noted that "we are poor, happy people, and industrious beyond example. Our gracious King gives us land gratis and furnishes provision and clothing, farming utensils, etc. until next September; after which, the generality of people will be able to live without his bounty."

The greatest satisfaction for Stuart during these early years was the decision to move his flock out of the barracks and into a real church. The merchants raised some money and on 25 October 1791 the vestry resolved unanimously that the money subscribed for the purpose of erecting a church shall be immediately applied to that use." J. Douglas Stewart and Ian E. Wilson, in their excellent book, *Heritage Kingston*, quote an early source: "In consequence of this resolution, a carpenter [was] to be employed to erect a frame building of 40 by 32 feet in the clear, to weather board, shingle and floor it, also to ceil and sash it." The carpenter so employed, it might be noted, was Archibald Thomson, whose son, Hugh, was the founder of Kingston Penitentiary. This is the same family that more recently produced Lord Thomson of Fleet.

The church, styled St. George's, was indeed built and was ready for use in 1792. Rev. Stuart was pleased and described his church as "a decent commodious Edifice, [it] was plastered last of all and a temporary pulpit and reading desk erected in it. The whole expense of which was 172 pounds currency, but 28 pounds remains to be raised by subscription."

Some observers were less than complimentary. The Duke de la Rochefoucould-Liancourd looked at St. George's when it was very young and dismissed it thus: "There is but one church in Kingston, and this, though very lately built, resembles a barn more than a church." Bishop Jacob Mountain (the first Anglican bishop of Quebec, and as such Stuart's bishop) visited Kingston in 1813. He should have been more sympathetic than our French duke, but he had this to say about the first St.George's: "The church is a long, low, blue, wooden building, with square windows, and a little cupola or steeple, for the bell, like the thing on a brewery placed at the wrong end of the building."

The first St. George's might not have been beautiful but it was open for business in 1791, and for almost 200 years that building and its successors have been the heart of a vibrant Anglican community.

IV

IT IS NOT POSSIBLE in a few paragraphs to recreate the tone of the early congregation, to explain the natures of the early leaders, or to analyse the larger role played by the church in its formative years. Rather, I will present a brief series of images that might evoke some of these things.

First, a description of John Stuart by John Beverley Robinson, one of the gigantic figures in the history of Upper Canada: "There was something in Dr. Stuart's appearance that could not fail to make a most favourable impression. He was about six feet two inches in height – not corpulent, and not thin – but with fine masculine features, expanded chest, erect figure, well-formed limbs, and a free, manly carriage, improved by a fondness in his youth for athletic exercises, particularly fencing. From my recollection of him at this moment, "continued Robinson, "I should say that I have seen no one who came so fully up to the idea one is led to form of a fine old Roman – a man capable of enduring and defying anything in a good cause; incapable

– absolutely incapable of stooping to anything in the least degree mean or unworthy." Clearly Rev. John Stuart was a powerful force in the little pre-War of 1812 Kingston.

The second image implies much about the relationship between priest and congregation. J.R. Carruthers, who has written an excellent study of Stuart, tells us that he "loved to sit on the shore of Lake Ontario and play his flute." Bishop Mountain wrote that late in "the little gentleman's" life some members of his flock "brought up in the puritan school objected to a minister's 'whistling tube' as a worldly variety … he laid it aside forever – not without indulging in a smile at their absurdity – but influenced by I Cor viii 13." That particular Bible passage reads as follows: "Therefore, if food is a cause of my brother's falling, I will never eat meat, lest I cause my brother to fall."

The third image relates to Molly Brant, Joseph's sister and a powerful Mohawk leader in her own right. She had been the consort of William Johnson, who died in 1774. They lived on a 130,000-acre estate in the Mohawk country of northern New York. When the revolution broke out, she was the head of the Six Nations matrons and as such was a major leader of the the Iroquois Confederacy. She was also a fierce Loyalist who used her power to keep the Mohawks and the other components of the Six Nations loyal to the British Crown. A senior British official, Daniel Claus, described her influence: "one word from her goes farther with [the Iroquois] than a thousand from any white man without exception." When the revolutionary wars ended, she moved from Carleton Island to a house in Kingston built for her by the British authorities. Molly Brant was the only woman among the 54 "Benefactors of the Members of the English Congregation for erecting a church in Kingston." She was regular in her attendance at church, where she was described by a traveler shortly before her death in 1796: "In the church at Kingston, we saw an Indian woman, who sat in an honorable place among the English. She appeared very devout during divine service and very attentive to the sermon. She was the relict of the late Sir William Johnson … and mother of several children by him, who are married to Englishmen and provided for by the Crown: When Indian embassies arrived, she was sent for, dined at Governor Simcoe's and treated with respect by himself and his lady. During the life of Sir William, she was attended with splendor and respect and since the war, received a pension and compensation for losses for herself and her children."

The final image is that of St. George's on Sunday, 8 July 1792. On that day Upper Canada was proclaimed a separate constitutional jurisdiction in St. George's church, Kingston. That is, the civil life of our province commenced in St. George's. W.R. Riddell, the biographer of John Graves Simcoe, our first lieutenant-governor, described the event: "Simcoe appointed the Protestant Church. (St. George's) as a suitable place for opening the Royal Commissions, and on Sunday, July 8, 1792, repaired thither, accompanied by Osgoode, Russell, Baby and White, the Attorney-General, together with the principal inhabitants – the commissions were read and Simcoe took the required oaths. The Executive Council did not function until the following day, July 9, when Simcoe, now fully clothed with his office, formally appointed Osgoode, Robertson ..., Baby, Grant ... and Russell, Executive Councillors."

George Lothrop Starr, once canon of St. George's Cathedral, paints a more imaginative picture in his little book, *Old St. George's*: "The new born town with its background of virgin forest; the wigwams of the Indians in the distance; on the steps of the little wooden church stands Governor Simcoe, resplendent in his uniform of office; about him are grouped the councillors, four of whom have come from England, appointed by the Crown, and the others representing the settlers ... [including Richard Cartwright, Jr. of Kingston]. These latter would probably wear uniforms of sorts, as they were either members of the militia or had taken part in the war. Indians too are there, in their aboriginal paint and feathers, and among them the great chief [Joseph] Brant ... then a resident of Kingston. Towering above them all we can see 'the little gentleman,' Dr. Stuart, in surplice and scarf. The troops form a hollow square before the steps, and in the harbour several war sloops lie at anchor, while beyond, the blue lake sweeps away to the westward. Could there have been a fitter setting for the consolidation of those principles for which the Loyalists had fought and bled?"

The Lieutenant-Governor's wife, Elizabeth Posthuma Simcoe, attended St. George's. Mrs. Simcoe was a diarist. She described this momentous event in Canadian history in the most laconic way possible. On July 8 she wrote, "The Governor went to church and took the oaths preparatory to acting as Governor." Perhaps she was not interested in civil affairs because she was absorbed by the hobby she discovered a day earlier – forest fires. Mrs. Simcoe explained: "I walked this Evening in a wood lately set on fire, by some unextinguished fires being left by some persons who had encamped there; which in dry weather often communicates to the trees. Perhaps you have no idea," continued the worthy woman, "of the pleasure of walking in a burning wood, but I found it so great that I think I shall have some woods set on fire for my evening walks. The smoke arising from it keeps the musquitoes [*sic*] at a distance and where the fire has caught the hollow trunk of a lofty tree the flame issuing from the top has a fine effect. In some trees where but a small flame appears it looks like stars as the Evening grows dark, and the flare and smoke interspersed in different masses of dark woods has a very picturesque appearance a little like Tasso's enchanted wood."

V

CLEARLY ST. GEORGE'S, led by an impressive priest, was a dynamic and important place from the outset. However, we all know that the clerical leader of a church cannot do everything. He needs assistance in the form of what we might call "a lay infrastructure." This was established at least by 1789. The elective or appointive procedures are not totally clear, but we know that in 1789 there were two wardens, Richard Cartwright Sr. and Thomas Markland, and two vestrymen, Joseph Anderson and Michael Grass. I will conclude with a few comments about these four officials of St. George's.

Richard Cartwright Sr. was the senior member of a family that became one of the greatest in the town's history, producing such notables as Hon. Richard Cartwright, Rev. Robert Cartwright, John Solomon Cartwright, and Sir Richard Cartwright. But although he moved here in 1784 he was not really the founder of the Kingston family. That honour belongs to his son, known usually as Hon. Richard Cartwright, one of the defining figures in Upper Canadian history. Hon. Richard was active in the area independent of his father. Richard Sr. did receive land as a Loyalist, land that almost certainly went to Hon. Richard, when he, the father, died in 1794. Richard Sr. was a member of the land board and served as a magistrate.

Thomas Markland, like the Cartwrights, acquired substantial amounts of land. Like other prominent Loyalists he held militia rank, served as a magistrate (Court of Quarter Session, 1794-1826), and acted as a commissioner from time to time. In addition to acquiring and selling land, Markland was a merchant and served as the local agent for the Bank of Montreal. He was also connected with numerous philanthropic and public-spirited institutions and movements, including the Lancastrian school, the Midland District School Society, the hospital, the Kingston Compassionate Society, the Frontenac Agricultural Society, the Union Sunday School Committee, the Society for the Promotion of Christian Knowledge, the Kingston Auxiliary Bible and Common Prayer Book Society, and the Wesleyan Missionary Society. One wonders how anybody could be so good!

Joseph Anderson, the vestryman, is not a well-known figure. He was, of course, a Loyalist and a captain in the militia. Like most upper-strata Loyalists, he held a variety of appointments – magistrate and collector of customs. Anderson died in 1813.

The most interesting member of this group of four is Michael Grass, and that might be because we know more about him than we do about the others. Michael Grass, according to one reliable description, was "hard-nosed, strong-willed and suspicious of those who fomented change." He was an Alsatian who immigrated to America and ended up in the Mohawk area of northern New York. He might have been a French prisoner during the Seven Years War. If this story is true, he was a prisoner in Fort Frontenac in 1756 or 1757. We do know that in New York he was a loyalist and was persecuted as a result. He fled the Mohawk country for New York City where, through an ad in the *Royal American Gazette* (27 May 1783) he began the process of organizing a group of Loyalists targeted for settlement at Fort Frontenac. Grass was successful and led a group of Loyalist settlers to Cataraqui in 1784.

The argument that Grass should be considered the founder of Kingston has been hotly contested, then and recently. But he was *a* founder and obviously a completely worthy person. Shortly before he died he noted in the Kingston *Gazette* that he had had his creative years and then he said: "strong in my attachment to my fellow subjects, I led the loyal band, I pointed out to them the scite [*sic*] of their future metropolis, and gained for presented principles a sanctuary [,] for myself and followers a home."

VI

THE RECTORSHIP and wardenships are, by Ontario standard, very old. The rectorship dates from 1785; the wardenships from 1789. There are no civil posts with a continuous history domiciled within this province that are older. The only competitors are church-related. The Anglican church at Cornwall claims an origin from 1784 – a claim that has received a sort of endorsement from Queen Elizabeth the Second. Nonetheless, that claim has been firmly, and almost certainly correctly, disputed. The Hay Bay Methodist Church was founded in 1792; it is clearly very ancient, but not as old as St. George's. Presbyterians were active in this area at a very early date, but not on a continuous basis, it would seem, as early as Stuart and the Anglicans. In fact, the only real competitors, in terms of age, are the Roman Catholics. The oldest institution in Ontario, continuous and domiciled within the province, is Assumption Parish Church, Windsor, which has at least a generation more of continuity than St. George's. Assumption's continuity includes both priest and wardens. This means that St. George's rectorship is the third-oldest institution in Ontario; the wardenships are the fourth. Certainly these are the oldest institutions in this community. This is indeed a first-rate reason for celebration.

Personalities

View of the building on Wellington (Quarry) Street that housed the law offices of John A. Macdonald, where Alexander Campbell and Oliver Mowat articled. Around the corner on Brock Street, James Richardson ran his first business as a tailor.

Sir John Alexander Macdonald

POLITICIAN OF NATIONAL UNITY

Sir John A. Macdonald is one of a small handful of truly great Cana-
dians because of his creativity. He was one of the most creative public
men in our history.

THE GREATNESS OF Sir John Alexander Macdonald has been established beyond doubt. His political longevity is impressive; Macdonald played a major role in Canadian public life from 1847, when
he entered William Henry Draper's government, until he died in office 44 years later. During most of that long period, he was in office
and was usually first minister or leader of the Ontario wing of the
Conservative Party. Along with this incredible ability to survive went
his famous warmth, wit, and humanity. We tend to concentrate too
much attention on these aspects of the great man's life. It is as tempt-
ing to explain Macdonald through the use of a virtually unlimited
supply of anecdotes as it is to turn to his tragic personal life. This is
understandable enough. Our twentieth-century leaders have tended
to be calculating (if not always successful) manipulators, transformed
civil servants, populist crusaders, vain millionaires, and aloof intellectuals. We can empathize with Macdonald and that perhaps is why we
so often discuss his humour, corruption, family turmoil, and bouts of

---

Sir John A. Macdonald was the focus of Professor Swainson's scholarship
following his graduation from University of Toronto and appointment to
Queen's University. The result was two biographies, *Sir John A. Macdonald:
The Man and the Politician* (originally published by Oxford University Press in
1971 and in revised editions by Quarry Press in 1989 and 2011); and *Macdonald of Kingston* (published by Nelson Canada in 1979 with a preface by John G.
Diefenbaker). This article appeared in *Historic Kingston*, Vol. 28 (1980), the
publication arm of the Kingston Historical Society.

Portrait of young John A. Macdonald circa 1861-63 (Library and Archives Canada).

drinking. These things are important and help to reveal a fascinating and essentially attractive personality; they do not, however, explain Sir John's historic role.

I

SIR JOHN A. MACDONALD is one of a small handful of truly great Canadians because of his creativity. He was one of the most creative public men in our history. Look briefly at the record. He was the architect of the first of our two truly national political parties. That work was accomplished in the main before Confederation, when he removed the racist teeth of Ontario conservatism and forged an enduring alliance between his group of Ontario conservatives and George-Etienne Cartier's *bloc* of moderate French Canadians.

This political instrument gave him immense power and he used it. He brought the Conservative Party to the support of federal union and then designed Confederation and saw his scheme made into law. His first Confederation government, 1867-1873, was easily the most successful regime in Canadian history. Nova Scotia was reconciled to union. Prince Edward Island, British Columbia, and Rupert's Land were added to the Dominion. The importance of these acquisitions cannot be stressed enough. Rupert's Land alone included what is now Manitoba, Saskatchewan, Alberta, and portions of northern Quebec, Ontario, and the North-West Territories. The new constitutional system was carried into practice during these years at both federal and provincial levels, and totally new constitutions were written for Manitoba and British Columbia. The Intercolonial Railway, designed to link central Canada with the Maritime Provinces, was started and brought close to completion. The North West Mounted Police force was planned.

At the international level Sir John participated in the negotiations that led to the signing of the Treaty of Washington in 1871. He signed that treaty in spite of its unpopularity in Canada. He then used his political authority to obtain parliamentary approval of the sections that applied to Canada. Macdonald obtained some financial concessions from Britain for those parts of the treaty that were adverse to our interests, but, essentially, he supported the treaty because he was statesman enough to understand its long-term implications. Had

Canada rejected a portion of the treaty, the entire treaty would have been in jeopardy. Macdonald knew that the Treaty of Washington was the key to Anglo-American détente, and he knew as well that détente was the key to Canadian security. It became and remained the lynchpin in our external policy. Macdonald understood all this in 1871.

II

WHEN MACDONALD returned to power in 1878, he continued his creative work. The National Policy, with which he won the election, was implemented in the early budgets of his second Confederation government. The NP became the instrument that defined our federal economic structure. In 1880, Canada annexed the islands of the Arctic archipelago, thus establishing (with the exception of Newfoundland-Labrador) the opportunity for entrepreneurs willing and able to construct a transcontinental railway. The CPR was chartered and, with the active support and aid of the regime, completed in 1885. Sir John and his colleagues thus formulated the main outlines of Canadian transportation policy.

We all know about the failures and the abuses: the Riel Rebellions, the Pacific Scandal, the Gerrymander of 1882, the meetings in the Red Parlour, the inability to dispose of incompetent colleagues, the re-emergence of racism within the Ontario wing of the party, and the apparent reluctance to renew the leadership. These are important, but all of our prime ministers have made blunders and presided over disasters; however, not one can match Macdonald in the extent of success or the brilliance of creation. To use the jargon of the bureaucracy, Macdonald not only wrote the policy of federal union; he carried it through the implementation stage.

He also defended his union. From the beginning, Confederation was under attack. Nova Scotia was coerced into the union, and wanted out; huge secessionist majorities were elected in Nova Scotia in 1867, both federally and provincially. Sir John had to deal with that problem, and did. Politically he wooed Joseph Howe, and brought him into the government; financially he gave Nova Scotia "better terms." The re-arrangement of Nova Scotia's financial terms was of profound constitutional significance. Thereafter the terms of Confederation were no "fixed fact." Confederation has been under negotiation ever since. The Nova Scotia crisis was only the first. In 1869-70, Louis Riel led a provisional government at Red River. There was real fear in Ottawa that the annexation of the West might be blocked or that the United States might intervene in our affairs.

Ontario, led by Oliver Mowat after 1872, rejected the kind of centralized federalism desired by Macdonald, and waged constant political warfare against Macdonald's second government. The federal Liberal Party, in close alliance with the Grand Trunk Railway, attempted the ruin of the Canadian Pacific Railway, both politically and financially – and in London as well as in Canada. The tariff structure of the National Policy was subjected to a similar sustained assault, this one at the hands of the Liberal Party and its American allies. Louis Riel led a hapless and tragic rebellion in western Canada in 1885; his execution triggered a nationalist movement in Quebec that posed a major threat to national integrity. By the late 1880s, most of the provinces were controlled by governments dedicated to provincial rights and the erosion of the central authority necessary to a functioning federalism. The provincial premiers met in Quebec City in 1887 and argued that they possessed an authority similar to that of the Quebec Conference, and that they could re-write the terms of Confederation. All the while, the Judicial Committee of the Privy Council was ruling against a strong national government and helping to create a decentralized federal state.

Perhaps most ominous of all was the rise of an ugly divisive racism that threatened the basis of co-operation between English- and French-speaking Canadians. D'Alton McCarthy and Matthew Crooks Cameron rode the protestant horse in Ontario, while Honoré Mercier manipulated race hatred in Quebec for the benefit of the provincial Liberal Party. Prairie politicians like Joseph Martin and Thomas Greenway destroyed dualism in Manitoba and the Territories.

III

MACDONALD DEALT with each of these crises; the results were mixed, and to some of the problems there was no solution. Historians have examined these events and analysed Macdonald's solutions. Interestingly enough, however, Sir John A. Macdonald has never really been perceived as a politician of national unity. We have relegated that role to leaders like Wilfrid Laurier and Mackenzie

King. Macdonald did not, of course, wear the issue on his sleeve as has been the case with too many of his successors. Perhaps also Macdonald's Canada was too young for "unity" politics. During the generation after 1867 these things were viewed within the framework of "nation building." Historians who have studied Macdonald have adopted this perspective and have dramatized many of Macdonald's actions that might be viewed in a somewhat more mundane light.

Nonetheless, "unity" politics did not wait for the twentieth century. Sir John was a very important and often successful politician of national unity. This aspect of his career is of particular importance today when Canada is in the midst of a profound and deepening crisis of unity. What, we should ask today, were the characteristics of such politicians and the system that they constructed in the last third of the nineteenth century?

Macdonald himself was a successful lawyer and businessman who became a professional politician with a long-term commitment to public life. He was neither a visionary nor an idealist. In approach, he was infinitely pragmatic with a near perfect instinct for reality and power. His legendary ability to manage men is historically accurate. This is not to suggest that he possessed neither principles nor morals. But his principles were parameters, not a harness. He was dedicated to Canadian social structure and monarchical institutions; he was willing to be extremely flexible in the methods he employed to attain objectives that remained general and subject to redefinition. The colleagues that he attracted to his standard, men like Cartier, Tilley, Tupper, Langevin, and Campbell, shared these characteristics.

His party, upon which his success was based, was built upon these and similar men. Macdonald was not a plebiscitary leader. He surrounded himself with the best men he could get. They represented their regions and interests, and they ran their departments. The public knew who ran the show and dealt with a government that could be understood. Policies were not laundered through royal commissions, task forces, green papers, inter-departmental administrative study groups, the PMO, and a maze of cabinet committees. The cabinet was kept reasonably small, and the ministers represented their interests and regions vigorously. There were winners and losers within the Tory leadership, but the system was one that forced politicians back to those they represented.

A nineteenth-century government could atrophy, but that process was not abetted by a system that tended to isolate politicians from reality and that was based on an unseemly concentration of authority in a single leader. By what was a recognized convention, cabinet membership was related to the population of the provinces. Hence the government formed in 1867 included five Ontarians, four Quebecers (of whom three were Francophones), two Nova Scotians and two New Brunswickers. The corollary of this convention was that these ministers must be drawn from truly national political parties. Macdonald devoted vast quantities of time to the maintenance of the national nature of his party, which in turn forced the opposition to retreat from the politics of sectionalism and compete in a truly national fashion. This is why in 1887 the Liberal Party made the daring and dangerous decision to go to its area of weakness, Quebec, for a new leader. Wilfrid Laurier became Macdonald's real successor in terms of policy and leadership.

Canada was created by practicing and pragmatic politicians. They sustained it during its early years. Macdonald exemplifies the breed. This point cannot be over-emphasized. Confederation was not much influenced by generals, philosophers, messianic leaders, rebels, exiles, nationalists, intellectuals, or moralists. It was the achievement of politicians of the line, who then went out and designed political structures that enabled them to represent the people, respond to the people, and lead the nation. The system that Macdonald built was far from perfect, but it was impressive in its capacity to deliver. Modern politicians should study it; they have much to learn.

Sir John Alexander Macdonald was the architect of his country. For a generation he strove to complete and protect his design. In this crucial area, he was remarkably consistent. His views were well summarized in 1861 when he spoke about the province of Canada:

> *"Whatever you do, adhere to the Union – we are a great country, and shall become one of the greatest in the universe if we preserve it; we shall sink into insignificance and adversity if we suffer it to be broken."*

Macdonald's Legacy

THE POLITICAL STATE

Our country was created by old-fashioned pragmatic politicians, the most important being Charles Tupper, Samuel Leonard Tilley, George-Etienne Cartier, Alexander Tilloch Galt, George Brown, and John A. Macdonald. These men were members of the political elite. Not one had a strong commitment to democracy.

P RESSURE GROUPS and historical societies throughout Canada are involved in a campaign to convince the government to declare a heritage-oriented national holiday in February. Some want the holiday to be named Macdonald Day, or, perhaps more appropriately, Macdonald-Cartier Day. Others prefer the broader Heritage Day label, which can become an umbrella for virtually anything. (The City of Kingston has already declared February 15 Sir John A. Macdonald Day, and Queen's University celebrates a Heritage Day on February 22.) Still others might want to commemorate the patriation of the Canadian constitution with a Canada Day or Constitution Day.

Some of this sentiment, of course, involves little more than a desire for a long weekend during February, which is usually a dreary month. But most groups lobbying for such a holiday have a much stronger motivation. They sincerely believe that great leaders from the past and our heritage in general deserve more attention and reverence. Such people, and their numbers are increasing, represent the growing passion for knowledge about our origins, our ancestors, and our communities.

Professor Swainson returned to the subject of Kingston's foremost personality in this article published in the *Whig-Standard Magazine*, 13 February 1982, where he ingeniously connects Macdonald's personality with the defining characteristics of Canada as a nation.

Portrait of Sir John A. Macdonald by the Topley Agency, 1883 (Library and Archives Canada).

In Kingston, it is natural that such sentiment should focus on John A. Macdonald. He ranks as the leading Father of Confederation and one of our greatest prime ministers. Without doubt he is the most celebrated of all Kingstonians. When we commemorate the life and achievement of this man, what are we celebrating? What is the Macdonald heritage? What did he leave to Canadians as a legacy that can guide us, define us, and unite us?

I

A CLUE CONCERNING Macdonald's place in the Canadian imagination can be found in recent scholarly writing about Sir John and his activities. In spite of his serious shortcomings, virtually everything written about him is positive. And his shortcomings were major. His drinking was an embarrassment that weighed heavily against his effectiveness. The evidence here is particularly impressive concerning two crucial occasions.

In 1862, the government led by George-Etienne Cartier and John A. Macdonald fell when defeated on a bill to increase the strength of the Canadian militia. During the debate preceding the collapse of the administration, Macdonald was incapacitated much of the time. Donald Creighton, a very sympathetic biographer, described the situation thus: "Macdonald suddenly ceased to be the captain of the ship and became an irresponsible stowaway. He was drinking heavily; and he went on drinking heavily in complete and cheerful disregard for the Militia Bill, the Canadian government, the Conservative party, and the military necessities of the British Empire." Creighton describes this singularly ill-timed bout as a "prolonged relapse into irresponsibility."

An even more serious incident occurred in 1872-73. Macdonald, now Sir John, was prime minister leading his party in a crucial election campaign. His partner, Cartier, was ill. The annexation of British Columbia was a key issue in the campaign, as was the question of a transcontinental railway. After the election, and the results were less than definitive, the Pacific Scandal erupted. The very existence of the government was at stake. Macdonald's ministry fell on 5 November 1873.

Shortly after the regime collapsed, Alexander Morris, a former cabinet colleague of Sir John's, asked Alexander Campbell for an explanation of the fall of the government. Campbell was well placed to explain the problem. He was a member of the cabinet, a Senator, and a father of Confederation. A leading Kingstonian, he had been Macdonald's law student and partner. Senator Campbell managed several of Macdonald's Kingston campaigns. In short, he was a leading Tory insider who knew whereof he spoke. His letter to Morris is an amazing document that explains that after Macdonald won personal re-election in June 1872, he started to drink and continued to drink throughout the remainder of the campaign (elections then were staggered) and until the fall of the ministry in November 1873.

"From the time he left Kingston, after his own election," wrote the Senator, "I am very much afraid he kept himself more or less under the influence of wine, and that he really has no clear recollection of what he did on many occasions at Toronto and elsewhere after that period … I am very sorry to say that the same reason which impeded his management of the election was operating during the whole of the days the Parliament remained in Session, and we never had the full advantage either of his abilities and judgment or of his nerve and courage. A night of excess always leaves a morning of nervous incapacity and we were subjected to this pain amongst others."

This problem, which was a kind of structured irresponsibility, was by no means Sir John's only major weakness. He abused constitutional convention, as in the "double shuffle" affair of 1858. The electoral system was shamelessly manipulated; the great Gerrymander of 1882 is only the most famous of a series of such manipulations. It is generally agreed amongst historians that a major cause of the rebellion on the Saskatchewan in 1885 was the woeful neglect of the department of the interior by Macdonald, who was the responsible minister, 1878-83. His refusal to deal with the question of a successor as Tory leader helps explain the collapse of the Conservative Party in the 1890s.

These are serious matters. They are known to biographers and historians, and can be easily documented. It is not that Canadian historians have shown any hesitation about writing critical material concerning our prime ministers. Alexander Mackenzie, who replaced Macdonald for a brief period (1873-78), has been devastated. We take great delight in publicizing the quirky side of Mackenzie King. John Diefenbaker has received unfavourable attention. But for Sir

John Alexander Macdonald the blemishes are ignored, forgiven or, explained: the good press continues.

II

THE EXPLANATION might lie in the very nature of the Canadian state, and Macdonald's relation to its origin. We can all point to distinctive aspects of our country. But in one major respect it stands alone. Britain, France, and the United States, the three countries closest to Canada in tradition and culture, were created or defined by revolutions, charismatic figures, military geniuses, word-important poets, major political philosophers, and instantly recognized national documents.

This is not true of Canada, except for the influence that we absorb from other countries (as with, say, Magna Carta). Our country was created by old-fashioned pragmatic politicians, the most important being Charles Tupper, Samuel Leonard Tilley, George-Etienne Cartier, Alexander Tilloch Galt, George Brown, and John A. Macdonald. These men were members of the political elite. Not one had a strong commitment to democracy. They refused to admit the press to the conferences that drafted the Confederation agreement, and they were adamant in their position that the voters need not be involved or consulted.

Our central Canadian political leaders recorded their views of Confederation in the *Confederation Debates*, a massive volume of 1,032 pages. Many of the speeches are able and astute. Much can be learned about the origins of Canada by reading these speeches. But not one is a statement of political philosophy that matches the contents of the *Federalist Papers*, a document that constitutes a major statement of American political philosophy. Among those who fathered Confederation, there is not a single major writer, general, or charismatic leader.

Similarly our national tradition has not been shaped by Canadian Shakespeares, Paines, Cromwells, Miltons, Washingtons, Napoleons, De Gaulles, Churchills, and Robespierres. Canada has produced fine writers and brilliant thinkers, but we have no documents that impinge on the national consciousness along the lines of the *Declaration of the Rights of Man*, the *Declaration of Independence*, *Areopagitica*, *Fabian Essays*, the *Gettysburg Address*, or the *Social Contract*.

Canada was created by politicians, sustained by politicians and defined by politicians. The main line of their development, at least at the national level, has involved organizational skill and ideological pragmatism. Their chief concerns have been economic development, national units, and the largest degree of autonomy consistent with our relationship with Great Britain and the United States. Unity has been viewed from a federalist perspective, which was nicely put by George-Etienne Cartier in the *Confederation Debates*: "We could not do away with the distinctions of race. We could not legislate for the disappearance of the French Canadians from American soil, but British and French Canadians alike could appreciate and understand their position relative to each other, and their contact produced a healthy spirit of emulation. It was a benefit rather than otherwise that we had a diversity of races."

The great names in our modern period (post-War of 1812) are Robert Baldwin, Louis La Fontaine, Francis Hincks, Joseph Howe, Macdonald, Cartier, Wilfrid Laurier, Mackenzie King, and so on. Most provinces have produced similar lists. Our key documents are the *British North America Act*, the *Rowell-Sirois Report*, the constitutions of the Prairie Provinces, the *Confederation Debates* and, more recently, *the Charter of Rights* with the amending formula for the revised constitution. This is hardly the stuff of drama, and is material that is not widely read even by well-educated Canadians.

It can be argued that the system here described has been overdrawn. There are exceptions. Louis Riel is hardly a managerial politician (although during his early and creative period he was much more a typical Canadian politician than we often wish to acknowledge). Riel, who was perfectly correct when he noted, "I know that through the grace of God I am the founder of Manitoba," can be seen as a father of Confederation. William Aberhart was a rare Canadian politician who was genuinely charismatic. Numbers of French Canadian leaders have espoused a nationalist ideology that has shaken Canada to its roots. Socialist leaders, such as William Irvine and James Shaver Woodsworth, have challenged the basic tenets of Canadian society. Leading Anglophones, such as Robert Borden, Arthur Meighen, and J.L. Ralston, have pushed the cause of conscription to the point of damaging national units to the point of no return.

But these apparent exceptions really prove the point. In such sister democracies as France, the United States, and Britain, great traumas can actually help define traditions in ways that promote national cohesion. That is not true in Canada. Such traumas simply illustrate weaknesses and breakdowns in the political system. They are examples of the periodic failure of the politics of management.

There is no positive legacy from the conscription crisis – only an intensification of Francophone and Anglophone nationalisms that are mutually antagonistic. Louis Riel might be the most written about of all Canadians, but the Riel cult does nothing to pull Canada together. William Aberhart might have been a folk figure on the prairies, but his influence has led to an intensification of the Alberta garrison mind, which hardly conduces to national well being. Even the most casual observer can see that Francophone nationalism is a threat to Canada, and that it must be contained if the country is to function successfully.

The recent revisions to the constitution, which are of fundamental importance to the future development of Canada, are characteristic of the Canadian way. The amending formula and charter of rights are sufficiently unreadable to be safe from popularity as documents of national definition. We can be sure that future generations of Canadians will ignore them. They will be known only to politicians, judges, lawyers, and academic specialists. These crucial documents, like the original Confederation agreement, were drafted by senior political leaders and advisors with neither public involvement nor approval. The press was not allowed to view anything that was really crucial; the electorate will have little opportunity to say anything. Of course, all of this was done for the most traditional and noble of Canadian motives: Our political leadership moved to contain dangerous pressures, prevent breakdown within the system, and enable increased federal supervision of the economy.

III

IT IS THIS tradition of Canada that explains Macdonald's position in the Canadian psyche. He is the most visible and important of those who created this political nation. To denigrate John A. Macdonald is to cast in doubt the legitimacy of the Canadian state.

His perennial good press is perhaps not explained quite so

blatantly. We are reluctant to accept the centrality of politics in our system and have been less than explicit in much of our historical analysis. Our understanding of the nature of the Canadian state has often been as much intuitive as analytical. Nonetheless, the fact remains that without Macdonald the origins of Canada become inexplicable. A ravaged Macdonald is a shaky foundation upon which to build an understanding of Canada. We need a positive Macdonald in order to have a nation sanctified by legitimate origins.

This then is the key to the Macdonald heritage. We are a political nation and in all likelihood can be nothing else. Certain implications flow from such a definition of Canada.

A recurring Canadian theme is the quest for our cultural identity. We are constantly at work in this area. We have a Canada Council to endow the arts. Recently, the government moved to save Canadian periodicals. Radio and television are regulated in the interests of Canadian content. From time to time we mount an agitation to maintain the national purity of our universities. We seem to be on the brink of cultural annihilation, and it would seem that we have been in that uncomfortable situation for eons.

Subsidizing Canadian culture is perfectly reasonable; if anything, we should amplify such programs. But the health of the Canadian state is not dependent on the creation of cultural forms and standards that are distinctively Canadian. That is not why Canada was founded. On the contrary, a key motive for the founding of a political state was a desire to accommodate cultural diversity. And, be it noted, much of that culture was directly imported from Britain, France, and the United States, or heavily derivative of the cultures of those countries. We do not know a great deal about the reading habits of some of our leaders, but we do know a bit. John A. Macdonald was an omnivorous reader; so was Pierre Elliott Trudeau. Their reading lists are both massively foreign in content. It is almost a certainty that Trudeau has read more good Canadian literature than had been written by the time Macdonald died in 1891. Does it matter? Not likely; the two men share something far more Canadian – an intuitive understanding of the nature of the Canadian state.

We should not begrudge the CBC its budget. It should be encouraged to foster Canadian talent and produce Canadian shows. But those who prefer *Lou Grant* to *The National* are not weakening the

Canadian fabric. They are simply responding to foreign stimuli as Canadians always have and always will.

The nature of the Canadian state has serious implications for various types of scholarship, and especially for historical research. Much Canadian research about Canada is methodologically derivative; in fact, for some Canadian historians innovation consists of little more than slipping some Canadian content into a borrowed interpretation. A few years ago numbers of our historians began to react against what they felt to be an excessive concern with politics. The "limited identities" school emerged, and all sorts of scholars devoted themselves to studying regions, towns, children, ethnic groups, workers, working class culture, women, and strikes.

All of this is perfectly reasonable; such themes merit attention and it is healthy that they are now the subject of rigorous analyses. For our purposes, the interesting aspect of this development is the absence of politics. Without politics there is no Canada, and that became increasingly obvious as members of this school published ever increasing quantities of books and articles. They could find no way to define or describe Canada once politics had ceased to be the centre of analysis. J.M.S. Careless, one of the founders of this school, reviewed its work in 1980. In an article entitled "Limited Identities – ten years later," he noted: "Altogether, limited identities threaten to take over, and settle the matter of a Canadian national identity, by ending it outright, leaving perhaps a loose league of survivor states essentially existing on American outdoor relief."

Needless to say, the intensely political nature of our country has its influence on our thinking about politics and politicians. At the present time we tend to be cynical about our leaders, or even angry. The current consensus is perhaps summed up by a comment made by Bod Edwards of the Calgary *Eye-Opener* more than 50 years ago: "Now I know what a statesman is; he is a dead politician. We need more statesmen." This sort of view is reiterated in a variety of formats. Our politicians are often presented as over-paid louts who protect their salary and pensions while the rest of the country goes to hell. Cartoonists ridicule them; those who call open line programs abuse them. Joe Clark is the butt of dozens of nasty jokes; many Canadians hate Pierre Elliott Trudeau with a passion usually saved for the leaders of invading armies. Allan MacEachen is regarded as a mindless predator bent on destroying the economy in one swoop. During the recent constitutional crisis, the intemperance with which we described politicians we oppose was appalling. One fears that unless we exercise some restraint we will wreck the parliamentary, judicial, and bureaucratic instruments that are the basis of our ordered democracy.

It might be that our politicians simply get the abuse that they deserve. On the other hand, it might be that we over-react for reasons rooted in our political culture. Our cynicism might be the reverse side of hope; anger and bitterness the reverse side of positive expectation. Perhaps we become so nasty about our leaders because we expect so much from them. When we experience collective difficulty, we turn as if by instinct to the prime minister and the premiers. The control the governments of Canada and we expect the state to solve our problems. The state and the political system play an enormous role in our society because Canada is so much a political nation.

A similar analysis might explain our peculiar attitude toward Prime Minister Trudeau. It is doubtful that Canadians have been so ambivalent about any national leader. During his first campaign as prime minister, he was mobbed by adoring crowds. The word "Trudeaumania" was added to Canadian English. In 1970, Canadians were united in admiration when he dealt firmly with the FLQ crisis and invoked the awesome authority of the War Measures Act. His popularity then plummeted and he came within an ace of losing the election in 1972. Two years later, armed with a young, beautiful, and apparently ingenuous wife, he was restored to public favor and won a decisive majority in a general election.

His career after 1974 was checkered. The election of Rene Levesque and the Parti Quebecois in Quebec in 1976 made Trudeau appear indispensable, but that credit was quickly shot, and by 1979 his unpopularity was a major issue in the election. He lost, and after a bit announced his retirement from public life. Then occurred the most amazing political resurrection in Canadian history. The Clark government fell; Trudeau cancelled his retirement and was restored to the leadership. He went on to win a Liberal majority in the House of Commons. The ambivalence continued. Virtually all Canadian federalists were filled with admiration when he intervened in the Quebec referendum on independence in 1980. His intervention was highly successful. But his constitutional initiatives and energy policy have provoked much opposition, and the recent management of the economy has resulted in apoplectic rage in many quarters. Trudeau is now as unpopular in English Canada as he was in 1972 or 1979.

Of course, there is nothing unusual about popular politicians losing their popularity. Both Margaret Thatcher and Jimmy Carter shed substantial popularity and trust. What is unusual about the Canadian case is the combination of unpopularity and political success. Trudeau has at crucial times been as unpopular as any of our national leaders. At the same time he has won four general elections. Only John A. Macdonald, Wilfrid Laurier, and William Lyon Mackenzie have equaled or bettered that record.

It would seem that Canadians expected enormous results from Trudeau, and go on expecting such results. Their anger is disappointment at his inability or unwillingness to deliver. Perhaps this anger becomes irrational because of the intuition that Trudeau's failings are Canada's failings. In a grudging sort of way we have made a politician who is representative of much in our political tradition a symbol of the modern Canadian state. We keep electing him to office because we have faith (or want to have faith) in our system. When he fails, the system fails and our disappointment and fear become irrational.

Has all of this taken us too far from Sir John Alexander Macdonald? Not really. The real Macdonald heritage is the Canadian state and his relationship with that state during its birth and formative years. Canada was created by a particular group of people for specific reasons. Once we understand our origins, we will function in a much more mature and sensible manner. Canada is more the creature of politicians than any of those sister democracies with whom we share cultural traditions. The politicians of the 1860s hammered out the Confederation agreement so that the northern portions of this continent (the residue of Britains's North American empire) could have unity and order under a strongly centralized national government. The primary function of the state was to promote prosperity and economic growth. Cultural pluralism was assumed. The Fathers of Confederation had no intention whatever of creating a Canadian culture that could define Canadians in ways that Englishmen and Frenchmen have been defined by their cultural traditions.

This kind of state involves certain very clear necessities. Without the kind of cultural cohesion prevalent in such countries as France and

Britain, Canadians cannot be mobilized into a national entity. When this has been tried, especially during the First World War, the result has been massive disunity and major danger to our national existence. Ideological agitations are threats because they rarely (if ever) grip more than a few groups of citizens. The quest for cultural identity is fruitless, because it defies the nature and purposes of Canada.

This is not the stuff of epic history, but our tradition should not be denigrated. When Canada functions well it is as a prosperous and pluralistic society. Pluralism permits a wide variety of thought and opinion, and helps assure the maintenance of substantial freedom within a society that must be ordered in the interests of cohesion.

More than any other Canadian, Sir John A. Macdonald serves as the embodiment of the Canadian state. By all means let us celebrate his achievement and heritage. In the process, we should learn a little about who we are and how our country functions.

Sir Henry Smith

AND THE POLITICS OF THE UNION

Because these political groups were cadre organizations, the individual members are worth studying in their own rights. One such man was Henry Smith of Kingston, who left behind enough evidence to permit an episodic study of his career.

THE POLITICAL process in pre-Confederation Ontario often involved a socially democratic give and take between politicians and the limited number of men who possessed the franchise. John A. Macdonald, for example, is well known for the practice of a kind of politics that had certain democratic characteristics. He was a warm, friendly man who was easily accessible, personally or by correspondence, to a large number of persons through the province. He asked all sorts of people, from a variety of walks of life, for favours – and reciprocated whenever possible. When an election was called, he sent out dozens of his famous little letters to men with votes or influence, regardless of their social standing. He remembered the names of thousands of humble Canadians, who were consequently assured that he and they were one. During a campaign, he mingled with the general public, drank with the men, and made all sorts of voters feel that they were intimates with the powerful. Throughout his life Macdonald wore lightly the trappings of high office and great power. Informality was the mark of the man, as it was of several other leading pre-Confederation figures.

This article first appeared in *Ontario History*, Vol. 66, No. 3 (September 1974) and shows Professor Swainson's fascination with this remarkable generation of politicians, statesmen, and businessmen who came to prominence in nineteenth-century Kingston.

Portrait of Sir Henry Smith (Library and Archives Canada).

This appearance of social democracy should not be allowed to confuse us about the essential nature of the exercise of political authority in pre-Confederation Canada. The politics of the Union were not democratic, at least not in ways implied by that word today. Parties and leadership groups were cadre in nature. They were not based upon extensive extra-parliamentary organizations, nor were they managed along internally democratic lines. Parties or groups were dominated by established personnel, whose rise was by no means occasioned by democratic influences or procedures. Once entrenched, such men often retained positions of authority for long periods of time. These men were, of course, receptive to societal pressures; they managed each other, engaged in factional warfare, modified their thinking, and were on occasion forced to adopt new policies. The personnel changed as men died, retired, or were defeated. Backbenchers might be simple tools of powerful regional leaders; often, however, they were men of substance and local power who could and did challenge their party leaders, sometimes successfully. The number of men active in politics at the parliamentary level was relatively small. Because these political groups were cadre organizations, the individual members are worth studying in their own rights. One such man was Henry Smith of Kingston, who left behind enough evidence to permit an episodic study of his career.

I

HENRY SMITH JR. was born in London, England, on 23 April 1812.[1] His family, whose motto was "Pour Bien Agir Il Faut Bien Penser,"[2] immigrated to Canada before 1818, and settled in Montreal , where young Henry was sent to Dr. Workman's private academy.[3] Other relatives also settled in Canada. One of his uncles immigrated at the same time and became "the first manager of the Bank of British North America, in Toronto."[4] Another uncle moved to Canada because he was unable to find employment in London. A relative explained to Henry Smith Sr.: "This will be conveyed to you by your brother Benjamin who has been ineffectually trying to get into employment here, but such is the difficulty, owing in a great measure to the distress of the times, that he has resolved to try his fortune in Canada."[5] The Smiths left England for economic reasons, and regarded Canada as a land of opportunity.

After a brief sojourn in Montreal, the Smith family moved west to Kingston. Henry Jr. completed his formal education at the district grammar school, where he commenced a long-standing friendship with John Alexander Macdonald.[6] Henry Jr., like most Kingstonians of the day, was a committed Conservative at any early age. As a teenager he served as a campaign worker for the local Family Compact leader, Alexander Hagerman, who was impressed by the boy's qualities. As a result, Hagerman took young Henry into his law office as a student in articles.[7] When Hagerman "was temporarily elevated to the bench,"[8] Smith was transferred, at least for a time, to the office of Thomas Kirkpatrick, an influential lawyer and local politician.

These were difficult days for young Henry, who found his life painful. For a while he was bitterly estranged from his family. In 1831, he wrote a pathetic letter to his mother:

> I am afraid I have taken a cold … I care little for this, as bodily pains are of little consequence in comparison to mental. I have not been at the office since Monday nor do I intend to at present. Mr. H[agerman] informed me that my dear brother is unwell but I am deprived of the pleasure *at present* of seeing him … I cant [*sic*] inform you where I put up at present as I have promised secrecy, my bed is very good but I dont [*sic*] sleep, my meals are here, there, and everywhere … I am anxious to make a reconciliation with my father, as it is my opinion a separation equally painful for us both, should I not be able to do so, I shall leave this place and endeavour to serve out my time with some obscure country lawyer to whom my services will be more valuable than they are considered at present. As for Mr. Kirkpatrick, he is a mean base fellow … Instead of our family motto "pour bien agir il faut bien penser" I shall adopt the following "mihi pax non est." I did not think my dear mother I could have written such a letter to you after the manner in which you scolded [?] me on Monday.

An even more pathetic P.S. follows:

> don't fail to send me trousers socks and [illegible] or something else to put on my feet as they are cramped with wet … destroy this sheet.[9]

Henry survived the horrors of adolescence and was admitted to the bar of Upper Canada in 1834.[10] He became a very successful lawyer, "noted for his ability in addressing a jury;"[11] his standing was recognized in 1846 when he was made a Queen's Counsel.[12]

As early as 1836 he attended "term" in Toronto, which he described as "this dirty place."[13] In due course he acquired the Kingston business of the Grand Trunk Railway.[14] Like many of his fellow lawyers, he speculated in land, with holdings as distant as Prince Edward County, and as early as 1841 he was "a holder of landed property in several parts of [Frontenac County]."[15] He "acquired a good deal of property as a Trustee as well as for his own behalf ... For example, he took out Patents for a number of his constituents, and, having in many instances, advanced part of the money for the purpose, occasionally took the Patents in his own name."[16] When he died his mortgages and land holdings were so large that he was obviously a man of considerable wealth.

Smith was a professional, political, and social confidant of John A. Macdonald. As early as 1838 they collaborated in the representation of John Ashley against Colonel Henry Dundas. In this spectacular case, which was an extremely unpopular suit for illegal arrest, Smith was the senior counsel, with Macdonald acting "in support of Smith."[17] They won £200 damages, in spite of the fact that Christopher Hagerman represented Colonel Dundas.[18] In 1848, Smith cooperated with Macdonald and others in the formation of a literary club, modeled on the Wistar Association of Philadelphia, "for the cultivation of literature – for the discussion (under proper restrictions) of the various subjects which ought to interest society – and for the formation of a library." They agreed "to unite themselves in such an Association under the name of The Cataraqui Club."[19]

Macdonald and Smith were political intimates throughout the 1840s and most of the 1850s. Macdonald regarded Smith as a "confidential man"[20] and regularly confided to him private information about government policy and ministerial colleagues. The two men showed a great affection for Kingston and boosted their town whenever possible. In 1855, for example, Macdonald proudly reported to Smith: "As soon as the Court House is finished we will build a Custom House and Post Office, thus getting up three fine public buildings in old Kingston."[21] On another occasion, Macdonald bragged to Smith:

"I am going to carry all we want for Kingston, if the people have common sense."[22] Smith was trusted with most irreverent comments: "We are to have a *short sharp and decisive* session, like a jackasses gallop."[23] So close were the two men in the mid-1850s, that in 1856 Smith agreed to assist Macdonald in an affair of "honour."

Macdonald had engaged in a nasty public quarrel with Colonel Arthur Rankin, MPP for Essex, but felt that his possible responses were constrained by a promise he had made to the speaker. He asked Smith, as "my friend," to intervene and to explain to Rankin that if he would repeat outside the House "any of the injurious expressions" used in the House, "you will take notice of them on my behalf and make the necessary arrangements with any friend he may refer you to. I need scarcely say that circumstanced as I am, any meeting must take place out of Canada."[24] Macdonald's quarrel with Rankin was settled in another way, but this incident reveals the degree to which the two men were friends. Another revealing incident occurred in the same year. Late in 1856, Sir Allan MacNab was forced out of the premiership and out of the cabinet. This was a controversial and bitterly debated manoeuvre. It is interesting to note that Macdonald unburdened himself to Henry Smith: "I might, as you know have been Premier but I refused, and insisted on Tache's claims, lest it might be said that in putting McNab out, I was exalting myself."[25]

Once a member of the bar, Smith prospered professionally and became a member of John A. Macdonald's circle of close friends and political cronies. His domestic life reflects this affluence and prestige that came at a young age. An Anglican who belonged to the "Church of Saint George,"[26] Smith was married to Mary (1813-82), "eldest daughter of Robert Talbot … of Kingston [by] the Venerable Archdeacon Stuart."[27] His father-in-law was a member of the local upper crust. In 1851, Smith bought Roselawn, an "elegant country home … [in] a fashionable area, north of the Governor General's residence ."[28] This beautiful home, now owned by Queen's university, remained in the Smith family until 1888. Henry and Mary proceeded to have numerous children, at least two of whom, Henry Maud and Mary Elizabeth, died as infants.[29]

Smith was not involved in local politics at the electoral level, but he did serve his old district grammar school as a trustee and as secretary to the board.[30] He was part of the group that planned "an imposing reception for Governor Sydenham"[31] when he arrived in Kingston in 1841, and he was active in the militia, receiving an appointment as "Lieutenant Colonel of the 1st Battalion Frontenac" in 1848. [32] For recreation, Smith hunted, and was "completely wedded to his gun."[33] His regular "sporting excursions in the distant townships"[34] of Frontenac county brought him into contact with a number of usually ignored voters, and strengthened him in his electoral contests.

II

HENRY SMITH entered Union politics in 1841 when at the age of 29 he was elected MPP for Frontenac in a factionalized contest between several contenders. He held the seat without interruption until 1861,[35] when he was defeated. *The Globe* described Smith as "a Conservative of the extreme school,"[36] but he was really a moderate of the Sydenham-Draper-Macdonald school. This was made clear in his first election address: "Hitherto the affairs of the Province have been greatly mismanaged ... In the appointment of a Statesman to preside over our destinies, under whose able administration this fine Province has already attained a degree of prosperity heretofore unknown, may be seen the watchful care of the Home Government for our welfare."[37] Smith also campaigned (regularly) on the policy of agricultural protection: "I pledge myself to use my utmost exertions to protect the agricultural interests of the Province against the losses now sustained by it in the introduction of American Produce free of duty, whereby the farmers of our country are subjected to the mortification of witnessing the departure of large sums of money to a foreign state, which ought to reach the pockets of our fellow subjects."[38] As a member of the Assembly, Smith was reasonably prominent. He rarely gave lengthy speeches, but intervened in debate on innumerable occasions – usually on items relating to disputed elections, local problems, agricultural protection, game preservation, the management of the assembly and legal administration.[39]

III

ALTHOUGH HENRY Smith was never a major politician, he did
obtain prominence (or notoriety) on several occasions. Henry
Smith's name first achieved province-wide notoriety because of his
father, Henry Smith Sr., who was appointed warden of the provincial
penitentiary near Kingston (in his son's riding) when the institution
opened in 1835. Henry Sr. was a public servant, but he was also an active Conservative. As he explained to Macdonald: "With regard to the
election for Kingston it was proved that I asked a Keeper to prevail on
his brother to vote for one of the Candidates who was at the time a
member of the Government,[40] which it was my duty to support. There
is no law to prevent the warden from interfering at elections, but of
course it would not be tolerable that he should [use] his influence
against the existing government."[41] The warden also worked closely
with his son, who in turn defended the interests of the penitentiary
(as defined by his father) and its warden in the provincial assembly.
The power of the Smiths was enhanced by their close friendship with
John A. Macdonald, the rising star of the Conservative Party. The
Smiths used their power crudely and for personal benefit; in 1846
Henry Jr. succeeded in pushing a Penitentiary bill through Parliament. This strengthened Warden Smith against his many enemies
within the prison system by increasing "the power and salary attached
to the Warden's post, while decreasing those of the Deputy Warden."[42]
As a consequence, the prison inspectors resigned, enabling Smith and
his allies to appoint friendly inspectors.

Conditions within the prison were grim. Appointments were made
on the basis of favoritism, dismissals were often designed to stifle criticism and punish enemies, salaries of enemies were arbitrarily reduced,
the financial administration was in shambles and prisoners were regularly given punishments that revolted even that callous age. One illustration will explain why a twentieth-century observer described Smith
and his colleagues as "sadistic, grating, illiterate ... monsters."[43] On
Christmas eve 1844, an eleven-year-old French Canadian was given
twelve lashes. His offence? Speaking French![44] It is hardly surprising that this barbaric, corrupt, and highly politicized prison administration should become a target for Reform attack, especially after

conditions deteriorated to the point that the highly respected prison doctor irrevocably split with Smith and provided damaging evidence to prison reformers. The result was the appointment of an investigatory commission after the electoral triumph of L.H. La Fontaine and Robert Baldwin in 1848. The commission, dominated by its secretary George Brown, carried out its work in 1848-49. The result was a series of lurid disclosures that shocked observers and led to the dismissal of Warden Smith.

John A. Macdonald defended the Smiths in Parliament, and in the process became the mortal enemy of George Brown. This feud between the Smiths and the Reformers (who were assisted by local allies) helped to poison the already bitter politics of the union. Needless to say, Henry Smith Jr. would never again be an obscure, if influential, backbencher. During the penitentiary controversy, he and his father received an enormous amount of usually adverse press exposure.[45]

IV

HENRY SMITH JR. was a controversial figure, but he was politically useful to Macdonald and the upper Canadian Conservatives during the grim period of Reform ascendancy after 1848: he was one of the few moderate Tories able to hold his seat between 1848 and 1854. He was useful in the House and seemed to enjoy baiting Reformers, especially Francis Hincks. He also worked closely with Macdonald in the management of the eastern Ontario district.[46] If the degree of fervor of opposition attack was evidence of Smith's usefulness to the Conservative Party, he must have been very useful indeed. In 1851, his opponent, Kenneth Mackenzie, referred to "the UTTER, the TOTAL uselessness of HENRY SMITH as a public servant" and applied to Smith such descriptive words as "Treachery," "Neglect," "Hypocrisy," "Total Incompetency," "Deceit" and "Degradation."[47] Smith's loyalty to the party was rewarded in 1854 when he entered the Allan MacNab – A.N. Morin ministry as Solicitor-General West. He served from September 11, 1854 – February 24, 1858,[48] but was never given cabinet rank. He won the required by-election on 28 September 1854 with ease.[49]

Henry Smith was not a distinguished solicitor-general, and it is safe to assume that Attorney-General Macdonald exercised close supervision over the junior justice portfolio. While in office, Smith rarely spoke, and when he did, his concern was usually a mundane administrative matter.[50] There were some exceptions. Twice in 1856 he delivered vigorous attacks against George Brown because of Brown's earlier assaults on Henry Smith Sr.[51] In March 1857, he introduced an Independence of Parliament Bill, explaining that "it would ultimately have the effect of removing from the House any honorary gentlemen receiving payment for his services, under the Government," except, of course, in the case of ministers.[52] It was an obscure provision of this act that permitted Macdonald and several of his colleagues to return to office without by-elections after the summary defeat of the George Brown – A.A. Dorion government in 1858. This statute made the famous "double shuffle" possible.

Smith easily won re-election to the sixth union Parliament, after which he was removed from the ministry and installed as Speaker of the Assembly. He served as speaker, 25 February 1858 – 10 June 1861.[53] This was a controversial appointment. Macdonald moved that Smith be elected speaker, justifying his choice with the comment "that Mr. Smith was one of the oldest [that is, most experienced members now sitting in Parliament."[54] Cartier, who seconded the motion, observed that Smith "spoke French sufficiently well to be able to follow the drift of a discussion, however long and intricate."[55] It has been traditional under responsible government to attempt to select speakers who hold the confidence of opposition and government parties alike. This tradition was by no means fixed during the Union, when the speakership was often the subject of partisan dispute. The decision to impose Henry Smith on the Assembly was flagrantly political. The opposition was aghast. *The Toronto Globe* spoke for Upper Canadian Reformers when it was rumored that Smith was to be the government's nominee. His elevation to the speakership, argued the *Globe*, was a confession that he could not survive another session as solicitor-general:

> The selection shows a lamentable lack of material, for one less
> qualified to fill the chair could hardly be found ... He is a rash,
> hot-headed partizan [*sic*], the foremost in every fight, who would
> not only be very objectionable to the Opposition, but would not
> command the respect even of his own side of the Assembly. As a
> member of the House, he has been famous as the ringleader of

those who defied its rules ... It is confidently asserted that he was the happy inventor of that peculiar sound, produced by scraping the edge of the sole of hon. Members' highblows against their desks, which added so much to the liveliness, if it detracted from the dignity of the House.[56]

Brown opposed his election on the floor of the Assembly: "There were many other members who, by position, temper and general demeanor, would be much better entitled to the office."[57] When the vote took place on February 25, Smith was elected by a margin of seventy-nine to forty-two.[58] Profound humiliation was caused by the fact that a majority of Upper Canadian members voted in the negative.[59]

Smith was not properly qualified for the post, but he tried his best. At openings, he adorned himself with lace ruffles, and he "ordered a full bottomed wig from England."[60] He was also able to create an impression of authority and control: "his voice ... loud and ponderous ... penetrated to the utmost recesses of the house."[61] It is also clear that he was willing to make at least some non-partisan appointments; he appointed a son of William Lyon Mackenzie to an assembly clerkship.[62] Unfortunately, Smith was not a successful speaker. The opposition disliked him intensely, as would be expected of anyone connected with the regime that perpetrated the notorious "double shuffle," and he alienated several legislative councillors who regarded him as "rude and harsh."[63] His "reign [was made] memorable by an ill-judged collision with the members of the press:"[64] "Mr. Speaker Smith ... has managed to tread – and we dare say pretty heavily – upon Mr. Correspondent's favorite corns ... [I]f his temper has sometimes been too much tried by correspondents, and others difficult to satisfy, it is not to be wondered at."[65] His speakership ended in a quarrel with the government that led to a public breach between Smith and Macdonald.[66]

V

LITTLE DIRECT evidence relates to Smith's personal social aspirations in 1859-60. Circumstantial evidence makes clear, however, that either Smith strongly pushed a personal claim or was publicly humiliated because it was widely assumed that he was in the grip of personal ambition.

In the 1850s, Canadians were possessed by railroad mania. The decade saw a tremendous boom in railroad expansion, and great pride in what was regarded as a major national achievement. The most important enterprise was the construction of the Grand Trunk Railway, which ran from Detroit through Canada to Portland, Maine. Perhaps the most impressive single component of this great railway system was completed in 1859. This was a two-mile long bridge across the St. Lawrence at Montreal.[67] Many Canadians felt that this achievement should be suitably marked. What could be more suitable than to invite Queen Victoria herself to come to Canada to open this great bridge, which would be named in her honour?

Almost certainly with Smith's connivance, the matter was brought before the assembly in 1859, and an address was passed inviting Queen Victoria to come to Canada to preside at the official opening of the Victoria Bridge. Instead of forwarding the address through Governor General Sir Edmund Head, the assembly resolved that Speaker Smith should deliver the address in person. He did, and that was the beginning of his downfall.

During the summer of 1859, Smith spent several months in Britain. On the face of it, the visit was a success. Smith, a hometown boy who had made good, enjoyed himself, and was pleased and impressed by the reception he received as Canada's first commoner.[68] He saw the sights, visited Paris, and bought £1250 worth of books for the parliamentary library.[69] His visit was capped by a successful meeting with the Queen. The London *Times* described the scene: "Before the Levee Her Majesty received … a deputation from Canada composed of the Hon. Henry Smith, Speaker of the Commons of Canada, Mr. Hector Langevin, Mayor of Quebec … The deputation presented an address to Her Majesty that she may be graciously pleased to visit Canada on the occasion of the opening of the Victoria Bridge in 1860."[70] The Queen declined the invitation but agreed that her son, the Prince of Wales, would tour Canada in 1860 and represent the Crown at the official opening of the bridge.

Henry Smith's travels occasioned considerable controversy in Canada. Some were displeased at the expense involved; others claimed that his purpose was to obtain a knighthood. Smith became the butt of a considerable quantity of nasty publicity. One newspaper put it this way: "Pickings – Mr. not-to-be-knighted Speaker Smith has been debited with $2,000, in compensation for his expenses out of the late trip to England, when he hoped to rise up Sir Henry, but did not. The sum of $401 has been appropriated in payment of the expenses of the Governor to St. Maurice."[71] Smith was subjected to crude humour. W.F. Powell, M.P.P. for Carleton, suggested: "It had been contended that there was not much good in a title, but he thought there were some names so very common as to need a little to save them from oblivion. Jones, Brown and Smith, were all names to which a title would lend a little dignity."[72]

This sort of reaction was embarrassing, but the real sting was in another place. The evidence makes clear that Smith wanted a knighthood, and that the Canadian government refused to support him in his desire for elevation. A document in the *Newcastle Papers*, probably written by Sir Edmund Head, makes this clear: "At this moment [Smith] is very angry because the ministers [illegible] will not recommend his appointment." An attached letter continues, "I am decidedly of opinion that it is better *not* to confer on [Smith] the honour of knighthood. He is a vain ... man." Even his own friends did not support his claim.[73] This rift between Smith and his Conservative colleagues was exploited by Conservatives and Reformers alike. J.B. Robinson bluntly asked whether the government requested a knighthood for Smith.[74] He received no useful reply. D'Arcy McGee, still a Reformer in 1860, blandly suggested that Smith had been slighted by being denied a knighthood while in London. Why was this a slight? Because while Smith was in England the Speaker of the Barbados House was knighted. Why was he knighted? Because Smith's old enemy Francis Hincks was the Governor of the Barbados. This led McGee to a conclusion that was very embarrassing to Smith: either the Canadian government had declined to recommend that Smith receive the coveted honour, or Francis Hincks had more influence in London than the Canadian government.[75] Smith was no doubt mortified by his predicament.

In the late summer of 1860, the Prince of Wales arrived in Canada to commence his royal tour. His arrival involved the usual pomp, ceremony, and splendor. The Parliament Buildings in Quebec City were transformed into a royal palace. He took possession on 21 August 1860 and held a levee on the same day. The scene is well worth describing in the words of a contemporary witness:

The Council Chamber, in accordance with the original designs, has been fitted out as a reception-room, in which the levee is to be held. A velvet carpet covers the floor: a costly affair. Upon a white ground, are worked groups of flowers in many brilliant colours, purple and yellow predominating. The Speaker's gilded chair stands upon its accustomed scarlet dais ... There he took his seat upon the throne, surrounded by high Civil, Military, and Naval Personages, all in uniform.[76]

Dignitaries were presented to the Prince. First came the Legislative Councillors, led by their speaker, Narcisse Belleau. Speaker Belleau presented an address, to which the Prince replied. He then did an unexpected thing: he knighted Narcisse Belleau. "No one was certain that this great event was really going to take place, and those assembled were somewhat surprised."[77] Next in order of precedence were the members of the legislative assembly. They appeared, led by their speaker. The inevitable address was presented. "Then the Honourable Henry Smith ... knelt and was also knighted."[78] Poor Smith. He had obtained the honour he wanted, but only after suffering public humiliation and a great deal of very damaging publicity. He must have been a very bitter man as he contemplated the ironic story of his transformation into *Sir* Henry Smith.

VI

SIR HENRY WAS so politically dissatisfied by 1861 that he was ready to terminate his long association with the Conservative Party. More was involved than personal pique, although the knighthood incident was probably the final straw. Political life began to sour for Smith in 1858. From 1854 to 1858 he was Solicitor-General West. In 1858, he was elected Speaker. This was a demotion, and an expensive one: "Mr. Smith gave up an office worth, one way or another, some £1,500 a-year for the arduous position of Speaker ..., the entire emoluments of which do not exceed £800 a-year."[79] Politically, it was not only a demotion but a dead end. Smith had been rejected from the ministry and was not even successful as Speaker. He was also on bad terms with the government over his knighthood. Consequently, he knew in 1861 that his political career was over. The back benches had no attractions for Sir Henry.

In addition to these sources of discontent, Smith had a policy disagreement with the regime. He had always had a tinge of Upper Canadian sectionalism and concomitant anti-French sentiment. In 1846, for example, he explained "that the hon. Member for Berthier had stated that the people of Lower Canada were not represented in the ministry, he (Mr. Smith) thought that they could only blame themselves for this, for they had identified themselves with the minority of Upper Canada ... if the members from Lower Canada have made so bad a selection as to unite with the hon. Member from the Fourth Riding of York, they must suffer the consequences."[80] Upper Canadian sectionalism, combined with a profound suspicion of French Canada, has usually been associated with George Brown and his followers. Numerous Conservatives, however, shared these sentiments, and they helped contribute to the factionalism that wracked Upper Canadian conservatism during the Union.

In the 1850s, Brown made "representation by population" a popular rallying cry, and in the process put Upper Canadian Conservatives on the defensive. It is hardly surprising to discover that a number of Macdonald's followers adopted rep-by-pop, especially after the census of 1861 proved that Upper Canada's population was substantially and irrevocably larger than that of Lower Canada. It is even less surprising to learn that in 1861 Sir Henry Smith was one of those "plainly all in favour of electoral reform."[81] After all, he had sectionalist urges; he was at odds with his party; if he was to have a political future he needed a new party; and, much conventional wisdom in 1861 was to the effect that Macdonald, Cartier and their Liberal-Conservative coalition were doomed.

Smith knew that he was loathed by the opposition, but he probably also knew that if he secured re-election he (or anybody else with a parliamentary vote) would be acceptable to the Reform leaders. In the spring of 1861, he began to build a bridge to the Reformers. William McDougall explained the process to George Brown:

> I give you a few stories bruited about here ... The Census Returns have worked wonders [concerning rep-by-pop]. Even Cauchon admits that the present regime is at an end. Speaker Smith is also among the prophets of evil. He says the game is played out, that reconstruction is impossible[,] that John A. is done – that *he* can

beat him if he pleases in Kingston. He seems to be bitterly hostile to John A. [S]ays they have not spoken for some time. [W]ishes to know what we intend to do about the Sarnia Business[82] and is very communicative in the matter. No knowing whether he might act [illegible] secretly in John A.'s interest and wishing to push me in order to see if we had any settled plan of attack so as to give warning[,] I have kept him at arms length but picked up all the information I could. I am inclined now to think his enmity is sincere. He suggests a Committee and says we can disclose transactions that will ruin John A. and Ross for ever. He offers to give hints etc [?] with that view ...[83]

The general election, called for the summer of 1861, had reached the stage of name calling and epithet throwing by early June. Sir Henry publicly entered the fray by publishing an election address that placed him squarely in opposition to the Liberal-Conservative coalition. He proclaimed himself "a true and liberal conservative" and then went on to make six critical points:[84]

1. Rep-by-pop must be implemented.
2. The coalition's education policy was vigorously attacked: "A question of paramount importance is the endowment of University College, by which all the advantages of that institution are concentrated at Toronto, to the manifest injury of all other parts of Upper Canada which do not participate in the endowment. I am in favour of legislation on this subject."
3. The government was attacked for advancing funds to the Grand Trunk Railway and for handling public finances improperly: "The present administration has been making further advances to this company, without the consent of the people or their Representatives in Parliament, and the consequence has not only been serious to our finances, but a principle has been established which is subversive of all good government, namely the spending of the public money without the sanction of Parliament."
4. Smith adopted a key Reform policy: "economy and retrenchment are required."
5. The personnel of the ministry was assaulted in a crude and self serving way: "The qualifications for office under the present administration

appear to have been based on the political delinquencies or bankruptcy of the parties who have obtained it. No regard is had to past services or merit."

6. Smith firmly identified himself with the sectionalist and anti-French Canadian line of the Brownite group. He notes that the government has refused to consider rep-by-pop while favoring French Canada in many areas, and comments: "it is no wonder we are said to be under French domination."

Sir Henry's defection was one of the minor sensations of the campaign. After all, for "twenty long years [he] had represented good old Frontenac and the Conservative interest." Reformers might have loathed Smith, but they could not resist the opportunity to capitalize on his defection. This attitude was well represented by the *Globe*, which listed him as "Conservative Oppositon"[85] and used his testimony to attack the regime: "There are few people so well able to judge the merits of the present administration as Mr. Speaker Smith, and it is with great pleasure therefore, that we transfer to our columns his address to the electors of Frontenac, in which he handles the ministry without kid gloves."[86] George Brown, however, wanted no close public association between Smith and the Reformers during the course of the election. When a Conservative newspaper accused Smith of entering a "secret compact" with Brown,[87] the *Globe* was quick to react: the basic point relating to Smith's testimony was that it illustrated the disintegration of the Liberal-Conservative party. The *Globe* explained:

> Sir Henry Smith perfectly well understands that there can be no unity of political action between himself and Mr. Brown, even as opponents of the same ministry. The member for Frontenac ... is only following the lead of a very large section of the Conservative Party ... It is a matter disheartening to the Ministerialists to find John A.'s favorite Central Canada idea [i.e. opposition to rep-by-pop and the alliance with French Canada] repudiated by his right hand man ..., but John A. has many more rebuffs of the same kind in store for him.[88]

Needless to say, the ministerial press was bitter and personal in its assault on Sir Henry Smith, traitor. The Montreal *Pilot* had little time for rational argument: "we will admit that there is one crime against the country of which the Ministry cannot be acquitted, and that is the appointment to the Presidency of the Commons House of the Parliament of Canada, of a vulgar ignoramus, who, at once, made the office ridiculous, and less desirable as an object of ambition to men really worth to fill it."[89]

The Quebec *Chronicle* was just as curt: Smith "owes his social and political standing to the Hon. John A. Macdonald and his colleagues ... [and] should be the last to turn ungratefully against his friends, and declaim against their extravagance, because they find it impracticable to have him re-elected as Speaker and impolitic to admit him into the Cabinet."[90] Some of the roughest comments came locally. The Picton *Gazette* regarded him as grossly ungrateful for all that he had received, and then itemized his gains from the public treasury since he joined the Ministry in 1854. The result, including his official salary, legal fees from the Grand Trunk, payment as an MPP, routine expenses and expenses for his trip abroad, came to an impressive $96,000.[91] If an inflation multiplier of five is used to translate this sum into 1974 dollars, Smith had garnered $480,000 in seven years for an annual average of $68,600 per year. At that rate some gratitude probably was in order! Later, in crowing over his defeat, the *Gazette* explained his behaviour: "[I]t will be remembered that the cry was echoed and re-echoed throughout the length and breadth of Canada that the Ministry would be nowhere ... [C]onsequently it became evident that there were those who had before strenuously supported the Ministry who were afraid to go to the country upholding that, as was reported and believed by many, unpopular and dishonest government. It was at this juncture that Sir Henry Smith bethought himself of the idea of abandoning his former principles ... in order to bend to what he imagined would be popular opinion, and in so doing he was gloriously defeated." [92]

Macdonald and his advisers took Smith seriously. Oliver Mowat tried to defeat Macdonald in Kingston in 1861. This was the first serious personal threat Macdonald had received. Donald Creighton quotes Macdonald during the campaign: "Gentlemen, I am on my trial – I feel that I am on my trial."[93] But Macdonald was on his "trial" not only in Kingston but in Frontenac, where a seasoned Conservative veteran was running in opposition to the government. The threat was yet more extensive, for Sir Henry was attempting to marshall opposition strength in neighbouring areas. To John Stevenson of Napanee he wrote: "I hope you will be able to show up McDd and his Sarnia speculation where he made $25,000 and took the title ... Give your own confidence to Hooper and the result will be certain [.] David [Roblin] is the mere [illegible] of John A and has got his family well provided for."[94] Mowat and Smith thus threatened the Conservative ascendancy in the old Midland District, the base of Macdonald's personal strength and the most reliable Upper Canadian Conservative district.

Macdonald took no chances with Frontenac. He had the county polled during the last phase of the campaign, indicating that he was worried about the result. His candidate was a very popular, if bankrupt, Kingston brewer named James Morton. The campaign was hard fought and dirty, with both sides using every available weapon. It is clear that John A.'s impressive Kingston-based organization worked hard to defeat Smith's opponents."[95] Macdonell was active throughout the riding and used money extensively in Morton's favour. Smith, for example, complained that Macdonell bribed voters, which was doubtless true, and that he relieved several voters of notes due to Smith. The suggestion was that in return for such financial relief, voters were required to vote against Smith.[96] Sir Henry, of course, intended to coerce his debtors into voting for himself! Smith also sought to obtain the details of Morton's financial problems for political use.[97] In the end, Macdonald won his own seat and held most of the Midland district. It was another painful moment for Sir Henry Smith. His old Conservative friends regarded him as a traitor; Reformers would claim him only if he was successful. The *Globe* jeered: "Smith: Knighthood has not saved him. Morton is elected by 110 majority."[98] He tried to stage a comeback in 1863, but was defeated in Frontenac by William Ferguson.[99] Smith's career in Union politics had come to an inglorious end.

VII

NINETEENTH-CENTURY Canadian politicians often had an unswerving devotion to public life. Once committed, they usually retained their commitment to the bitter end. Henry Smith was no exception, and returned to politics when Confederation provided a new political arena. In 1867, he contested the provincial seat of Frontenac. The "softening influences of time having obliterated old antagonisms."[100] He won an easy victory (1187-710) over John Fraser[101] and commenced a new phase of his career.

Sir Henry went to Toronto "as a Conservative member, to give a very liberal support to [John Sandfield Macdonald's coalition regime]."[102] His interests in provincial politics were similar to those he had earlier espoused in relation to the Union.[103] He presented the petitions of constituents and allies, and was very interested in the conduct of legislative business.[104] He was a member of the general committee on elections, and chairman of the private bills committee. Sir Henry opposed dual representation, campaigned to abolish the system whereby newly appointed provincial ministers were required to seek re-election through a by-election, supported electoral reform, legal reform, more progressive land settlement policies and the passage of legislation designed to ensure the legislature's independence of executive influence. He continued to agitate for better game laws, with some success: "we certainly owe to him the new Game Act of Ontario."[105]

One aspect of his new political role must have brought with it profound personal satisfaction. Early in 1868, he renewed political relations with Sir John A. Macdonald: "I have a bill prepared on the subject of our Parliamentary Privileges but before introducing it I thought I would write you on the subject."[106] Smith must have received an early response, because a week later he wrote: "I was glad to see your old familiar hand again and coincide entirely with your views on the Privileges question."[107] After a considerable period of silent animosity, the two men had restored reasonably amicable working relations.

Sir Henry was only 56 in 1868. Although no available evidence relates to his intentions or hopes, it is safe to posit that Smith was an ambitious man and certainly did not regard his career as approaching termination. He may have realized the instability of the Conservatives' provincial base and made overtures to the Liberals, as he had done in 1861. In any event, he was held in some esteem by at least some Liberals, as this statement in a Liberal newspaper indicates:

[T]he measures he has advocated and submitted to the House have been, on the whole in consonance with the principles of the Reform party. His bill for having all the elections to take place on the same day, for securing the independence of the legislature, for amending the law of evidence, and his Homestead Bill, are all progressive in their nature. They are all very defective, but the principles which underlie them are, for the most part correct,[108]

This new-found political promise was almost immediately cut short. Early in 1868, "he took cold, and was prevented from being present at the close of the session."[109] His kidneys became "affected," and he never recovered. As the Kingston *Daily News* expressed it on 18 September 1868, the day he died: "The unfortunate gentleman has been for some months a sufferer from a painful and exhaustive disease, and although at one time hopes of his restoration to health were entertained, these hopes gave way within the past few days in consequence of untoward symptoms which set in, and he died to-day in the forenoon."[110]

VIII

SIR HENRY SMITH left a widow, eight children, "a considerable fortune,"[111] and a problem that proved embarrassing to his family and friends. The operative portion of his will was ambiguous: "I give, devise and bequeath to my wife, Mary Smith, all and singular my estate, real and personal, to have and to hold the same and every part thereof, to her heirs and assigns for ever and I appoint her my sole executrix."[112] The problem was that the will was made in 1837, and that "the words employed by him to express such intention are open to a doubt in respect of property and rights, acquired by him subsequent to the date of said will."[113] This problem was accentuated by the nature of his business affairs, which were heavily involved with land. Lady Smith and Sir Henry's friends were convinced that Sir Henry's intent was that Lady Smith receive all of her husband's property on his decease.

Consequently, Lady Smith asked for legislation to remove the ambiguity and, in effect, to change the will by bringing under its provision all property acquired by Sir Henry between 1837 and his death. R.W. Scott moved the second reading of the bill, and explained its need. Smith had acquired much property in partnership or as a trustee. In some cases, he held patents on a property he had gained as a trustee.

Scott feared that unless "the will was legalized, there would be a great deal of litigation. These parties, to obtain their rights, would have to bring a Chancery suit in each instance. By this Bill, all this needless litigation would be prevented."[114] In other words, Scott and Lady Smith wanted to prevent the bulk of this complicated estate from being divided between Sir Henry's eight surviving children, five of whom were minors. The bill was strenuously opposed by Edward Blake, who defended the sanctity of the law and the rights of Sir Henry's children. Characteristically, he finally reduced the issue to one of freedom *versus* tyranny.[115] The bill in an amended version nonetheless passed, and Sir Henry's undoubted wishes became law.[116]

Sir Henry Smith was not a major politician, but his career is significant in some respects. Like many politicians of the Union period, he was by profession a businessman-lawyer. In Smith's case, he confined his business activities almost exclusively to land speculation. He was also a member of his town's elite and operated from a strong personal and political base. Smith was for years a trooper in the Conservative army, but he was willing to accept that role only as long as it was consistent with his own interests. It must be assumed that he was a man of influence, whose views, when he had any, carried weight.

His career illustrates some of the problems of factionalized parties. He came from what was essentially a one-party district. This led to problems that repeat themselves over and over again in the Kingston district. Ridings tend to be safe Conservative seats. Hence members usually hold seats for long periods of time. Very senior persons tend to dominate the party in the district, and as a result advancement for more junior men becomes difficult or impossible. This has had a profound influence on the careers of several nineteenth-century Kingston politicians: Alexander Campbell, Richard Cartwright, G.A. Kirkpatrick, and Henry Smith are examples. Had these men operated in a two-party district their careers would almost certainly have evolved in different ways.

A one-party district produces another phenomenon: political differences tend to find expression with a party, rather than between parties. Consequently, the Conservative Party in the Kingston district was (and is) highly factionalized. John A. Macdonald emerged as the district leader, but his position was never totally secure. Before Confederation both Campbell and Smith represented alternative regional leadership possibilities. During the immediate post-Confederation years that role was played by Richard Cartwright.

When the Conservative Party could no longer contain factionalized discontent (whether caused by a policy dispute or personal ambition), the discontented were required to accommodate themselves to the party or move into open opposition. Alexander Campbell before Confederation, and G.A. Kirkpatrick after 1867, made the necessary accommodations and had significant careers within the framework of their party. Sir Henry Smith and Sir Richard Cartwright could not make those accommodations and drifted into open opposition. They both mounted serious challenges to Macdonald's district leadership. Smith overestimated the strength of his local base and was crushed in 1861; Cartwright might have succeeded during the mid-1870s, but failed along with the first Liberal regime and was driven out of eastern Ontario.

Determining the motivation of public men is difficult. The case of Sir Henry Smith is no exception. It is clear, however, that he wanted certain things from politics: prestige, office, and income. He got all of these when he entered the Ministry in 1854. His position was considerably diminished when he was demoted in 1858. By 1859-60 he was under no illusion. Rather than deriving prestige through his elevation to knighthood, he suffered severe public humiliation. Smith knew that he was no longer a candidate for any type of preferment.

Coincident with these personal setbacks came a policy difference with the regime over rep-by-pop, and, in all likelihood, an acceptance by Smith of a widely held belief that the Cartier-Macdonald coalition was virtually finished. These factors intermeshed with Smith's belief that he was strong enough to hold Frontenac regardless of his political persuasion. He probed the possibility of an alliance with the Reform Party. This accounts for his decision to run as an oppositionist in 1861. Oliver Mowat's campaign against Macdonald in Kingston in that year is well known. The threat, however, was far more serious. Augustus Hooper, a Reformer, defeated David Roblin in Lennox and Addington;[117] Smith came within 110 votes of holding Frontenac. Prince Edward remained loyal to the Liberal-Conservative coalition. Had Frontenac and Kingston joined Lennox and Addington in electing oppositionists, Macdonald's regional base would have been shattered and the history of the Kingston district, and of the Conservative

Party, would have entered a new phase. A knowledge of Smith's activities in the 1861 election adds a new dimension to this interesting episode in Union politics.

Sir Henry Smith was not a very attractive figure. He would have scoffed at the concept of conflict-of-interest guidelines. Politics existed in order that a politician could help himself, his family, his friends, and his neighbours. He abused his position to help all those people. As a politician, he was neither creative nor inspiring; as an official, he cannot be rated a success. As a personality, he hardly merits serious attention. He was, nonetheless, an influential man who belonged to a powerful group. Such men must be understood if our knowledge of the Union is to be complete.

$\mathcal{A}$lexander Campbell

GENERAL MANAGER OF THE CONSERVATIVE PARTY
(EASTERN ONTARIO SECTION)

Campbell's real role in politics was as a Conservative "fix-it-man." He acted as a sort of party general manager for the Ontario section. Often he was Macdonald's legate.

As the most famous Kingstonian, Sir John A. Macdonald always over-shadowed Sir Alexander Campbell. This was true in nineteenth-century politics, and it is true today. Macdonald is now a national legend; few have ever heard of Campbell. This is unfortunate because without an understanding of the activities of Senator Campbell we cannot really understand the politics of Kingston, of Eastern Ontario, or of the Conservative Party during the early years of Confederation.

I

ALEXANDER CAMPBELL was born in 1822 and was of Scottish ancestry in spite of the fact that his birth-place was Hedon in Yorkshire. His father was a physician who moved his family to Canada in 1823. The Campbells lived in Montreal until 1832, when they went to Lachine. In 1836, Dr. Campbell and his family moved again, this time to Kingston.[1]

Alexander received a good education. Initially, he was taught by a Presbyterian minister. Then with his brother Charles he went to the Roman Catholic College at St. Hyacinthe. He later attended the Royal

---

Published in *Historic Kingston*, Vol. 17 (1969), this article derives from Professor Swainson's PhD thesis, where he began to study individual biographies, which, when placed side by side (as in this book), reveal the substance and spirit of the age.

Portrait of Sir Alexander Campbell (Library and Archives Canada).

Grammar School in Kingston. When he was seventeen, he began the study of law as John A. Macdonald's second articled student; Oliver Mowat was the first. In 1843, he was called to the bar of Upper Canada.[2] Although he received part of his education from a Presbyterian clergyman and another part at a Catholic college, Campbell was an Anglican.[3]

Campbell became Macdonald's law partner in 1844. The legal partnership did not last long, but the two men formed a political association that lasted until Campbell left active politics in 1887. Campbell entered electoral politics in 1850 as alderman for Victoria Ward, and held the seat for two years.[4] In 1858, he was elected to the Legislative Council for Cataraqui, a district which included both Kingston and Frontenac County. For a few months in 1863 he served as speaker in the upper house. The resignation of the Sandfield Macdonald-Dorion government in 1864 precipitated a major crisis. A.J. Fergusson-Blair was asked to form an administration, but failed. Campbell was then asked, and he too failed.[5] A final attempt to play the old politics of the Union was made by E.P. Taché and John A. Macdonald. Campbell was included in their government as Commissioner of Crown Lands, a post he retained in the great Confederation Coalition formed later in 1864. Campbell was thus a delegate to the Quebec Conference, and hence a Father of Confederation.

In 1867, Campbell was appointed to the Senate, where he remained until 1887. When the first dominion government was formed, Campbell was transferred from Crown Lands to the Post Office Department and given the leadership of the Conservative Party in the Senate. Years later, *The Week* commented on his appointment as Postmaster-General: "The new position did not call, to the same extent as the previous one, for the exercise of legal acumen, but it involved dealing with large public interests and a very extended patronage."[6] The patronage will be discussed later; it was indeed extensive!

On 1 July 1873, Campbell left the Post Office to become Minister of the Interior and Superintendent General of Indian Affairs. The Pacific Scandal drove him and his colleague from office in November 1873. During the dull and hapless Mackenzie interregnum (1873-78), however, he retained the Conservative leadership in the Senate.

Campbell, Sir Alexander after 1879, re-emerged as a minister in 1878 and held four separate portfolios in the subsequent nine years.

He was Receiver General, Minister of Militia and Defence, Minister of Justice and, on three different occasions, Postmaster-General. He was appointed Lieutenant-Governor of Ontario in 1887 and held the post until shortly before his death in 1892.

II

CAMPBELL DID not limit his activities to politics and the practice of law. During the early years of Confederation he was also Dean of the Queen's Law Faculty.[7] More interesting was his very broad involvement in business. During the early 1870s, for example, he was vice-president of the Isolated Risk Fire Insurance Company and a director of two additional firms: the Kingston & Pembroke Railway and the London and Canadian Loan and Agency Company.[8] He was also active in the Boiler Inspection Insurance Company and in the Canadian Express Company. The Intercolonial Express Company, under Campbell's presidency, was organized when the Intercolonial Railway was opened. At about the same time, he became Chairman of the Board of the Toronto Branch of the Consolidated Bank. In 1873, Campbell, John Beverley Robinson, and Richard Cartwright purchased a coal area in Nova Scotia; it was not successful. During the 1880s, he speculated in western Canadian land. This business activity dates, in large part, from 1873 and after. The fall of the first government freed much of his time and made extensive business activity more feasible. When he died, he was still president of two firms: the Imperial Loan and Investment Company of Canada (Limited) and the Boiler Inspection and Insurance Company of Canada.

Campbell invested in companies other than those he helped to direct. In 1870, the Ives Mining Company informed him that it was making "a further call of $220 per share." Campbell owned two shares in the company, which was presided over by Senator James Ferrier. C.J. Brydges of the Grand Trunk was vice-president, and A.T. Galt was a director.[9] In 1872, he sent James Domville of St. John $1,000 as the second call on his shares in the Maritime Bank of the Dominion of Canada.[10]

James Domville (1842-1921) is worth an aside. He was Vice-President of the Maritime Bank and Conservative MP for King's New Brunswick. Also a merchant and an industrialist, Domville sat in

Parliament from 1872 to 1882 and from 1896 to 1900. He was called to the Senate in 1903, by which time he was a Liberal. In 1919, he supported Mackenzie King for the Liberal leadership and was thus probably the only important Canadian politician to be both a Macdonald Conservative and a King Liberal.[11]

It is important to note that a minister like Campbell could work with an oppositionist like Cartwright, in spite of the latter's political activity in 1873. Campbell also worked with C.F. Gildersleeve of Kingston, an important Liberal and businessman. They were active together as directors of the Kingston & Pembroke Railway, and Gildersleeve felt no compunctions about asking the Senator to use his political influence to aid the line:

> The Tête du Pont Barracks is vitally necessary as a depot for the Kingston & Pembroke ... [A] meeting of the City Council is called for tomorrow evening to petition government on behalf of the city to grant the barracks to the railway Co. Sir George Cartier should be seen about it as application has been made by Montreal transportation Co. for it. [O]blige us by staying proceedings until our application can reach Govt.[12]

Again in 1872, Gildersleeve appealed to Campbell. Is it, he asked, "settled whether or no Calvin & Breck get the Tug Contract again. I have sold the *Bay of Quinte* conditionally to them on that event."[13] The most dramatic example of business co-operation between political foes was the Isolated Risk Fire Insurance Company. Alexander Mackenzie, the Liberal leader, was president. Campbell was vice-president, and the Board included Edward Blake, George Brown, Matthew Crooks Cameron (Ontario Conservative leader), Adam Crooks (Mowat's Provincial Treasurer), Senator William McMaster (a Liberal and president of the Bank of Commerce), Robert Wilkes (Liberal MP for Centre Toronto), and Hon. Col. Shaw (U.S. consul in Toronto).[14]

Campbell also received business requests from his political confidant, Senator John Hamilton of Montreal, an important lumberman and railroader. In May, 1872 he wrote Campbell: "The enclosed petition of the Ottawa, Vaudreuil & Montreal Ry Co was forwarded to me here ... May I ask you to be good enough to present it for me on Monday or get someone else to do so."[15] Gildersleeve and Hamilton were

Campbell's friends. They doubtless knew that a request for a favour, at the very least, would obtain a sympathetic hearing.

Through politics, business and social activity, Campbell was in contact with a host of people. He was at the centre of a web of inter-relationships. Miss M.K. Christie only scratched the surface when she described it thus:

> Campbell's brother Charles, later in life a prominent Toronto Conservative, began his banking career in the Commercial Bank under ... Mr. Francis Harper who was Macdonald's cousin ... With the Strange family Campbell was connected by marriage. With Kirkpatricks and Gildersleeve he formed close associations which were to last all through his life. With Richard Cartwright he was for many years to co-operate in a number of business enterprises ...[16]

III

CAMPBELL'S REAL role in politics was as a Conservative "fix-it-man." He acted as a sort of party general manager for the Ontario section. Often he was Macdonald's legate. His activity in this area was very important, especially during the first government, 1867-73. After the general election of 1874, Campbell became less and less active. During the late 1870s, he gave up all interest in electoral politics and confined himself to cabinet and administrative work. John Graham Haggart was his successor, at least as Macdonald's lieutenant for eastern Ontario. Nonetheless, Campbell was an important politician and manager during Macdonald's first administration. This role can be explained only by illustrating his activities. Most of these illustrations are drawn from the early 1870s.

As a minister, Campbell was cool and conscientious. On 14 August 1873, for example, when he was Minister of the Interior, he wrote Lieutenant-Governor Morris of Manitoba a ten-page letter concerned with such administrative problems as the policing of Fort Whoop-Up, a treaty for the Blackfeet and Crees, an Indian commission, proposed Indian negotiations at the North West Angle, and an aspect of U.S. Indian policy. He closed with a promise to send additional dispatches on several other problems.[17] This letter was written on the day following the climacteric and extended prorogation crisis of 13 August 1873. Campbell was probably the only minister at his desk on August 14! It was very important to Macdonald and to the government to have a key ministry, like the Interior, well administered regardless of political tension and rancor. Both western rebellions could perhaps have been avoided had Campbell administered the West at more crucial times.

At election time, Campbell assumed responsibility for a variety of tasks, and his concern was broader than for Ontario. Early in the 1872 campaign, he asked Lieutenant-Governor Morris for a "paper on Manitoba." He informed Macdonald that J.G. Bourinot had prepared a study of the relations between Nova Scotia and Canada; he asked the prime Minister to dictate "a paper on the general achievements of the government."[18] After conversations with Henry Nathan and Donald A. Smith, he advised Macdonald to call the B.C. elections for the "earliest possible period" and the Manitoba elections for "the last half of August or the first week of September."[19]

His close friend, Senator Hamilton, asked him to intervene in the Quebec riding of Ottawa county: "I hope you did not faile [sic] to bring what I mentioned with respect to the County of Ottawa under M. Langevains [sic] notice, for I think it is only fair and *right* to Wright that the Govt should do what it can to prevent his having more trouble than is unavoidable, for in such a county as Ottawa, the very least amounts to a great deal."[20] If Campbell, in fact, intervened he was successful; Alonzo Wright won by acclamation.

Even before becoming Minister of the Interior, Campbell concerned himself with the detailed work of political management in Manitoba.[21] Useful information was gathered and passed along to Macdonald. Assistance was given in securing Cartier's 1873 by-election victory in Provencher, and he was involved in the fight for the seat when Cartier died later in the same year. The Manitoba Metis (and especially Riel) were a problem. Campbell advised on this sensitive problem: "What do you say to my proposition to pay the loyal French half breeds the £500 recommended by Donald Smith out of the secret service fund?"[22]

When Campbell testified in 1873 before the royal commission of enquiry into the Pacific Scandal, he claimed only a dim knowledge of Hugh Allan's massive campaign contributions of the previous year.[23]

Most Conservative leaders suffered from poor memory in 1873. Regardless of his disclaimer, Campbell knew a lot about campaign funds. In July 1872, William Cleghorn at the Office of the Commissioners of the Trust and Loan Company of Canada (Toronto) told him that he and his staff would contribute to the election fund.[24] Later in the campaign his brother Charles appealed for help. His letter to the Senator describes a remarkable incident:

> I was yesterday persuaded by Sir John to do a thing which I very much regret. John Shedden & I became parties to a joint note for $10,000 at the Merchants Bank to enable him to supply funds to the several constituencies which he hopes to carry, the only security we have being "Sir John's undertaking in writing as a member of the Government to recoup us the amount loaned him." It is a very foolish thing in me to do but it is too late now to regret, my object in writing is to make you aware of the circumstances so that steps may be taken for my protection when the subject comes up, pray write me as soon as you can & let me know how far official promises are reliable.[25]

The problem of the $10,000 was solved, but poor Campbell must have reeled after reading his brother's letter. Fortunately, he understood Macdonald and knew the reason for such a dangerous indiscretion.

In an important letter, Campbell explained the fall of the government in November 1873: "From the time [Sir John] left Kingston, after his own election, to go West [i.e., Western Ontario], I am very much afraid he kept himself more or less under the influence of wine, and that he really has no clear recollection of what he did on many occasions at Toronto and elsewhere after that period."[26] Macdonald was fortunate to have for a colleague a man like Campbell, who understood him, was discreet, and was able to solve innumerable problems of this sort.

It is clear that Campbell understood how his party raised money; he was, after all, intimately involved. Judging by his brother's plea in 1872, and his own analysis of 1873, Campbell must have understood the dangers inherent in the system. In a letter from Alexander Campbell to Alexander Morris, 29 November 1873, he observed:

Ottawa,
29th Nov. 1873.

Private & Confidential

My dear Morris,

I received a day or two ago your letter of the 12th inst., and thank you very much for the kind things you say in it.

Our upset was unexpected and resulted partly from misfortune and the treachery of *soi'disant* friends and partly from, I think, mis-management. This last fault, looking back on events, I think, may be said to have commenced in the Session of last winter when the Pacific slander was first put forward in the House by Huntington. Macdonald was then excessively alarmed and persuaded us all that there was no alternative save that of putting the investigation off until the return of Allan and Abbott who were then in England. His argument was specious enough and substantially was that until their evidence should be given it was impossible to predict what Allan might state on the subject, and that until he had made his statement it was unsafe for Macdonald to make his and therefore unwise and unsafe for us to allow the investigation to be proceeded with. I believe now, although I yielded to Sir John's views at the time, that it would have been better to have gone on last Winter and had the investigation proceeded with and to have taken the evidence of Allan and Abbott on their return. Then again when the House met in August we might have been in a position to have gone on. We did not try to be. Macdonald then urged that he would have a Royal Commission issued and that its sittings would be prolonged and the public mind would be wearied of the subject before the Session, which he then thought would be held in December or January. It would, looking back, have been better to have gone on in August as we had not done so last winter. The delays have all worked against us and for the enemy. The public were fed with exaggerated stories

Alexander Campbell   117

untrue in almost everything but still with a grain of truth
which made other parts of the stories seem specious. Notwithstanding all this when we met on the 23rd October we
had a majority of *twenty* had we taken a vote at once, that is
after the first two or three days of the Session. This we might
have done but Macdonald was again for delay. He postponed
the reply to the address unnecessarily from Thursday until
Monday and then when the "Ball" was opened he refused
to speak for a great many days in the hopes that he could
drive Blake to precede him. In the meantime the Opposition were working on our friends with all sorts of promises
and all sorts of representations and from day to day we had
the painful experience to which I at all events was quite new
of hearing each morning that some supporter had dropped
away and was about to vote against us. We had every reason
to count upon the *six* votes from Prince Edward Island. They
were all pledged to us, and the terms of Union which we had
granted to the Island were considered by them so favorable
that they professed at their elections to be very grateful to
the Dominion Gov't. As it turned out we have only got *two*
votes out of the *six* thus losing *four* which on a division would
count *eight* as compared with our calculations beforehand.
We also would have lost the following upon all of whom we
had counted and had the strongest reasons for doing so, viz:
Shibley and Lewis of Ontario, Tourangeau and Langlois of
Quebec, Pearson, Killam, and perhaps Ray from Nova Scotia,
Cutler and Appleby of New Brunswick, Donald Smith of Manitoba, and so our majority dwindled away until we were satisfied that upon a vote we should be defeated. It then became
a question with us whether it was best to meet the vote or to
resign without having it taken. Pope, Tilley and Langevin
were all very strong in favour of the policy of resigning, their
argument being that many of our friends would be weakened
in their Counties by voting to sustain the Government in this
Pacific matter, and that such a vote would be taken advantage
of by their opponents at the next elections and made use of
to their injury, and that there was no object in forcing friends

into a position which was one of disadvantage to them. This view prevailed and Sir John tendered our resignations and Mackenzie was sent for. If I have seemed in my narrative to have blamed Sir John Macdonald for the delays which I think injured us, I do not forget, nor do our friends, the valuable service which he has rendered to the country and to the party which he has so long led to victory. We both of us know in the past that his policy of delay has very often succeeded and we know also how partial he always is to that course, and how difficult it is to persuade him or to bring reasons of sufficient weight to change his views, and also how apt one is to yield ones own judgment to that of a colleague whose ability and political experience are so universally honored. In this particular instance I am persuaded he was haunted by an idea, which turned out to be utterly without foundation, that there were some telegrams behind which would be published and this dread paralyzed his action. I do not believe up to the last moment that he felt sure, or now feels sure, that all he telegraphed during the Elections has come out. From the time he left Kingston, after his own election, to go West, I am very much afraid he kept himself more or less under the influence of wine, and that he really has no clear recollection of what he did on many occasions at Toronto and elsewhere after that period. I write all this in the *greatest confidence* simply to give you an idea of the inner history of the fall of the Ministry. No one has a higher opinion of Macdonald's abilities, or a more just sense of his many good qualities, than I have, and I would be the last man to say a word to his prejudice, either in reference to his conduct of this affair or his private habits to any one in the world, and if I refer to this last topic now it is only for the purpose of giving you the clue to much of the delay and paralysis of action which attended and helped to accomplish our downfall. I am very sorry to say that the same reasons which impeded his management of the elections was operating during the whole of the days the Parliament remained in Session, and we never had the full advantage either of his abilities and judgment or of his

nerve and courage. A night of excess always leaves a morning of nervous incapacity and we were subjected to this pain
amongst others.

I am

My dear Morris
Very truly yours
A. CAMPBELL

To His Honor
Lieut. Governor Morris
Fort Garry
Manitoba

Big contributions were politically dangerous if they became public.
They could be risky propositions even if they remained a dark secret.
The $10,000 loan is a case in point. The government would suffer
severe damage if it became known that Macdonald had agreed "in
writing as a *member of the Government to recoup us the amount loaned him.*"
If the loan was not quickly repaid, the result could be the alienation
of some important Toronto Conservatives. The political hazards are
clear. It is a great pity that we do not know how Campbell reacted to
the problem, or what solution he employed.

During the early period of his career, Macdonald was a member
of the moderate wing of his party. This brought him into conflict
with Toronto conservatism, which tended to be more extreme and to
draw more heavily on the traditions of the Compact. During the early
years of Confederation, Torontonians like Casimir Gzowski and D.L.
Macpherson were close associates of the Prime Minister, but the government was often suspect because of its banking and railway policies.
In fact, Toronto businessmen often regarded the first government as
excessively friendly to Montreal.

Under these circumstances, Alexander Campbell was very useful
to his leader because he was close to Toronto business. He was allied
with the traditional conservatism of the provincial capital when he
made his bid for leadership in 1864. His brother became an important city businessman, and Charles and Alexander were close political
colleagues. Alexander Campbell had many associations with Toronto.
Thus he often served as a link between the government and Ontario

big business. Late in 1872, Charles wrote his brother about making "a raid on Sir John," in spite of Macdonald's desire not to see Charles Campbell and his associates. They assumed that Alexander would help.

A bit later, Charles Campbell, Senator Frank Smith, J.B. Robinson, Angus Morrison, and George Laidlaw wanted to see Macdonald on business "related to the Pacific." In the fall of 1872, this was the most sensitive problem before the government, and the Torontonians counted on Alexander Campbell's assistance. These incidents merely illustrate another of Campbell's many roles.[27]

Although he sat in the Senate, Campbell took part in the management of the lower house. It was Campbell, for example, who was authorized to offer Dr. James Grant of Russell a senatorship in return for loyalty during the parliamentary crisis of 1873.[28] Campbell was also heavily involved in the manoeuvres designed to prevent the defection of Donald A. Smith immediately prior to the fall of the government in November 1873.[29]

During his first six years as Postmaster-General, he dispensed patronage all over Canada, and administered much of the patronage handed around by MPs and defeated candidates. This was work crucial to the success of a nineteenth-century party. Campbell was required to approve pay raises for postal workers, leaves-of-absence and appointments.[30] Important party members asked him to obtain patronage, even if another department was involved. Hence, in 1871, G.A. Kirkpatrick (MP for Frontenac) wired: "Please get Captain Hunter 47th battalion a commission in regiment going west."[31] On occasion it was necessary to search out a man to handle patronage for a given county. On one occasion, Campbell suggests that this be done for Glengarry County. He wrote Macdonald: "Can you give me the name of any one in Glengarry to refer to in the future? H.R. Macdonald to my mind should not have our confidence he got himself beaten by 1100."[32]

Newspaper management was another of the indefatigable senator's interests. This was an important and difficult problem because the Conservative Party in Ontario faced the powerful *Globe*. Attempt after attempt was made to counter the influence of George Brown's paper, but during the Confederation era, the Conservatives were always outclassed. Nonetheless, the press war was waged, and Campbell was a chief campaigner as long as he was Postmaster-General. He controlled Post

Office advertising and could, therefore, provide the revenue needed to keep a fractious editor loyal to the party, and an insolvent newspaper in business. In fact, he kept a master-list of loyal newspapers. To obtain government advertising or printing contracts, a newspaper had to be on what an Orangeville newspaperman called "the List."[33]

The *Daily News* of Kingston was a problem. It operated with a deficit, and its editor, James Shannon, wanted patronage assistance from the government. He saw Macdonald, who made a promise of some sort, and then failed to provide the help. Shannon then turned to Campbell, who solved the financial problem and kept a loyal newspaper alive.[34] At about the same time, another Kingston newspaper, the *British Whig*, was disciplined for being insufficiently fervent in its loyalty to the party. Campbell cut off its subsidy. The editor was mortified and appealed to Campbell: "I have not sold to the Grits – on the contrary I have bluffed them off & yet on the mere rumor of so doing, the Government Offices ... [have stopped advertising in the *British Whig*]."[35] In this instance the editor won, but not for long. Advertising was restored to the *Whig*, but stopped for a second time a year later.[36]

Campbell received numerous requests for help from impecunious newspapermen. Occasionally, he acted rapidly. During the 1872 campaign, J.G. Moylan of the Toronto *Freeman* asked for an advance on a "few thousand dollars worth of printing."[37] The request was granted within five days, doubtless because Moylan threatened to suspend publication.[38] At any cost, that sort of disaster had to be avoided during an election campaign. It is interesting to note that the *Ontario Workman*, Ontario's first important labour newspaper, was on Campbell's list. During the campaign of 1872, the Conservative Party obtained labour support, and Macdonald and Campbell provided revenue for the *Workman*.[39]

III

I T HAS ALREADY been demonstrated that Campbell's role in the Election of 1872 was crucial. As Miss Christie described it:

> Macdonald seems to have committed to Campbell's charge not only the task of insuring his own re-election in Kingston, but that of directing the battle in a number of the old Midland counties.

It was to Campbell that the leading lights in Hastings, Prince Edward, and Addington were accustomed to report and appeal.[40]

Macdonald had started his career from the base of the Midland counties. For years he had carefully managed the ridings in the Kingston area. But after Confederation the Prime Minister operated on a far broader stage. The base of his power widened and the Midland district became less important. He thus delegated large quantities of work to Alexander Campbell – not only in the Kingston district but throughout Ontario and especially in eastern Ontario. In the crucial election of 1872, Campbell was Macdonald's legate.

Of all the ridings he managed, however, Kingston was the most important because it was the Prime Minister's constituency. Campbell was an ideal campaign manager for Kingston. As a Kingstonian and former law partner of Sir John, he was well known and in turn knew Kingston well. For years he had handled part of the area's patronage, and he had represented Kingston and Frontenac County in the elective legislative council of the Union. In 1872, Campbell managed Macdonald's personal election in detail. He kept Macdonald informed about what happened in the riding, and he arranged his nomination.[41] On July 20, he urged Macdonald to return to Kingston, for he felt that the seat was in danger from "some of the Catholics, some of your former friends and a lot of younger men." Campbell, of course, was working hard to prevent defeat, and described to Macdonald a successful meeting with the Bishop of Kingston: "The Bishop promised me today that he would speak to his people tomorrow – he is much pained at the disaffection particularly at this moment when half a dozen Catholics are running by your instrumentality – he says that he does not adopt the course of speaking in church but on the most important crises but he feels this to be one and will do it."[42] Numbers of voters were employed at jobs which took them out of town. Campbell was usually able to arrange their return to Kingston on election day, if, of course, they were Tories. If they supported John Carruthers, the Liberal candidate, he arranged that they be kept out of town during the poll.[43] Out-of-town voters were asked to come to Kingston on election day and help elect Macdonald.[44] After Macdonald won, by over a hundred votes, Campbell wound up the Kingston operation. From out-of-town voters and various kinds of campaign workers, he received requests for payment.[45] Unusually good service could even produce a recommendation for a patronage job.[46]

While managing Macdonald's election, Campbell was active in many other constituencies: East Hastings, Prince Edward, Addington, South Renfrew, and a variety of other difficult ridings stretching from Toronto to the Ottawa River. He encouraged candidates and offered advice, found campaign money, disciplined insufficiently partisan civil servants, convinced men of their duty to work in the campaign, appealed to religious leaders, and attempted to restrain factionalism.[47] It is clear why Senator Hamilton in a letter to Campbell referred to those elections "which you manipulate in Kingston."[48] To neighbouring politicians, Campbell's presence was real and his power considerable. J.S. McCuaig, the Conservative candidate for Prince Edward, regarded Campbell as a major leader. He wrote: "I look upon it in time you will become the Leader of the Ottawa Govt ... I have great confidence in your word & ability."[49]

Although unusual in some respects, Campbell's political career fits one standard nineteenth- century pattern. Through politics he rose to the highest level of the Ontario social structure and joined the elite of Ontario. But it should be pointed out that Macdonald and Campbell were not close personal friends. The break-up of their law partnership was extremely unpleasant, and Sir Joseph Pope (Macdonald's private secretary) commented: "Sir John and Sir Alexander were not kindred spirits, but any want of cordiality between them was on personal grounds, and politically they were always ... closely united.[50] This political union was exceedingly useful to Macdonald; the very able Campbell performed a host of invaluable functions. Senator John Hamilton, the important Montreal business leader, was his friend. His brother Charles linked him to the Toronto business community. Contacts with the opposition were maintained. Richard Cartwright was a friend, regardless of their serious political differences, and this friendship persisted even after Macdonald and Cartwright had become such bitter personal enemies that they rarely spoke. Cartwright was a pallbearer at Campbell's funeral in 1892.

While useful to Macdonald, Campbell represented no threat to his chief's leadership. He was not the type of politician able to compete successfully with Macdonald at the personal level. Campbell was an aloof man, contemptuous of the mass and somewhat scornful of popular politics.[51] He was more suited to the Senate than to the House of Commons. All the while he understood the weakness of the Senate and the necessity of basing a government on popularity and strong electoral politicians. Hence this comment to Macdonald: "No appointment [to the cabinet] from the Senate can add any thing to the strength of the Government with the Commons or the Country but the reverse ."[52] Campbell had tried a more public role during the Union, but his attempt failed.

Perhaps his most serious political weakness was the lack of an independent power base. Because he operated from Kingston, he operated from the centre of Macdonald's strength. During the Union, he came close to possessing a power base of sorts. When he was an elected councillor, he had a constituency, albeit simply Kingston and Frontenac county. More important was his pre-1864 alliance with some of the old guard of the Conservative Party.[53] Within the delicately balanced politics of the Union, when governments and leaders were used up with frightening speed, this strength was almost sufficient to obtain for him the leadership of the Upper Canadian Conservatives. After 1867, the elective upper house was gone and it was impossible for small groups to wield the tremendous power they possessed before 1864. Campbell accepted the change, and during the first government acted as a loyal and important lieutenant. His very inclusion in the first cabinet is testimony of Macdonald's esteem. Ontario had only five ministers in the government, and the Ontario wing of the cabinet was officially a coalition. Three of the ministers were Liberals; both Conservative members were residents of Kingston! That kind of concentration was dangerous, but it indicates how highly Macdonald regarded Campbell's assistance.

Campbell was useful and safe. He could not threaten Macdonald's leadership, but he could further it. Under the presidency of Sir John A. Macdonald, he was ideally suited to the post of General Manager of the Conservative Party (Eastern Ontario Section).

Oliver Mowat

ONTARIO ON THE RISE

He began as John A. Macdonald's protégé, but it did not last. To Macdonald's chagrin, Oliver Mowat turned Reformer, and as Liberal premier of Ontario for almost a quarter of a century, he became the father of the provincial rights movement.

OLIVER MOWAT may have learned his law from John A. Macdonald, but he looked elsewhere for his political inspiration. Repelled by the Tory leader's blatant use of political patronage and corruption, Mowat set up as a Liberal to practice the politics of "virtue." And as premier of Ontario for twenty-four years, he fought John A.'s centralizing view of federalism and championed provincial rights, establishing a solid claim to be considered Canada's most famous and most important provincial premier of the nineteenth century. Oliver Mowat was one of the Fathers of Confederation, but his view of the country differed from centralists like his old friend, John A. Macdonald. During his years as premier of Ontario, Mowat was the acknowledged leader of the provincial rights cause, and his impact on the shape of the country was profound. In 1897, Mowat retired from politics to become Lieutenant-Governor of Ontario. He held the position until his death a year and a half later.

Like Macdonald, Mowat grew up in the Scots Presbyterian community in Kingston, Upper Canada, where he was born in 1820 – the year Macdonald arrived in the area as a five-year old immigrant from Glasgow. Young Oliver was educated at Rev. John Cruickshank's private

---

This article was first published in *Horizon Canada*, Vol. 6, No. 66 (1985), with captioned illustrations. Professor Swainson was always quick to recognize Oliver Mowat's role as the champion of provincial rights in face of Sir John A. Macdonald's staunch federalism.

Portrait of Oliver Mowat (Library and Archives Canada).

school, graduating to Macdonald's office to study law. As a young man, he worked along with Alexander Campbell in Macdonald's office. Unlike Mowat, Campbell remained a Conservative all his life, serving in the Senate and in the federal cabinet in several positions. But the two remained close personal friends. The triumvirate of Macdonald, Mowat, and Campbell was remarkable for its predominance in Canadian political life. During one period, Macdonald was Prime Minister, Mowat was Premier of Ontario, and Campbell was its Lieutenant-Governor.

I

THE PRODUCT of a Conservative town, a Conservative family, and Conservative legal training, Mowat showed little interest in politics as a young man. On being called to the bar in 1841, he moved to Toronto where he quickly established a large and lucrative practice. In the early 1850s, he regarded himself as an Independent, but he maintained his ties with Macdonald, then the rising Tory star. The connection proved useful – John A. made him a Queen's Counsel in 1855 and a government commissioner in 1856.

Mowat now made a decisive career decision. He concluded that acting as a lone gun was no way to win the political influence he desired. He also decided that he preferred not to be a Tory because he was appalled by Macdonald's brand of politics. So he joined George Brown's Reform party. Oliver Mowat's decision to become a Reformer shocked his Tory friends and relatives in Kingston. He sought to justify his action in a careful letter to his old friend Alexander Campbell, an active Tory politician.

"In making up my mind that I should go into complete opposition," he wrote, "one of the most powerful considerations which influenced me was the conviction that the Ministry would do anything to keep in office; that nothing was too bad in legislation or government for them to adopt if it helped to secure their places."

He saw the Tory government as complacent, corrupt and cynical, and he placed much of the blame on John A. Macdonald: "Our friend Macdonald does not pretend to patriotism. In private he laughs at it, as you must have heard him do yourself. There is nothing that sustains his Government but his own popularity ... It did seem to me that opposition to such a government had become the duty of every one. It corrupts public men and the public itself."

Mowat thought men like Macdonald should never be allowed to govern. He also knew he was burning his bridges: "I dare say I shall find I have lost Macdonald's friendship ... I shall be very sorry for this; but one must not shape one's political course by friendship."

Once a friend and political ally of Macdonald, Mowat went his own way, and relations between the two men soured. Mowat was very serious, unusually dour, and totally convinced of the rightness of his opinions. He promised his electors that he would behave like "a Christian politician," not like Macdonald and his followers, "to whom it would be a farce to ascribe political virtue, or any higher motive than the love of office with its prestige and power."

Elected to the Parliament of the United Canadas, Mowat's obvious abilities and his capacity for hard work immediately made him a Reform leader. He served in George Brown's pathetic two-day "Short Administration" in August 1858, and in the government of John Sandfield Macdonald and Antoine-Aimé Dorion in 1863-64.

He followed Brown into the great Confederation Coalition of Reformers and Tories in 1864, serving as Postmaster General. He attended the Quebec Conference in October 1864, thus becoming one of the Fathers of Confederation, but in November, he retired from politics to become a judge as Vice-Chancellor of Upper Canada.

Needless to say, John A. Macdonald was less than amused by the emergence of his former pupil and protégé as one of George Brown's most influential and effective lieutenants. John A.'s resentment boiled over in April 1861 when Mowat had criticized him in Parliament. "You damned pup," he roared, "I'll slap your chops for you!" John Sandfield Macdonald had to step in bodily to prevent a fistfight on the House floor.

But now Mowat had withdrawn from all that. He remained away from politics for several years. Confederation came, Sir John A. Macdonald became Canada's first prime minister, while John Sandfield Macdonald took over as the first premier of Ontario. And after being routed in 1867, the Liberal party, as the Reform movement was known after Confederation, was rejuvenated by Edward Blake and Alexander Mackenzie.

The first major Liberal success came in 1871 with the toppling of the Ontario government of J.S. Macdonald. Blake became premier, with Mackenzie as his provincial treasurer. But these two had bigger fish to fry. Their major objective was the overthrow of Sir John A. Macdonald's national Conservative government. Establishing a Liberal power base in Toronto was but a step in the strategy; that task completed, they wanted to leave the provincial scene and focus all their energies on national politics.

Of course, they wanted to leave a trusty Liberal in charge in Toronto, so they sought a first-rate public figure who could step into Blake's shoes as premier and govern Ontario with ability and success. Mowat was their choice.

II

ON 21 OCTOBER 1872, Vice-Chancellor Mowat received Premier Blake, Treasurer Mackenzie, and his former leader, George Brown, at his home on Simcoe Street in Toronto. They offered him the leadership of the Ontario Liberal party and the post of premier. He considered the offer with care, accepted, and was sworn in as Ontario's third premier. A riding was opened for him, and by the end of the year, he was premier, attorney general, and member for North Oxford in the Ontario legislature.

Mowat – Sir Oliver after 1892 – never again left public life. He remained premier of Ontario from 1872 to 1896, easily winning six successive general elections. Sir Wilfrid Laurier made him a Senator and federal Minister of Justice in 1896, but the following year, he returned to Toronto as Lieutenant-Governor of Ontario, a post he retained until his death in 1903.

Mowat's long tenure as premier of Canada's largest province is enough to make him an important Ontarian and a major Canadian public figure. But his importance goes beyond that normally associated with a powerful premier. Mowat played a key role in structuring the country as a whole.

John A. Macdonald conceived of Canada as a highly centralized state. Financially and politically, he saw Ottawa's role as dominant. The provincial governments were to be minor affairs, with little money and little authority. He explained his position to a friend in 1864: "If the Confederation goes on, you, if spared the ordinary age of man, will see both local parliaments and governments absorbed in the general power. This is as plain to me as if I saw it accomplished."

That was not Oliver Mowat's view of Canada, or of Ontario's place in Confederation.

Mowat wanted Ontario to develop into a modern society with a sophisticated economy, and as premier he set out to bring that about. Agriculture, for example, was modernized. Mowat's government was very imaginative in educational and scientific areas related to agriculture, and he himself took this sector of the economy so seriously that he did not hesitate to pursue improvements substantially in advance of public opinion.

Hence he proceeded to permit the provincial agricultural college to award degrees, even as *The Globe*, powerful supporter of Mowat and Liberal party, scoffed: "It would strike a farmer as a ludicrous thing to have his son come home as a full blown 'Doctor of Agriculture,' or 'Master of Artificial Manures,' or 'Bachelor of Livestock.'"

While farmers were becoming substantially more competitive and productive, Ontario underwent tremendous urbanization, industrialization, and population growth. Major adjustments were required to meet these fundamental shifts. Big-city problems had to be faced, and trade unions had to be accepted as a fact of life.

III

MOWAT'S GOVERNMENT moved further and further into the field of government regulation. Significant legislation was passed to protect industrial workers. By the end of the Mowat period, an embryonic welfare state existed, placing Ontario at least a generation ahead of the other provinces. Increasingly sophisticated forms of education were required, and in this area the Mowat record was brilliant. The judicial system was reorganized and the law of the province codified, reforms reflecting the growth of statute law and the need for a more efficient administration of justice. Statistics began to be collected in a systematic way, providing the kind of material that was of enormous use to a government that was becoming increasingly rationalized and bureaucratic.

The Mowat regime did much to encourage economic growth. It was responsible for the completion of numerous railways in both northern and southern Ontario. These lines were extremely important: They stimulated development within the older part of the province and opened up large sections of northern Ontario; and they helped mold the province's diverse regions into a whole.

By the end of the century, the Ontario economy and social structure, as we know it, was emerging. At the same time, the provincial administration was becoming ever more modern, better able than any other regime in Canada, federal or provincial, to accommodate the tremendous and dynamic developments of twentiety-century Canadian society.

Mowat's liberalism, broad and pragmatic, performed an indispensable function in late nineteenth-century Ontario history, and materially assisted the province in its rise to dominance. It permitted the maintenance of a provincial consensus during a crucial period of economic and social growth. It set the tone for a party that could accommodate a variety of elements, which in other provinces, other governments, provoked discord and instability.

For example, after campaigning on the divisive slogan of "Mowat and the Queen," or "Morrison and the Pope," in his first election in 1857, Mowat, as premier, was able to incorporate into the Liberal party most types of Protestants and large numbers of Roman Catholics. During his premiership, he was also able to retain prohibitionists and representatives of the liquor interests within his party. Businessmen and trade unionists, farmers and urbanites, eastern Ontarians and peninsular Grits, promoters and unemployed, old-fashioned partisans and third-party advocates, liberals and conservatives – his party encompassed them all.

IV

MOWAT'S STUBBORN refusal to allow his Liberals to become at any time a single-issue party muted dissensions within the province. While the province of Quebec, to cite a dramatic example, was being torn apart by infighting within the Conservative party and vicious assaults on liberalism, Mowat was able to focus the energies of Ontarians on the basic work of adjusting to industry and urbanization, modernizing agriculture, opening the North, absorbing the political and social energies of trade unionism, and developing Ontario into the overwhelmingly dominant economic unit within the Canadian federation.

It is doubtful that Ontario society would have matured so quickly, or the economy grown so dramatically, without Mowat's consensus-style liberalism. At the same time, the most famous examples of strife in Mowat's day aided rather than harmed Ontario's development. Mowat is best known in Canadian history for his bitter feuds with Sir John A. Macdonald. The warfare between the two was particularly nasty in the years after Macdonald's return to power in 1878. The feud revolved around two broad problems – the nature of Canadian federalism, and lands and resources.

Mowat refused to accept Macdonald's notion of quasi-federalism, in which the provinces were to be subordinate to the federal authority. He held to the view that each level of government was sovereign within its sphere of jurisdiction as defined by Canada's Constitution. Mowat dealt with this problem through the courts, fighting all the way to the Judicial Committee of the Privy Council, which was then the highest court for all British colonies. He won a sweeping victory; his view, not Macdonald's, prevailed and became the basis for Canada's constitutional evolution.

Perhaps the most dramatic illustration of Oliver Mowat's anti-Ottawa stand was his chairmanship of the Interprovincial Conference at Quebec in 1887. The meeting was called "for the purpose of considering questions which have arisen or may arise as to the autonomy of the provinces, their financial arrangements, and other matters of provincial interest." Besides Mowat, the other premiers present were Honoré Mercier of Quebec, W.S. Fielding of Nova Scotia, A.G. Blair of New Brunswick, and John Norquay of Manitoba. Sir John A. Macdonald refused to attend what he knew would be a hostile session.

Guided by the deft hand of Mowat, the conference devoted its time to bashing the federal government: The provinces wanted more federal money, increased powers, and a say in some matters – like the appointment of senators – that were clearly federal responsibilities.

Macdonald ignored the conference, but it was successful to the extent that it publicized provincial grievances. And it set a precedent. Such conferences became ever more common and are now regarded as part of our Constitution. Not only do prime ministers routinely attend, they chair these meetings of "first ministers."

The second major point in dispute between Toronto and Ottawa concerned the physical dimensions of Ontario. Macdonald wanted

Ontario kept as small as possible in order to retain federal control over the lands and resources of as much territory as he could manage. Mowat wanted an enlarged Ontario, in order to obtain ownership of the wealth of the North.

The province, as it existed in 1867, was much smaller than it is today. It consisted essentially of what is now southern and eastern Ontario, plus an extension northward in the timber lands of the upper Ottawa River watershed, and a strip north of Georgian Bay and lakes Huron and Superior. The western frontier was in the Thunder Bay area, and the province did not possess the vast northern regions that are part of the watershed of Hudson Bay and James Bay.

Ottawa and Toronto both recognized that serious legal questions existed concerning Ontario's borders, so negotiations began. They were protracted and difficult, and ultimately failed. The matter was finally decided by the Judicial Committee of the Privy Council in important cases in 1884 and 1888. Mowat personally represented Ontario and won another sweeping victory.

In the west, Ontario's boundary was extended some 440 kilometres; in the northeast, the province's frontier was pushed all the way to James Bay. Mowat had secured for Ontario 285,000 square kilometres more, a resource-rich territory more than five times the size of Nova Scotia. Ontario has profited enormously from the valuable natural resources of its northern territory, much of which was secured in court cases during Mowat's period.

During Mowat's period in office, Ontario grew dramatically in size, economic power, and political influence. Much of the population growth was due to immigration Naturalists and outdoors enthusiasts remember Mowat for the creation of Algonquin Park in 1893. [2] Enlarged since his time, the park is now 7,600 km in area, larger than Prince Edward Island. Mowat also gave the province its Parliament building, Queen's Park, built from 1886-92.

V

MOWAT'S VICTORY over Macdonald was complete. Is it any wonder that the prime minister hated the premier of his home province and could say: "Mr. Mowat, with his little soul rattling like a dried pea in a too large pod – what does he care if he wrecks Confederation and interferes with the development of Canada so long as he can enjoy his little salary as Attorney-General?"

Mowat's legacy is modern Ontario and, to a substantial extent, modern Canada. His policies led to the development of a provincial society that was productive, advanced, well-educated, stable, and wealthy. Those attributes, plus the extension of the province's borders, made Ontario a resource giant and the dominant social, economic, and political unit within Canada. And he imposed on Canada his view of federalism as a system in which powerful and wealthy provinces could easily act as counterweight to federal authority. He was, without a doubt, a key architect of the Canadian nation.

James O'Reilly &
George Dormer

CATHOLIC POLITICS

*The history of the federal Conservative Party in Ontario during the
1880s and 1890s was complicated by a great deal of anti-Catholic
and anti-French-Canadian sentiment. It is interesting to speculate on
what would have happened had able and attractive politicians like
Dormer and O'Reilly lived.*

T HE POLITICAL history of Kingston is as rich as that of any city in
Canada. It is illuminated by towering figures. Christopher Alexander Hagerman was an important Tory during the pre-1841 period.
John A. Macdonald, Richard Cartwright, and Alexander Campbell
dominate the scene during the latter half of the nineteenth century.
Kingston did not cease to produce important politicians during the
twentieth century, as is indicated by even a cursory glance at the careers of Norman McLeod Rogers and Edgar Benson. Most of the politicians named are well-known and have received the attention of biographers or political historians. Kingston has also produced a number
of less important and lesser known politicians. Several of these men
merit study because of the inherent interest of their careers and because of what their careers demonstrate about Canadian politics. This
paper deals with two such politicians. James O'Reilly and George Dormer were close friends who were active in politics during the 1870s.
Both men had close ties with Kingston, although neither man was
ever elected for Kingston riding. There is a fair amount of material on
O'Reilly but much less information about Dormer.

First published in *Historic Kingston*, Vol. 21 (1973), this article on Catholic
personalities helps fill out Professor Swainson's portrait of nineteenth-century
political life in Kingston.

Portraits of James O'Reilly (left) and George Dormer (Parliament of Canada).

I

JAMES O'REILLY was elected to Parliament only once, but he had an interesting career that illustrates several facts of political life during the 1870s. A Roman Catholic, O'Reilly was born in Mayo county, Ireland, on 23 September 1823.[1] His father, Peter O'Reilly, immigrated to Canada in 1832 and settled in Belleville, where he established himself as a merchant. While a resident of Belleville, he was active in the militia and in politics. Peter O'Reilly was a follower of Robert Baldwin. During the nineteenth century, Hastings County was usually a Conservative stronghold. It is often forgotten, however, that the county contained a strong Reform element, which was powerful enough to elect Robert Baldwin as its MPP in 1841. Being a Reformer in Belleville during the early 1840s must have been both exhilarating and rewarding.

Patronage was an integral part of nineteenth-century politics. John A. Macdonald's use of patronage and corruption is well-known. Liberals and Reformers were equally willing to use political patronage to strengthen their position. Robert Baldwin was no exception to this rule and tried to solve even the most delicate problems through the astute use of patronage. Baldwin, for example, knew that William Hume Blake, when he appointed him to the bench, suffered from a mental disorder.[2] Blake's mental disorder was so serious that, while still a judge, he committed suicide in 1870.

James O'Reilly was almost certainly as aware of the political facts of life as any other nineteenth-century political activist and in due course received his reward for supporting Reform in the chilly atmosphere of Belleville. In 1847, he moved to Kingston, which Robert Baldwin once dismissed as an "Orange Hole."[3] There he received his reward for loyalty. He obtained several patronage posts – Clerk of the Crown, Clerk of the County Court, and Registrar of the Surrogate Court of the United Counties of Frontenac, Lennox and Addington. James O'Reilly was thus a member of a politically informed family.

James received his formal education at the Hastings Grammar School.[4] In 1842, (when he was 19) he began the study of law with Charles Otis Benson of Belleville, completing his studies with the Hon. John Ross and then Crawford and Haggarty. His training brought him into contact with several important public men, and this must have had a considerable influence upon him. John Ross, member of the Upper House, 1848-71, was a cabinet minister, 1851-56 and 1858-62. Ross succeeded Francis Hincks as the Upper Canadian Reform leader. He was both a director and president of the Grand Trunk Railway. A powerful figure in both politics and business, Ross fits very nicely into the businessman-politician category.

John Crawford was also a powerful figure. He was involved in all sorts of businesses. He served as president of the Royal Canadian Bank, the Imperial Building Savings and Investment Society, and the Canadian Car Company. He was the first president of the Toronto and Nipissing Railway and a director of the Toronto, Grey, and Bruce Railway. In 1861, he entered Parliament by defeating George Brown in Toronto east and he later served as an MP from 1867 until 1873 when he resigned to accept the Lieutenant-Governorship of Ontario. J.H. Haggarty was appointed to the bench in 1856 and was Chief Justice of Ontario, 1884-97. James O'Reilly was thus very well connected with influential businessmen and politicians. He was called to the bar of Upper Canada in 1847, and years later, in 1870, was called to the Lower Canadian bar as well.

Immediately after his admission to the bar, O'Reilly moved to Kingston to practice law.[5] Shortly thereafter, in November 1850, he married Mary Jane Redmond. He quickly became a successful attorney, involved with both civil and criminal cases. He developed a large practice, which included clients from as far away as Renfrew County, the southern part of which he represented in the second Parliament. He participated in a number of spectacular criminal cases, usually as defence attorney, and became a prominent Kingston lawyer and supporter of the Conservative Party. He was well known to Macdonald, and this probably accounts for his choice as prosecuting attorney against Patrick Whelan. Whelan, a Fenian, murdered O'Reilly's friend, D'Arcy McGee, on 7 April 1868 as the famous MP returned to his Sparks Street boarding house in Ottawa after a late sitting of the House of Commons.

The Whelan trial was a spectacular one, with several leading lawyers participating, including O'Reilly, J.H. Cameron, and M.C. Cameron. The trial was dramatic in its contradictions. O'Reilly, an Irish Roman Catholic, prosecuted a Fenian, while John Hillyard Cameron, Grand

Master of the Orange Order from 1859 to 1870, acted as defence attorney! The Whelan case was one of O'Reilly's most important and it revealed him as an able and aggressive, if somewhat vehement, attorney. These characteristics can be illustrated by two of O'Reilly's remarks during the trial:[6]

> God forbid that the man who committed the foul deed should not suffer the just punishment consequent upon his crime. The people of this country desire to see the murderer punished; the press unanimously agree that every effort should be made to lay bare the murder, and if I have been instrumental in drawing it to light I shall go down to my grave satisfied that I have tracked the felon who killed D'Arcy McGee.

A bit later he described the murderer at work: "Who saw him? – God in heaven saw him on that beautiful night when all heaven was lighted up, on that night when a dastardly deed was perpetrated which will bring down the vengeance of God and man." This was obviously a very sensitive case. Until the signing of the Treaty of Washington in 1871, Canadians lived in fear of an Anglo-American war which could be triggered by Fenian-inspired violence. Canadian leaders were afraid that McGee's assassination or the trial of Whelan might provoke violence of some sort and went to a great deal of trouble to avoid an incident.

That was probably why Macdonald selected O'Reilly as prosecuting attorney. As an Irish Roman Catholic, O'Reilly would be living proof for the argument that Whelan received a fair trial. O'Reilly secured his conviction, and Whelan was sentenced to death. He was the last man publicly executed in Canada.[7] John A. Macdonald was concerned with the implications of the case even after Whelan was dead and consequently refused to give up to Mrs. Whelan her husband's hanged body for fear of a Fenian demonstration in Montreal. Instead, Macdonald arranged for burial within the prison grounds.[8]

During the hectic years of the mid 1860s, the loyalty of Irish Roman Catholics was often suspect. Suspicions of this sort, often completely unreasonable, were inspired by fear of the Fenians. O'Reilly's prosecution of Whelan proved that he was eminently respectable and in no way sympathetic to the Fenian movement. The Whelan case was thus important to O'Reilly for both professional and political reasons.

There is no doubt that O'Reilly was a highly successful lawyer. His ability was recognized in 1864 when he was made a Q.C., and by his election as a bencher of the Law Society of Upper Canada. His professional career was doubtless well served by his wit, for which he was famous. Nicholas Flood Davin, a nineteenth-century student of Irish Canadians, provides an illustration:

> He was at one time entrusted with the brief for the plaintiff in a breach of promise case. His client was an elderly cook. She was fat as every good cook should be. Her face was red. She had lost one eye. Her lover was a man of humble station. O'Reilly had an inspiration. He proved that the defendant used to visit the plaintiff and sigh, protest and eat, that moreover during his acquaintance with the cook he had gained not less than forty pounds in weight. He put in two photographs of the defendant. One, taken before his days of courting, showed him lean and hungry; the other plump as a peach and fat as an overfed lap-dog. "To whom," asked the advocate who had evidently read the Merchant of Venice, "do these forty pounds belong if not to my client?" The jury convinced that the woman had a claim to at least a portion of the plaintiff and evidently estimating adipose [fatty] tissue at $5.00 a pound gave her a verdict of $200.00.[9]

A number of O'Reilly's witticisms were published in *Harper's Magazine*.[10]

While primarily a lawyer, O'Reilly was marginally active in business, serving as both a director and standing counsel of the Kingston & Pembroke Railway Company.[11] This interest brought him into association with such important business and political leaders of Kingston as R.J. Cartwright, C.F. Gildersleeve, G.A. Kirkpatrick, and Sir John A. Macdonald himself. Through business he associated with prominent members of both nineteenth-century political parties. The Kingston & Pembroke Railway was important in another way. It symbolized Kingston's metropolitan ambitions and ran from the lake north through what Kingston regarded as its hinterland. When O'Reilly contested South Renfrew he was running in a seat of considerable interest to Kingston and in an area in which Kingstonians possessed economic as well as political influence.

II

O'REILLY'S CAREER in federal politics was preceded by considerable political and community activity in Kingston.[12] After living in Kingston for only a brief period, he was elected an alderman in 1850 and held his seat for five years. He served as Kingston's recorder from 1864 until the abolition of the office in 1869. For a number of years, he was president of the St. Patrick's Society and active in the militia, in which he attained the rank of major. The people of Kingston honoured him for raising a company of volunteers during the Trent Crisis, an early proof of complete and un-Fenian loyalty.

O'Reilly's area of influence, however, was far broader than Kingston. This influence was based on his legal practice and close contact with the Bishop of Kingston. A letter from Alexander Campbell to Sir John Macdonald in 1872 illustrates what O'Reilly could do. In the general election of that year, two Conservatives were running against each other in Addington. The sitting member, one James Lapum, was being opposed by a Conservative named Schuyler Shibley. Lapum asked Campbell to see Bishop Horan about support in Addington. Campbell did as he was asked and later reported to Macdonald:

> The only hitch is in Addington where O'Reilly (in retaliation for Lapums [*sic*] old opposition to his being made a judge) had asked the Bishop not to help Lapum saying that Shibley is as good a friend of the Government as Lapum. I have asked O'Reilly by telegraph whether he has got or can get a letter from Shibley agreeing to support us or can advise him to write one. I will then see what is best to be done and may persuade Lapum to retire.[13]

O'Reilly was clearly regarded by senior Conservatives as a powerful Roman Catholic lay leader. His influence extended throughout eastern Ontario. Early in 1872, for example, he asked Alexander Campbell for the appointment of one John Roddy as postmaster at Chrysler post office, and commented: "I *can* & will help the Conservative Candidate in next election for Stormont if my request is granted."[14] At one point during the 1872 campaign he decided to contest Prescott, indicating confidence about his influence and reputation in that county.

At another point during the same campaign, John Haggart requested O'Reilly's assistance with the Catholic population of South Lanark.[15]

First elected to Parliament in 1872 for South Renfrew, O'Reilly declined to run in the general election of 1874, claiming that politics interfered too much with his profession.[16] He died the following year, on 15 May 1875. During his short political career he was a consistent Conservative, described in the *Parliamentary Companion* as "A Baldwin Reformer, and a supporter of Sir John A. Macdonald."[17] He thus preserved continuity with the politics of his father and indicated his membership in the tradition represented by such Baldwinites as his old law teacher John Ross. It was not, of course, unusual for Baldwinites to end up as Conservatives. Robert Baldwin himself had approved the formation of the Liberal-Conservative coalition of 1854, which was the origin of Macdonald's Conservative Party of the post-Confederation era.

O'Reilly wanted to be a judge, but a well-paid judge. As Richard Cartwright wrote Macdonald in 1867: "O'Reilly has been speaking to me about the judgeship of Frontenac stating that he is anxious to get it for Parker. I am not clear about his drift but think he means to try his hand for the House of Commons on the first opportunity, – always provided you do not intend to offer any increase of salary with the Frontenac appointment."[18] Campbell claimed in 1872, in a letter that has already been quoted, that O'Reilly opposed Lapum in Addington "in retaliation for Lampums [*sic*] old opposition to his being made a judge." His search for a judicial appointment was clearly active and well known. Nicholas Flood Davin, was confident that O'Reilly's judicial aspirations would eventually have been realized: "not long before his death, he expressed satisfaction of having been assured that had Sir John A. Macdonald's government remained in power, it was their intention to elevate him to the Bench whenever a vacancy should occur."[19] It is not surprising that a man so openly anxious for preferment should be identified as one seeking cabinet office. Thus in June 1873, Alexander Mackenzie, the leader of the federal Liberal party, commented: "O'Reilly was in Town last week and in speaking to his friends here he affects to believe that O'Connor was to be asked to resign and he (R) expected to be invited to take his place. I doubt if he has any grounds for such a belief."[20]

A cabinet post for O'Reilly was, of course, out of the question. Even if he was the ablest and most popular Ontario Irish Catholic Conservative MP, he could not represent the Irish Catholics in the Cabinet because he would have become the third Kingstonian in the Government (along with Macdonald and Campbell). John O'Connor, on the other hand, was from Windsor and represented Essex. In 1873, it was far more important to have a minister from Western Ontario than a third Kingstonian. Nonetheless, it is clear that O'Reilly sought preferment. This plus a Conservative need for Catholic candidates explains his brief career in federal politics.

III

THE ROMAN Catholic allies of the Conservative party were restive in 1872. The case was well stated by Archbishop Lynch of Toronto in a letter to a prominent Torontonian, Senator Frank Smith. Senator Smith must have passed it on to the Prime Minister. After a specific denial of his authority in politics, the Archbishop presented the case of his people. It is worth quoting at length:

> Now the majority of the Catholics of Ontario finding themselves for years past positively excluded with hardly an exception, from participation in all government offices of any worth, by every succeeding administration, whether Liberal or Conservative, justly complained & have formed themselves into a league for self-protection and advancement. This as a citizen and [illegible] man I must approve of. Hitherto I have used my influence with the Catholics, to give the Conservative Administration, which was so long in power, their hearty support, expecting that the government would some time or other treat them fairly, but now the Catholics after long experience, find their support and patience ill rewarded. I now consider it prudent not to exercise any pressure on the Catholics, the easier task, so that they may follow their own judgement [*sic*] in forwarding their public interest.
>
> The Catholics indeed have had a good deal of patience, and there is a little time yet before the election for the Commons, to conciliate them ... I am not ignorant of the difficulties the Conservatives have of giving Catholics justice. If they do they fear the

Orange Cry, which was so potent in the case of O'Reilly's projected appointment to the judgeship. It is indeed a dilema [*sic*] ... However, it seems to me if a little courage were displayed the same Orangemen ... would not abandon their old party. But a choice must be made and very soon. I have given up making any requests of the Conservatives, according to the old axiom "To attempt the useless is an ungrateful task."[21]

Macdonald propitiated the Archbishop, agreeing to give, in exchange for political support, a more adequate return, including the passage of a bill of interest to Lynch and the nomination of more Catholics in the forthcoming general election. These promises brought the Archbishop back into the fold.

"I have no doubt," he wrote Macdonald in a much quoted letter,

that if you will carry out your proposed measures in justice to the Catholic body, we will have no difficulty in keeping the Catholic vote as of old in your interest. But as I am frank I must urge on you the absolute necessity of showing to the Catholics that this time there will be no failure. Personally, you know, my dear Sir John, how much I esteem you ..., but only act vigourously now in the coming elections and politically we shall have the pleasure of being united. I cannot conceal from you the thought, that, (now that I am warmed up about you) I will have you a good Catholic yet.[22]

The kind of complaint made by Archbishop Lynch concerning the exclusion of Irish Catholics from public positions was presented early in 1872 by J.L.P. O'Hanly in a detailed and statistical pamphlet: *The Political Standing of Irish Catholics* (Ottawa, 1872).[23] O'Hanly, a Liberal railroad engineer, dedicated his pamphlet to the recently organized Catholic League. In page after page of statistics, he illustrated very effectively the under-representation of Irish Catholics in public places in central Canada and placed the blame squarely on the shoulders of the Conservative Party. O'Hanly was clearly attempting to turn to Liberal advantage the kind of discontent voiced by Archbishop Lynch to Senator Smith.

The situation concerning the Catholic vote was very delicate in

1872. The problem was rooted in provincial politics. Late in 1871, Edward Blake formed Ontario's first Liberal government, and persuaded R.W. Scott to enter. Scott, a Conservative, entered Blake's government for regional and economic reasons. Numerous Ottawa Valley politicians supported Scott's move because they were anxious to protect railroad and timber interests. Scott had also been for years an influential Roman Catholic leader, famous as the author of the Scott Act of 1863 – which is still the basis of Ontario's separate school system. His integration into the Liberal Party represented a real electoral hazard to the Ontario Conservatives. Of this Senator George Allen of Toronto was convinced. To Campbell he wrote, "[Blake's] appointment of Scott was skilful dodge, for it will carry the Roman Catholics."[24] Macdonald himself understood Scott's reasons for joining Blake and the implications of that decision. He confided to Campbell, "[Scott] telegraphed Skead and the other Lumbermen that he still preserved his Conservative position & his parliamentary allegiance as such – but wanted to take office to protect Eastern interests, viz: – Lumber Licenses & Canadian Central [Railway]." Macdonald explained that Scott had written him in this regard but had accepted Blake's offer of a cabinet place before receiving a reply because of fear that delay would cause the portfolio to be given to another. Macdonald continued, "the Lumbermen are all for him & the R.C.s, Banks, etc., so that there was only one way to beat him & that was by running agt him. I had half a mind to do so but I reflected that if I beat Scott I would lose the Western Catholics as Blake would find him a Constituency elsewhere." Significantly, Scott's juncture with the Liberals was approved by the leaders of his church. "Scott," concluded Macdonald, "had the approval of Bishops Lynch & Walsh. I don't know about Farrell."[25] The restiveness of many Catholics in 1872, combined with the juncture of Scott with the Liberals and the approval of that union by Lynch and Walsh (respectively, Archbishop of Toronto and Bishop of London), made imperative the conciliation of Irish Catholics, not only by legislative and patronage favours but by an improved representation in the House of Commons.

Roman Catholic complaints about lack of representation were well taken. One can cite examples of successful Catholic politicians during the Upper Canadian or the Union periods. Anthony Manahan, for example, had been elected for Hastings in 1836 and for Kingston in 1841. John O'Connor had been elected in 1863 and 1867. In general, however, Catholics had been hopelessly under-represented in Ontario. It was clearly necessary to field Catholic candidates in 1872. Macdonald and his Conservative colleagues recognized the urgency of the situation and arranged for the nomination for several Catholic Conservatives in Ontario in the general election of 1872.[26] The result was the election of three Irish Catholic MPs to the second Parliament: John O'Connor was re-elected in Essex; James O'Reilly and George Dormer were both elected for the first time. The Liberals elected one Irish Catholic, Darby Bergin in Cornwall. At the same time the Liberals defeated John Kidd in South Perth,[27] while Conservatives defeated John McKeown in Lincoln, John O'Donohoe in East Toronto, and Hugh McMahon in London.[28] Eight Irish Catholics ran for office in 1872. From their point of view, the Conservative Party was the most useful political instrument, and three succeeded in securing election as Conservatives. The fourth Irish Catholic member, Bergin, left the Liberal Party after the election of 1874.

IV

THE DECISION to run O'Reilly in South Renfrew was made relatively late in campaign planning by Campbell and Macdonald. In the ensuing campaign both John A. Macdonald and Alexander Campbell were active and extended considerable assistance to O'Reilly, who proved to be a very difficult candidate. On 9 July 1872, Campbell wrote to his chief:

> S. Renfrew
> If Robertson will not run or will not promise to support you let our friends there have a meeting and nominate O'Reilly and he will go down. Hincks can arrange this probably.[29]

Sir Francis Hincks, who was abandoning the representation of North Renfrew because he knew that he would not win the seat again, must have possessed more influence with the local Conservative organization than with the electorate! O'Reilly was duly nominated and the omni-present Campbell continued to assist. About July 20, he reported to Macdonald as follows:

S. Renfrew

    O'Reilly came back last night and today goes back – I have telegraphed French [?] to join him at Arn Prior – will you telegraph Richard Scott to help him with his private influence. I have advanced O'Reilly $500 for the fight which I probably will be a long time getting back but it cannot be helped – he has been very useful to you and there was no one here to whom he could apply though he has no claim on me.

    I have telegraphed [illegible] Abbot for him.[30]

Shortly thereafter Macdonald provided another $500. O'Reilly pressed hard for all the outside assistance he could get, writing Campbell: "I shall work hard but my main reliance for success will be the assistance you can send me."[31] He complained when Macdonald carried the Conservative campaign into western Ontario, arguing that he needed a great deal of help in Renfrew County. He clearly regarded Macdonald's departure as a betrayal of himself! Like most nineteenth-century politicians, he strongly emphasized the importance of election funds and argued that in his contest $2,000 would hardly be felt. Money was the key: "Oh if I only had the needful," he pleaded "I should triumph."[32] Not only was he short of money and in need of Macdonald's assistance, but he felt that Hincks was failing to give adequate cooperation. Campbell, however, came through with more help, O'Reilly writing him on 14 August: "I just received your cheque for one thousand dollars & many thanks for it." He explained that he had spent $700 of his own money and $300 he received from Ottawa.[33] Nonetheless, O'Reilly's depression continued. The Ontario Government was "putting out all their strength against [him]."[34] He ran out of money again and felt deserted by the party leaders.

    Not only was much money spent on O'Reilly's campaign, but A.P. Cockburn, Liberal MP from Muskoka, claimed that the conservatives were responsible for "the enrolment of hundreds of fictitious names as electors."[35] In spite of all of his complaining, O'Reilly won handily, by almost 300 hundred votes. The result was elation, described to Macdonald by Campbell: "O'Reilly went up on Saturday night and I got D'Arc Boulton to express him out to Lindsay that night – so that he might be at church on Sunday – I hope he will be of service. He is swelling with triumph. The Bishop is delighted and all our friends amongst the R.C.s [*sic*] with O'Reillys [*sic*] victory."[36]

V

A FEW CONCLUDING points should be made about James O'Reilly. Like other prominent Irish Roman Catholics of the day, he was of immigrant stock, but was not from a poor family. His father was first a merchant then an official. James O'Reilly was a very successful lawyer who came into early contact with leading politicians and businessmen. Before becoming an active politician, he was an influential Catholic, and he was able to capitalize on the unrest among Ontario's Irish Catholics, caused by the Liberals' provincial breakthrough in 1871.[37]

Alexander Campbell was very active in O'Reilly's campaign in South Renfrew. He had a major share in arranging his nomination. He used his very considerable influence on O'Reilly's behalf. It is interesting to note that an attempt was made to obtain for O'Reilly the influence of Richard W. Scott. If Scott did assist him it must have been for religious reasons because the evidence indicates that Scott opposed Conservative candidates in the Upper St. Lawrence area in the election of 1872. Campbell also donated money of his own, and arranged for the donation of further sums. The Conservative campaign in South Renfrew was expensive, costing a minimum of $3,000: $500 from Campbell personally, $500 from Macdonald, $1,000 forwarded by Campbell, $700 from O'Reilly himself, $300 from "Ottawa": $3,000 is the barest possible sum. O'Reilly felt very depressed during the campaign and had spent this sum several days before polling. It is almost certain that he obtained additional money. Nineteenth- century campaigning was obviously expensive. Three thousand dollars in today's money would be at least $15,000 and this sum was spent for a riding that included only 1,785 voters in 1872 (1,564 of whom voted).[38]

James O'Reilly was one of the few Irish Catholics elected to Parliament for an Ontario seat during the immediate post-Confederation period. He was an ambitious man, in politics for reasons of patronage and because he was an influential layman acceptable to the Conservative leaders. Had he not died in 1875 he, rather than John O'Connor, would doubtless have become the first Ontario Roman Catholic judge.

VI

FAR LESS IS known about O'Reilly's friend George Dormer.[39] Like O'Reilly, George Dormer was an Irish Catholic, but unlike O'Reilly he was born in Canada. Dormer was born in Kingston on 11 October 1838. His father, a medical doctor, practiced here. Dormer received a very unusual education by nineteenth-century standards. He attended Regiopolis College in Kingston, Laval University, and the University of Toronto, obtaining a B.A. from Laval in 1856 and a B.A. "*ad eundem*"[40] (that is, with "credits given from another university")[41] from Toronto in 1858. He then studied law in John A. Macdonald's office in Kingston. This was doubtless the beginning of his career as a Conservative politician, and the fact that Dormer studied law with Macdonald raises an interesting point. Most students of nineteenth-century politics are familiar with the fact that Oliver Mowat and Alexander Campbell studied law with Macdonald. It is clear, however, that Macdonald had several students over a period of years and that some of these relatively unknown men became active in politics. It would be most instructive to have a study of Macdonald's law students.

In 1862, Dormer "was admitted as an Attorney, U.C. but was not called to the Ontario Bar until 1872.[42] For a time he was a civil service clerk. This part of his career must have occurred while he was an attorney but before he was admitted to the bar.

Dormer, who married Sarah Marsh in October 1859, moved from Kingston to Lindsay, where he became active in municipal politics. Lindsay is often regarded as an orange centre, perhaps because its most prominent nineteenth-century figure was Sir Sam Hughes. One would not assume that a Roman Catholic politician would have met with much success in Lindsay during the mid-nineteenth century, but Dormer's career belies this assumption. He was elected mayor in 1871 when only 31 years of age, and retained that post until 1872. Evidence in the personal papers of Alexander Campbell indicates that while he was mayor, Dormer was active as a Conservative and that he controlled at least some of his area's patronage.[43] In 1872, when he ran successfully for Parliament for South Victoria, he had Macdonald's personal endorsement. Macdonald went to his assistance in Victoria County and commented on one occasion that "he had come to Lindsay for the purpose of doing what he could in his humble way for his personal and political friend Mr. Dormer."[44]

Dormer's federal career was limited to the second Parliament (1872-74). In 1874, he refused to contest the seat because of ill health. In the following year, he was with James O'Reilly in Kingston when O'Reilly died.[45] They had been fellow members of the second Parliament and were close friends. It was to Lindsay that O'Reilly rushed, after his own election success in South Renfrew, to help Dormer secure the Catholic vote. On 24 June 1875, Dormer himself died of consumption. These two old friends died within a few weeks of each other and both men died prematurely.

A few points concerning George Dormer's career should be emphasized. He was an Irish Catholic with an unusually good education. Although he moved to Lindsay, he had numerous close ties with Kingston: his family, his early training at Regiopolis, his experience as a student in Macdonald's law office, and his friend O'Reilly. His ties with O'Reilly and Macdonald were active. He must have been politically ambitious to become Mayor of Lindsay when he was 33 and an MP the following year. Like that of his friend O'Reilly, his parliamentary career was limited to one parliament.

The history of the federal Conservative Party in Ontario during the 1880s and 1890s was complicated by a great deal of anti-Catholic and anti-French-Canadian sentiment. It is interesting to speculate on what would have happened had able and attractive politicians like Dormer and O'Reilly lived. They might have been able to offer constructive leadership within the Conservative party and prevented much of the internal strife that bedeviled the party during the latter part of the century and that helped to cripple it during the 1890s.

Richard Cartwright's
Tory Phase

While political differences did not preclude business co-operation, business commitments exercised no undue influence on Cartwright's political judgment.

RICHARD JOHN CARTWRIGHT was a giant of nineteenth-century Canadian liberalism. He was a pillar of Alexander Mackenzie's hapless Liberal regime (1873-78). During the 1880s, he was a major figure within the party, and after Laurier became party chief in 1887, he served briefly as the effective leader of the powerful Ontario wing of the federal Liberal Party.

Cartwright's hour of glory came in the late 1880s and early 1890s when his continentalist policies were the main planks in his party's programme, and he led the agitation for Unrestricted Reciprocity with the United States. The failure of the continentalist agitation destroyed Cartwright as a major figure within the Liberal Party. After Laurier's triumph, he functioned as a secondary leader. Nonetheless, he served for 15 years, from 1896 until 1911, as Minister of Trade and Commerce. He was still a member of the Senate when he died in 1912. For 40 years, from 1873 until 1912, Cartwright was an important Liberal. It was during these years that he made his really important contributions to public life. While there is a deficiency of published material on Sir Richard, the basic facts relating to his career from 1873 to 1912 are well enough known. Not so much is

This article was published in the *Lennox and Addington Historical Society, Papers and Records,* Vol. 15 (1976). Richard Cartwright was first elected to the Union Parliament for Lennox and Addington in 1863.

Portrait of young Richard Cartwright as a Tory (Library and Archives Canada).

known about his pre-1873 career. For ten years before he became Alexander Mackenzie's Minister of Finance, Cartwright sat in the House of Commons as a Conservative or Independent Conservative. His career thus had a lengthy Tory phase. The purpose of this paper is to look at Richard Cartwright's Tory years, specifically two areas: his background and early business associations; and his early career in politics, including the reasons that finally occasioned his departure from Sir John A. Macdonald's Conservative Party.

I

RICHARD JOHN CARTWRIGHT was born in Kingston in 1835. Of United Empire Loyalist stock, he was the scion of a powerful Conservative family, "as nearly the equivalent of the English landed gentry as one can find in Canadian history."[1] His great grandfather emigrated from England to New York in 1742; his grandfather, Hon. Richard Cartwright, was a Loyalist and the founder of the Canadian family. He was a wealthy man, important in both the business and political life of Upper Canada.[2] Richard's father was the Rev. Robert David Cartwright, an Anglican clergyman; his mother was Harriet Dobbs.[3] Like his father, Richard was an Anglican. In 1859, he married Frances Lawe of Cork, Ireland; they had nine children.[4]

In 1851, at the age of 16, Richard was sent to Trinity College, Dublin, doubtless after a secondary education at the Midland District Grammar School. He remained at Trinity until 1856,[5] but in spite of a residence of five years took no degree (for reasons that are unknown).[6] Other pre-Confederation Ontarians were educated at Trinity. William Hume Blake (as much as an aristocrat as any Cartwright) graduated in 1830 before his move to Canada, and G.A. Kirkpatrick of Kingston followed Cartwright to Dublin. This was obviously a type of education available to only wealthy Canadians.

After his return to Canada, Cartwright "began the study of law but was never called to the bar".[7] Instead, Cartwright became a businessman-investor with extensive and varied interests. "Cartwright," noted Roger Graham in his excellent Ph.D. thesis, "lived by investing his own and other people's money in this and that."[8] His grandfather owned the site on which Napanee was built. This was the basis of Richard Cartwright's considerable wealth. To quote Roger Graham again: "This proprietary interest … passed on in large measure to R.J. Cartwright who owned extensive property in and around the village and also certain water rights on the Napanee River"[9]. His interests were broader than these and although "a man of no fixed profession, aside from politics … he managed to find a good many pies worth dabbling in".[10]

Before Confederation Cartwright's most important commitment was to banking. He was president of the Commercial Bank and has been described as "an up and coming figure in the financial world."[11] This phase of his business career ended in 1867 when his bank folded after an unsuccessful appeal for aid to the government, an appeal supported by Alexander Tilloch Galt, the Minister of Finance. This bankruptcy was at least in part due to poor management, and must, therefore, be placed at the door of the young president.[12] The refusal of the government to aid the Commercial Bank doubtless annoyed Cartwright, then a young Conservative backbencher. Aid, however, would have placed Macdonald in a vulnerable position because it would have involved aid to himself; he was a director of the bank and his law firm both acted for the bank and owed it the staggering sum of $79,000.[13] Macdonald, whose name is intimately associated with corrupt politics, was so heavily influenced by political considerations that he permitted the Commercial Bank to go under, even though it mortified an influential local Conservative family, wrecked his law firm, and precipitated his personal bankruptcy.

Cartwright, however, had other irons in the fire during the pre-Confederation years. In 1864, he explored the possibility of establishing a Canadian Express Company.[14] Lumbering was another interest and he attempted to purchase lots for "Cook and Cochrane."[15] He seems also to have used his political influence on behalf of this or another firm. Hence, this comment by Alexander Campbell, one of Macdonald's most important lieutenants in eastern Ontario: "I have yours of the 21st inst. and will with pleasure see what can be done for your American lumbering friends"[16] In view of Cartwright's later career as an agitator for continental economic integration, it is interesting to note this remark. As early as 1866, he was involved with American business interests and felt it appropriate to use his political influence on their behalf.

During the early years of Confederation, Cartwright co-operated with Alexander Morris in a number of business enterprises.[17] In

1867, the Bedford Navigation Company was organized with Morris and Cartwright as senior directors, each owning $3,200 out of a total investment of $10,000. The firm, established to improve navigation on part of the Rideau system, was re-organized in 1868 with Morris and Cartwright still the senior directors – each owning $10,000 worth of stock out of a total of $35,000. In the same year, Morris led in the formation of a company to do iron and plumbago mining in Bedford Township and at Chaffey's. Cartwright was also involved. Again in 1868, Morris and Cartwright agreed to form a company to manufacture tannin from hemlock, oak and other trees. Cartwright put up $2,000, and $50,000 was quickly raised. In 1869, the Ontario Concentrated Tannin Company was in operation at Perth, under the presidency of Alexander Morris. The tannin factory was destroyed by fire in 1871, at which point Morris and Cartwright sold out. The Chaffey iron properties, owned by two Morris brothers, John Manion and two Cartwright brothers, were sold to Americans in 1873, by which date all the joint Morris-Cartwright operations but the Bedford navigation Company had been sold.

Cartwright retained his interest in finance.[18] In 1868, the Canada Life Assurance Company elected him a director, a post he retained until September, 1873. He served for many years as either a director or president of the Frontenac Loan and Investment Society. By 1872, he owned at least 60 shares of the Bank of Montreal, worth $12,000. Later in his career, he was vice-president of the Trusts Corporation of Ontario, and one of the three trustees in Canada for the Equitable Life Insurance Company.

With other leading Kingstonians, Cartwright was heavily involved in the affairs of the Kingston & Pembroke Railway. He joined such men as James O'Reilly (Conservative politician and local lawyer), C.F. Gildersleeve (Liberal politician, local lawyer and business leader), and G.A. Kirkpatrick (Conservative politician, local lawyer and businessman) to petition John A. Macdonald to apply pressure to Sandfield Macdonald, Ontario's first premier "to empower municipalities to grant bonus to railways without special charter."[19] This is an interesting example of contemporary business practices. Men from both parties combined to manipulate the federal and provincial levels of government in the interests of their business affairs and community. Cartwright became a provisional director of the Kingston & Pembroke

Railway (K and P), then a director of the line, and purchased 100 shares (worth $5,000) in the line.[20] Macdonald was interested in the management of the line, and, in February 1872, asked Cartwright to vote for the previous year's Board of Directors because, as Macdonald put it: "The Robinson-Livingston-Fraser clique are intriguing and I want to checkmate them. If you can't attend personally Wednesday send your proxy like a good fellow to O'Reilly."[21] Alexander Campbell immediately added to the pressure applied by John A.[22] Cartwright quickly informed the Prime Minister that he doubted if he was "aware of all that has passed," stated that he was not "disposed to help the clique to whom you refer" and agreed to "bear your note in mind ... and defer action for the moment."[23] Macdonald was clearly working closely with Campbell and O'Reilly.

Cartwright, in spite of fundamental disagreements with the Conservative party in 1869, could still be a "good fellow" and was assumed to be willing to co-operative with the O'Reilly faction, a group that worked in close alliance with Macdonald's Conservative organization. Political differences, either within the Conservative Party or between the parties, in no way precluded business or civic co-operation. Cartwright's close involvement with the K and P, or the Kick and Push as it was called locally, illustrates another point. The basic strategy behind the line was simple: "It is the shortest route between the principal lumbering rivers of Ontario and the American market, and throws open for settlement a large agricultural area."[24] In other words, the line was not conceived as a component of a transcontinental communications system for Canada, but as a tool with which to exploit American markets. It was thus continentalist in conception. This is another early indication of Richard Cartwright's continentalist outlook. His later activities in the field of economic policy are consistent with his early business practices.

Mining speculation was another interest.[25] Cartwright purchased 10,000 shares worth $4,000 in "The Kingston and Sherbrooke Gold Mining Company (Nova Scotia)" in 1868 and paid for them with promissory notes. In 1869, he purchased 1,000 shares worth $1,000 in the Canada Gold Mining Company of Nova Scotia, a firm capitalized at $100,000. Cartwright was president of this firm, which must in some manner have been connected with the Kingston and Sherbrooke Gold Mining Company. Alfred Patton was an officer of both firms, and in each case Cartwright was extensively involved. The Cornwallis Magnetic Iron Mine in King's county was investigated for him in 1872, and in 1873 Campbell, J.B. Robinson (a prominent Conservative from Toronto), and Cartwright purchased a coal area in Nova Scotia. Although unsuccessful, it was an extensive venture. Campbell explained the financial situation to Cartwright: "I have drawn on you for $7,021.54 to yield $6,837.50 on account of the purchase money as agreed of one fourth of the Coal Mine and $337.50 your contribution to the preliminary expenses including the reports which you have seen. The balance due upon the lot [?] is $18,500 with interest payable next August, one forth of which you will be liable for."[26] This letter was written in October, 1873, less than a month before the fall of the first Macdonald government. It and other evidence from the same month, illustrates not only the Nova Scotia mining venture, but also something of the nature of nineteenth-century politics.

By the fall of 1873, Richard Cartwright was a renegade Tory. He was one of the key figures in the opposition that was on the verge of destroying the government of which Campbell was an influential member. In the eastern Ontario district, they were bitterly competing for the support of the same MPs, yet in non-political affairs it was business as usual.

On a day-to-day basis, Cartwright was an active Kingston businessman, concerned with a variety of problems and interest: office rentals, purchasing land, selling land, financing mortgages, trading shares, participating in firms of which he was a director, exploring business possibilities, and managing in detail his considerable properties.[27]

While political differences did not preclude business co-operation, business commitments exercised no undue influence on Cartwright's political judgment. Such is the inference drawn from a letter by G.W. Simpson, written during the summer of 1873. Simpson's concern was the accounts of the Merchant's Bank, which were not satisfactory. Cartwright owned 100 shares in the bank, 25 of which Simpson had sold. These shares, however, were declining in value. Simpson explained: "Subject of course to minor fluctuations, I fear the general course of the Stock will be towards a further decline, unless indeed we hear something positive and trustworthy about a sale of the Railway Bonds and the raising of the capital needed for the Can. Pacific R.R. either of which events would give rise to an active speculation for an advance."[28] It is true that Cartwright was attempting to sell these shares. Nonetheless, his political activities militated against the success of the Pacific railroad, and thus against the value of his bank shares. A similar situation developed during his later career. In the 1880s, he acquired "large properties" in Manitoba: a townsite renamed "Cartwright" and 300 acres flanking Portage Avenue on the then western outskirts of Winnipeg.[29] A successful National Policy would certainly have enhanced the value of this property. His support for continentalism and his strong opposition to the National Policy was thus contrary to his known economic interests.

Cartwright was a wealthy businessman-investor, a multiple-interest entrepreneur, to use today's jargon. Between 1867 and 1873, his traceable investments, as referred to above, totaled $41,000. In addition, he owned shares and interests in other properties, directed several firms, and owned property in the Kingston district and in Lennox and Addington. Professor Graham suggests that the "acquisition and management of land seems to have been his chief preoccupation, outside of political warfare, and his chief source of income."[30]

II

FOR THE FIRST 15 years of his political career, 1863-78, Cartwright sat for Lennox and Addington or Lennox. He was, of course, a prominent Kingstonian with numerous business activities centred in Kingston. It should be noted that he also had extensive and important associations with his constituency. His family had a traditional involvement with the county, based on the ownership of extensive property. As Richard Cartwright himself put it, "we had large material interests in the county. Its principal town was built entirely on our lands and we had direct business connections with many persons all over the county."[31] During his first campaign in 1863, he fought on the very local issue of whether Napanee or Newburgh was to be the county seat. Cartwright supported Napanee and the first bill he introduced was to incorporate Napanee as a town.[32] His wealth enabled him to spend a minimum of $5,596.08 securing his 1863 return.[33]

Once elected, his relationship with his constituents was normal by nineteenth-century standards. Patronage was dispensed; the Napanee Cricket Club elected him an honorary member. He guaranteed press support for himself. For example, before the election of 1872, he loaned $200 to T.S. Carman of the *Weekly Express*. Carman assured his creditor that he had "always taken any opportunity to look after your interests."[34] Cartwright also concerned himself with such typical problems as improvements for the Napanee harbour.[35] Cartwright and his brother James possessed one unusually useful set of relationships with residents of Lennox and Addington. They held many mortgages within the county, a factor which could be important not only to Cartwright but, after 1867, to any county colleague (the member for Addington) he chose to assist.

III

WITHOUT THE benefit of a municipal career, Cartwright was first elected to the last Union Parliament for Lennox and Addington in 1863, when he was 28. He was, of course, a Conservative. Virtually all pre-Confederation Kingston politicians were Conservatives; certainly, virtually every successful Kingston politician was a Conservative. Cartwright thus grew up in a profoundly conservative atmosphere. Like other Kingstonians of his generation, he had no need to articulate a political philosophy or choose between competing ideologies. He simply breathed the Tory air of the limestone city and adopted the political philosophy held by the vast bulk of his friends, business associates, and townsmen. His initial political affiliation requires no explanation.

During the last Union Parliament (1863-67), he was a fairly typical Conservative backbencher. Like many of his Upper Canadian colleagues, he found the lure of representation by population irresistible, and supported that issue on at least one occasion – despite the fact that John A. Macdonald and George Etienne Cartier were intransigently opposed to any concession on the rep-by-pop question. Again, like most of his Upper Canadian colleagues, he fell into line when the Confederation coalition was formed in 1864 and supported Confederation during the ensuing debates.[36] After the division of Lennox and Addington in 1867, Cartwright contested Lennox and held it until defeated in 1878. He was then returned for Centre Huron (vacated for him), which he lost in 1882. Another seat, South Huron, was made available and he was elected again in 1883. In 1887, he obtained South Oxford (a safe Liberal seat), which he held until appointed to the Senate in 1904. He remained in the Senate until his death in 1912. Of the 40 years Cartwright spent in the House of Commons, he sat for an eastern Ontario riding for only 15. His interest in the area continued, however, and as late as the 1890s he served as president of the Eastern Ontario Liberal Associaton.[37]

In spite of the fact that Cartwright was first elected to Parliament at the tender age of 28, he rose quickly. By 1869 he was able to oppose the government publicly and retain his seat; in 1873, at the age of 38, he obtained the prestigious and powerful finance portfolio. He held the post until 1878 and proved to be one of Mackenzie's few useful ministers. During the 1880s, he continued his advance, succeeding Blake as Ontario leader in 1887. After 1891 his influence declined, and in 1896 Laurier appointed him not to Finance but to Trade and Commerce, a post he held until the fall of the government in 1911. Cartwright was made a K.C.M.G. in 1879 and a G.C.M.G. in 1897.

The most interesting aspect of Cartwright's first decade in politics was his shift from John A. Macdonald's Conservative Party to the Liberal Party of Alexander Mackenzie. This matter has attracted more interest than any other aspect of Cartwright's early career, and has been dealt with by several writers, including this writer.[38] It is a complex matter.

A number of historians have suggested that the real problem was one of personal pique. After 1867, the Ontario wing of the federal cabinet was a coalition of Conservatives and Reformers. Within a very brief period after the election of 1867, the coalition was a pretty tattered affair, but it continued to have utility to the Conservatives, especially at the grass roots level in a number of traditionally Liberal ridings that supported the Conservative dominated coalition in 1867. Macdonald was determined to maintain the semblance of a coalition, but found this increasingly difficult in the face of an aggressive Liberal Party in Ontario. In 1869, John Rose resigned as Finance Minister. Macdonald decided to take the opportunity to strengthen the cabinet by the appointment to the Finance portfolio of the old Reformer, Sir Francis Hincks, who had just completed a tour of duty as Governor of British Guiana. This was a truly incredible appointment, one of the worst Macdonald ever made. Hincks had left Canada fourteen years earlier under a cloud of disgrace. He had alienated the George Brown faction of the Reform Party. That group dominated the Ontario wing of the Liberal Party in the years immediately following Confederation, and loathed Sir Francis. He was out of touch with Canadian affairs, and had no following whatever. Hincks was also distrusted. This proved to be not unreasonable, as Sir Francis was instrumental in setting in train the events that led to the Pacific Scandal.

It goes without saying that the appointment of Hincks as Minister of Finance was not well received. It was opposed by Liberals and Conservatives alike. Richard Cartwright was aghast, and his opposition to the appointment has been used to explain his break with the Conservative Party. It has been assumed that he himself wanted the Finance portfolio, and that when spurned, he became sufficiently angry to leave his party. O.D. Skelton puts the proposition in bold terms: "One result of the appointment was to complete the estrangement of a rising young Conservative, Richard Cartwright. Cartwright, though young and comparatively inexperienced, had a just confidence in his own financial capacity, and considered that the post should have been offered to him."[39] R.O. MacFarlane was equally certain: "The appointment of Hincks drove Galt and Cartwright out of the party."[40] This plausible explanation originated at the time of Cartwright's juncture with the Liberals, but contains several weaknesses: Cartwright knew that he could not become Minister of Finance in 1869 and was not a candidate for the job; the appointment of Sir Francis did not "complete" his alienation from the Conservative party; his final break with Sir John did not come until 1873; and, Cartwright's motivation was complex, not simply a desire to be Minister of Finance.

A detailed examination of the situation reveals a very interesting picture. Prior to 1869, Cartwright was a rising Conservative backbencher, becoming more and more involved in party management and on very good terms with the Prime Minister.[41] His clash with Macdonald over the Hincks appointment was straightforward and was made before the appointment was final.[42] After Hincks was appointed, Cartwright explained to Macdonald: "[You] will probably not be surprised to learn that I fear I cannot support that gentleman … I cannot feel the same confidence as heretofore in an administration in which Sir F. Hincks holds office."[43] Macdonald argued the case with his young back-bencher, but to no avail. Cartwright was simply "unable to concur with [Macdonald] in this matter."[44] No evidence indicates that Cartwright's criticism of this appointment was based on personal disappointment. He was blunt and open in his criticism. "Sir Richard objected to this step," said Joseph Pope "in a manly, straightforward manner."[45]

And he had a fair amount of support. Alexander Galt agreed with him; so did Mackenzie Bowell.[46] Both were Conservatives of an independent type, but were nonetheless Conservatives. Other Conservatives disliked the appointment with various degrees of intensity, for example, men like Pope, Colby, Webb, Ross (Dundas), and Lapum.[47] Cartwright thus represented a fairly widespread sentiment within the party. Also, Cartwright did not know that his friend Alexander Galt had refused the portfolio before it was offered to Hincks.[48] For some weeks, Cartwright laboured under the misapprehension that Macdonald's real motive was "to keep [Galt] out of the Finance Ministership."[49]

In any event, Cartwright knew that he was ineligible for the Finance or any other portfolio. He was a ministerial impossibility. Of five Ontario ministers he would have become the third Kingstonian and third Conservative in an ostensibly coalition regime – a politically absurd situation. James Cockburn of Cobourg realized this and commiserated with his friend: You must go in bye and bye. Would not Campbell take the Judgeship? It is unfortunate that there are two Kingstonians already in the Cabinet."[50] Cartwright regarded the appointment as a political disaster, and he opposed it in order, as he put it, "to preserve the present Liberal Conservative Party, if possible, in spite of all their Leader has done to destroy it."[51] His strategy was not to strengthen the opposition, but to change the Conservative Party. Cartwright sought influence, not permanent alienation from his Party.

The evidence indicates that the quarrel of 1869 need not have produced a permanent rift between Cartwright and the Conservative party, or union with the Liberals. In the House, he often voted with the government between 1869 and 1873 and continued (to a lesser degree) to do so in 1873. He sat, of course, on the cross benches but was not regarded by all Conservatives as an oppositionist.[52] Senator Macpherson, for example, made this comment in December 1870: "I do not suppose that your disapproval of some of the Government measures of last session affect your personal friendship with Sir John A. I imagine that you and I occupy much the same ground in regard to him."[53]

In the election of 1872, the Conservatives made no real attempt to defeat Cartwright in Lennox, and he won by a large margin, 1,224 to 513.[54] During the campaign, the Toronto *Globe* assumed that Cartwright was just another Conservative, and described him as "a Tory and a corruptionist."[55] Cartwright stuck to his own riding during the campaign,[56] thus giving a minimum of offence to the Conservative Party.

After the 1872 campaign, the government probed his intentions in discreet ways. He maintained friendly personal and business relationships with numerous Conservatives, and was to co-operate in the House with a Conservative as influential as John Carling.[57] As 1872 closed, Cartwright was neither moving farther away from the Conservative Party nor again reconciling himself to Macdonald's leadership. What propelled him out of the party was the Pacific Scandal. In 1869, he believed that the Hincks appointment would seriously damage the party. In 1873, the problem was far more serious, and Cartwright determined to help defeat the government. His motives were doubtless mixed. An earlier attempt to reform the party had failed. Gaining office was more likely under the Liberals. The parliamentary crisis of 1873 would enable him to play a major role as an "Independent Conservative" – as he described himself after the election of 1874.[58] Cartwright was able to play the role of a third party leader, rallying dissidents and co-operating with the Liberal leaders, not as a colleague or follower but as an ally. While Cartwright was almost certainly influenced by the legitimate desire to obtain office, he could not seriously have anticipated being offered the Finance portfolio in the event that Macdonald was driven from power. Alexander Mackenzie reserved Finance for Luther Holton. Not even Mackenzie knew that Holton would turn down the crucial portfolio.

The decision to ally himself with the Liberal leaders was not an easy one. Alexander Mackenzie began the process of wooing Cartwright early in 1873. Cartwright, fully aware of the dangers involved, was reluctant, explaining to Mackenzie that while he had been elected "as an absolutely independent candidate," he was not in the same position as a member of the opposition.[59] Mackenzie persisted, but the results were minimal, until the Liberal leaders started to uncover the facts related to the Pacific Scandal. Here was something that might influence a waverer to change his stance. Mackenzie asked for a meeting with Cartwright on the day before the opening of the spring session of the House of Commons. At the same time Mackenzie explained an "extraordinary story" he had just heard: "It seems that Sir John made an agreement with Sir Hugh Allan and Jay Cooke and their Yankee Associates before the election that they were to have the contract, they engaging to furnish 3% on their capital or $300,000 to carry the elections. This money was actually [paid] and all the subsequent negotiations with Senator McPherson and others was a mere blind."[60]

Lucius Seth Huntington made his devastating charges on 02 April 1873, and in the following months the whole story of the Pacific Scandal came out. This convinced Cartwright that the government must be defeated, and he entered into close co-operation with the Liberal leaders. He became in effect the opposition leader in eastern Ontario. 1873 was an exciting, frantic year. Cartwright worked hard. He co-operated closely with Liberal leaders on day-to-day problems relating to political management and parliamentary strategy. He attempted to convince neighbouring MPs to desert the government. With Edward Blake, he discussed the possible composition of a new cabinet. By the fall of 1873, he was unquestionably a member of the opposition high command. As Edward Blake put it: "I suppose you will be at Ottawa on 22nd. It is of great consequence that those of us who have to do the headwork should have full time to concert and mature plans for every contingency."[61]

The opposition assault on the Conservative regime was successful. Macdonald and his ministers resigned on 05 November 1873. Mackenzie then went about the task of constructing a government. Cartwright was a logical person to include in a Liberal ministry. He was able and could be held to represent "independent" Conservative opinion in Ontario. In addition, he came from a staunchly Conservative area. It was hoped that he might emerge as a powerful regional leader in his own right.

Appointing Cartwright to the Finance portfolio was not quite so logical as his inclusion in the government. Finance was first offered to Luther Holton, who refused the post. Mackenzie seriously considered taking the post himself. As he explained to George Brown: "I would have liked to take the Finance dept myself, but I did not see who could take the Public Works."[62] Once Holton and Mackenzie were ruled out, Cartwright was an obvious choice for the portfolio and was so appointed.

Once sworn in, the ministers sought re-election, as was required by the law of the day. Cartwright was the only Ontario minister to meet opposition. This situation was not hard to explain. As a recent convert to Liberalism, he must have been extremely annoying to Conservatives. More important, he represented a major threat to the party in its most import Ontario bastion. Defeating him would thus have been both gratifying and useful. The by-election (which Cartwright won easily) was consequently hard fought, personal and very bitter.

The campaign was probably a major cause of the personal estrangement that developed between Macdonald and Cartwright. They never again had any normal non-parliamentary relations.[63] After 1873, Cartwright might continue to call himself an "Independent Conservative," but all the value of independence had vanished. He was in the Liberal Party and had no place else to go.

This early phase of Richard Cartwright's career is of considerable interest. Cartwright was a pre-Confederation Canadian aristocrat. A scion of a powerful Conservative family, he was well educated, an Anglican, a United Empire Loyalist, and wealthy. As a young man, he became prominent as a financier; but his post-Confederation business activities were more concerned with general investment and land management. The importance of understanding Cartwright the businessman should be stressed. He was not just a *rentier*. He was an active business leader, heavily involved in a staggering number of enterprises. This, of course, must have influenced his view of economic affairs, federal economic strategy, the role of business in the state, labour, and the whole gamut of problems he would deal with as Minister of Finance or as Liberal Finance critic after 1878. His business activities are suggestive of other things as well. Business brought him into contact with a variety of men in public life, including both friends and foes. It is evident that nineteenth-century politicians refused to allow mere considerations like personal hatreds to stand in the way of the pursuit of profit.

While Cartwright's role as a businessman must have influenced his intellectual makeup and his general outlook, it is clear that particular business concerns did not influence Cartwright's political judgment in cases of specific policies or incidents. It is also interesting to note Cartwright's early involvement with American businessmen, and with projects designed to tie in with the American economy. This, of course, is consistent with his later strong belief in the virtues of economic continentalism.

Between 1863 and 1869, Cartwright was a fairly typical Conservative backbencher, although a fairly important one. His cabinet prospects, however, were seriously limited by the concentration of Conservative talent in Kingston. In 1869 occurred the famous conflict over Hincks' appointment to the cabinet. R.O. MacFarlane argued: "This appointment of Hincks drove Galt and Cartwright out of the party."[64] This statement is misleading. These men were estranged from the party, but Galt was back in a few years. Cartwright became an "Independent Conservative," but his independence was not necessarily permanent. His concern in 1869 seems to have been the welfare of the party, not the obtaining of the Finance portfolio as has been suggested. Cabinet ambition in 1869 was clearly not a rational ambition.

It has also been suggested that Cartwright's alienation from the Conservative Party was caused by reasons that were essentially personal. That this quarrel was "personal" is open to the gravest doubts. That the 1869 quarrel made the Conservative Party an impossible political home for Cartwright is equally dubious. Between 1869 and 1873, he was an "Independent Conservative" and after the election of 1872 could have retained that status or rejoined his party. Either alternative was as reasonable as fusion with the Liberals. What made the Conservative Party an impossibility for Cartwright was not "1869" but "1873." As much is indicated by chronology. As late as 04 February 1873, he protected his independence with care,[65] although he was in contact with Mackenzie – a contact politically logical and almost certainly initiated by the latter. He learned of the scandal charges by February 21 at the latest. These charges made logical his move from independence to opposition. Again he had reason to doubt Macdonald's leadership, but this time he had no hope of exerting pressure within the party. The Pacific Scandal then was decisive in putting him out of the Conservative Party and propelling him into the Liberal Party.

During 1873, he rose rapidly as an opposition leader. His entry into the cabinet, the Lennox by-election, and his rise to real prominence within Mackenzie's government fixed his identification as a Liberal and he remained an important Liberal until his death in 1912.

Richard Cartwright

JOINS THE LIBERAL PARTY

The conventional view that resentment over the choice of Hincks as Minister of Finance in 1869 led Cartwright to forsake the Conservative Party is seen to be untenable. What chiefly led to his defection were the unsavoury disclosures of the Pacific Scandal in 1873.

RICHARD CARTWRIGHT is one of the dominant figures in the history of the Canadian Liberal Party. As Minister of Finance, 1873-78, he was a pillar of the first Liberal government. An important opposition figure after 1878, he emerged as the leading figure in the Ontario wing of the party when Laurier succeeded Blake as leader in 1887. His influence reached its zenith during the late 1880s and early 1890s when he led the forces of continentalism and campaigned for Unrestricted Reciprocity. His influence waned after 1896 as the National Policy succeeded and as Laurier remade the Liberal Party, but he nonetheless served for 15 years as Minister of Trade and Commerce. Cartwright was thus an important Liberal for 40 years, from 1873 when he entered Mackenzie's administration until his death in 1912. But he began public life as a Conservative. Why he became a Liberal has never been satisfactorily explained.

The second part of Professor Swainson's profile of this influential Kingston and Canadian politician appeared in the *Queen's Quarterly*, Vol. 25, No. 1 (1968). This article is among his earliest publications. Passages from this article also appear in his previous work on Cartwright's Tory years.

Portrait of Sir Richard Cartwright as a Liberal (Library and Archives Canada).

I

On three occasions, the Finance portfolio exerted a powerful influence on Cartwright's career, and on how his career has been judged by historians. While still a Conservative, he opposed the appointment of Sir Francis Hincks as Minister of Finance in 1869. Having become an "Independent Conservative," he entered Mackenzie's government as Minister of Finance in 1873, holding the post until the fall of the government in 1878. When a leading Liberal, he was denied his old portfolio in 1896, a denial which symbolized the party's temporary abandonment of continentalism and which marked the end of Cartwright's ascendancy within the Ontario wing of the Party.

In both 1873 and 1896, the disposition of the portfolio was crucial to his career. This has perhaps caused historians to assume that it was equally so in 1869. It has been argued that Cartwright left the Conservative Party and became a Liberal because of his opposition to the appointment of Hincks as Minister of Finance in 1869. "One result of the appointment," said O.D. Skelton, "was to complete the estrangement of a rising young Conservative, Richard Cartwright. Cartwright, though young and comparatively inexperienced, had a just confidence in his own financial capacity, and considered that the post should have been offered to him." R.O. MacFarlane was equally certain. "The appointment of Hincks," he said, "drove Galt and Cartwright out of the party." Roger Graham, the author of the most extensive study of Cartwright, argues in a similar vein. What was really at issue in 1869 was the disposition of the Finance portfolio, a post wanted by Cartwright. The "supposition is strong," says Graham, "that this was at least partly responsible for his course."[1]

Preoccupation by historians with the Finance portfolio has obscured this phase of Cartwright's career. He was not, in fact, a candidate for the post in 1869. The appointment of Hincks did not "complete" his alienation from the Conservative Party. His final break with Macdonald came in 1873; and Cartwright's motivation was complex, not simply a desire to be Minister of Finance.

Prior to 1869, the situation was simple enough. Cartwright was first elected for Lennox and Addington in 1863, defeating a sitting Conservative in a factionalized and intensely local contest. This necessitated a show of independence because of the importance of the Liberal vote in such a contest. Once elected, however, he quickly settled into the role of a Conservative backbencher, becoming more and more involved in party management and on very good terms with his leader, John A. Macdonald.[2] Six years later, a cabinet reorganization produced a public rift between Cartwright and Macdonald, but it was not the first time Cartwright had cause to disagree with his leader. In 1867, the cabinet, in spite of a strong plea from A.T. Galt, the Minister of Finance, refused to come to the aid of the ailing Commercial Bank, of which Cartwright was president. The bank went bankrupt, and the cabinet's refusal to help was a major reason for Galt's resignation in 1867. The dispute in 1869 was of a less personal nature. Macdonald needed both a new Minister of Finance to replace John Rose, and a Reformer, to keep alive the illusion that the ministry was a coalition. With a rare combination of poor judgment and bad luck he selected the old Reformer, Sir Francis Hincks, recently retired from the colonial service, and made him Minister of Finance.

Cartwright protested the appointment, both before it was made and after it was announced.[3] "I fear I cannot support that gentleman," he explained to Sir John.[4] Macdonald sent Cartwright a long and detailed explanation, but Cartwright was not satisfied and found himself "unable to concur ... in this matter." It is most unlikely, however, that Cartwright was after the post for himself. There is certainly no evidence to that effect. He was open and blunt in his criticism of the appointment. "Sir Richard objected to this step," said one of his harshest critics, "in a manly, straightforward manner."[5] He had considerable support.

Alexander Galt was strongly opposed to the appointment, as was Mackenzie Bowell,[6] both Conservatives of an independent type, but nonetheless Conservatives. Galt, in fact, was offered the Finance portfolio in September 1869 in succession to Rose.[7] Other Conservatives objected to the appointment with various degrees of intensity, including several MPs: John Henry Pope (Compton), C.C. Colby (Stanstead), W.H. Webb (Richmond and Wolfe), J.S. Ross (Dundas), and James Lapum (Addington). Cartwright's objection thus represented a widespread sentiment within the Conservative Party, although he did not know that Galt had rejected the appointment. As late as 06 November 1869, two and a half months after his initial opposition, he suggested to Galt that Macdonald's real motive in appointing Hincks may have been "to keep you out of the Finance Ministership." Galt was a far more likely candidate for the job than Cartwright, who knew he could not have the post.

He was an impossible choice. Had Cartwright entered the government, he would have become the third Kingstonian, along with Macdonald and Alexander Campbell, in the ministry, a politically unrealistic situation. This was realized by James Cockburn of Cobourg, Speaker of the House of Commons. Late in 1869, he commiserated with Cartwright: "You must go in bye and bye. Would not Campbell take the Judgeship? It is unfortunate that there are two Kingstonians already in the Cabinet." If the appointment of a Kingstonian was impossible from a sectional point of view, it was even more so from a coalition point of view. Ontario had five ministers in a cabinet of 13. Initially three were Liberals, two were Conservatives. Cartwright's appointment would have reversed the balance, with all three Conservatives residing in Kingston. Cartwright was not so naïve as to consider such a possibility within the realm of reason.

He regarded the appointment of Hincks as a political blunder. He opposed it, as Joseph Pope pointed out, "in a manly straightforward manner," doubtless because, as he himself said, it was necessary "to preserve the present Liberal Conservative Party, if possible, in spite of all their leader has done to destroy it." The strategy he devised to coerce Macdonald was designed not to strengthen the opposition but to transform the Conservative Party. He wished to apply pressure on the government, publicly or privately, from the heartland of Conservative Ontario. He explained his tactics to Galt. "[Bear] in mind," he wrote, "that the only section in Ontario on which Conservatives can really depend (apart from the Ottawa country which goes with the tide) is the central part lying between Cobourg and Prescott. Here we have 20 constituencies all represented by Conservatives and in this region which I know well and in which the 4 other Ontario men I named (i.e., self, Shanly, Ross and Bowell) have all for various causes a good deal of weight apart from our mere voting, Hincks' appointment is deeply and all but unanimously condemned."

Cartwright's personal ambitions were checked by the unusual concentration of Conservative talent in Kingston. At the same time he clearly felt that a similar heavy concentration of Conservative strength in eastern Ontario could be mobilized to influence the party. Influence was what Cartwright sought, not permanent alienation from his party. As Cockburn had commented, "You must go in bye and bye."

II

THE QUARREL OF 1869 need not have produced a permanent rift between Cartwright and the Conservative Party, or union with the Liberal party. Cartwright did not identify himself with the Liberals until 1873. In the House he often voted with the government after 1869 and continued to do so in the 1873 sessions.[8] While he sat on the cross benches, he was not regarded by the Conservatives as a member of the opposition. In 1870, for example, Senator David Macpherson asked him to make a donation to the Macdonald Testimonial, a fund designed to give financial relief to the prime minister. "I do not suppose," said the senator in his letter of request, "that your disapproval of some of the Government measures of last session affect your personal friendship for Sir John A. I imagine that you and I occupy much the same ground in regard to him."

In the election of 1872, the Conservatives ran a candidate against Cartwright, John Stevenson of Napanee, the speaker of Ontario's first legislature. His candidature was not serious. Senator John Hamilton, while pleased that Cartwright was opposed, doubted that Stevenson would be "any acquisition in the House,"[9] and Cartwright was able to crush him, winning 1,224 to 513. The contest in Lennox was not, in fact, a party fight. E.W. Rathbun, an inveterate Conservative factionalist, helped Cartwright in Lennox, as he worked to unseat the sitting Conservative in East Hastings in favour of a Conservative challenger more to his liking. In Lennox, his job was to help with the bribing of voters. After the election, he reported to Cartwright, "I send you all papers I have re last contest. I must say they are not as explicit as they should be ... It all goes to shew [sic] the depravity of the miserable things who must be bo't."[10]

While enjoying the support of Rathbun, who worked closely with Senator Campbell in the attempt to defeat John White of East Hastings,[11] Cartwright was opposed by the *Globe* as "a Tory and a corruptionist."[12] He remained in his own riding during the campaign,[13] thus giving a minimum of offence to the Conservative Party. Once he was safely elected for a third time, the government made discreet approaches to discover Cartwright's intentions. Between November 1872 and January 1873 he was three times asked to approve consular appointments or recommend a man to a post office job. At the same time, one correspondent in search of a job understood that Cartwright was not a regular Conservative, suggesting that "as the patronage belongs to the Dominion government you might not wish to ask any favours."

Cartwright was a businessman with extensive interests. He worked with numerous Conservative politicians after 1869, including Alexander Morris, Alexander Campbell, and John Beverley Robinson. He was involved in the affairs of the Kingston & Pembroke railway, along with such leading Conservatives as James O'Reilly, MP for South Renfrew, G.A. Kirkpatrick, MP for Frontenac, and John A. Macdonald himself. He was one of those who petitioned the latter to apply pressure on Premier John Sandfield Macdonald "to empower municipalities to grant bonus to railways without special charter." He became a director of the line, and purchased 100 shares, worth $5,000, in the company. The Prime Minister, interested in the management of the line, wrote Cartwright in February 1872 asking him to vote for the previous year's Board of Directors, because, stated Macdonald, "The Robinson-Livingston-Fraser clique are intriguing and I want to checkmate them. If you can't attend personally Wednesday send your Proxy like a good fellow to O'Reilly." Macdonald was seconded by Campbell. Cartwright informed MacDonald that he doubted if he was "aware of all that has passed" and assured him that he was not "disposed to help the clique to whom you refer," promising to "bear your note in mind … and defer action for the moment." Cartwright, in spite of his opposition to the appointment of Hincks in 1869 was still a "good fellow" and Macdonald was able to assume his co-operative with the O'Reilly faction in the management of the Kingston & Pembroke Railway. Personal and business relations were thus still fairly good in 1872.

III

NOTHING SUGGESTS that Cartwright was moving farther away from the Conservative party as 1872 closed, or that he had again reconciled himself to Macdonald's leadership. What propelled him out of the party was the Pacific Scandal. In 1869, he had opposed the appointment of Hincks, arguing that the party was being seriously damaged. The problem was far more serious in 1873, and Cartwright resolved to help defeat the government. His motives were doubtless mixed. His earlier attempt to reform the party had failed; the gaining of office, so difficult under the Conservatives, would be a real possibility under the Liberals; and the parliamentary situation would enable him to play a major role as an Independent Conservative, as he described himself after the election of 1874.[14]

MacDonald's first government was the only federal administration forced out of office during a parliamentary session without the intervention of a third party. Cartwright, in fact, played the role of a third party leader, rallying dissidents and co-operating with the Liberal leaders, not as a colleague or follower, but as an ally. While Cartwright may have been influenced by the legitimate desire to obtain office, he could not seriously have expected the Finance portfolio. It was reserved for Luther Hamilton Holton, twice Reform Minister of Finance during the Union, and a senior Liberal leader from Quebec. It was not until after the fall of the Conservative government that Holton indicated his unwillingness to accept any post in a new government.

Early in 1873, Mackenzie approached Cartwright, and the two men met in Montreal. What they discussed is not known, but Cartwright was wary about becoming too involved a political relationship. He agreed to another meeting with Mackenzie a month later but explained that while elected "as an absolutely independent candidate," he was not in the same position as a member of the opposition. He had certainly not coalesced with the Liberals when he said that in February 1873. Mackenzie would have been lacking in political judgment had he not realized the value of a convert to Liberalism from the eastern Ontario Conservative heartland. Cartwright would have been just as lacking in judgment had he not realized the dangers of conversion. He was wise to be on his guard. Mackenzie persisted. In February, he asked to see

Cartwright in Ottawa the day before the meeting of Parliament, "if you are not afraid of being seen in the company of Grits."

At the same time, Mackenzie explained an "extraordinary story" he had heard two days earlier. "It seems," he said, "that Sir John made an agreement with Sir Hugh Allan and Jay Cooke and their Yankee Associates before the election that they were to have the contract, they engaging to furnish 3% on their capital of $300,000 to carry the elections. This money was actually [paid] and all the subsequent negotiations with Senator McPherson and others a mere blind." Lucius Seth Huntington made his famous corruption charges in the House of Commons on 02 April 1873. In the ensuing struggle for power, Cartwright became, if not a Liberal, a member of the opposition high command. He conferred constantly with leading Liberals, Mackenzie, Holton, Blake, and A.J. Smith about a variety of problems.[15] Blake's approach to the parliamentary committee of enquiry was discussed, as were the tactics and strategy of parliamentary management. The search for support was a topic of concern, especially the quest of Cartwright's neighbours, Kirkpatrick and Shibley. Cartwright and Blake even corresponded about the sensitive problem of Blake's membership in an expected Liberal government, Blake admitting that he did not intend joining.

Cartwright was becoming an important leader of the opposition. He led the politically astute protest to the prorogation of 13 August 1873,[16] and was ideally suited for the task because he was not a straight Liberal and therefore lent weight to the argument that the opposition was broader than the Liberal Party. By the second session of 1873, he was a recognized opposition leader. "I suppose," wrote Edward Blake, "you will be at Ottawa on 22nd. It is of great consequence that those of us who have to do the headwork should have full time to concert and mature plans for every contingency."

It was just as evident, although not to Blake, that those who *could* "do the headwork" would have to join the cabinet formed on the defeat of Macdonald. Cartwright was a logical choice. Apart from his excellent performance he could be held to represent 'independent' opinion in Ontario. He was also an able and popular representative of the old Conservative heartland and thus potentially a very useful minister. While his inclusion in the Ministry was logical, it was not at all necessary that he become Minister of Finance. Finance was reserved for Holton, who refused it. Next to Holton, Mackenzie, a recent Treasurer of Ontario, preferred himself for the job. "I would have liked to take the Finance dept. myself," he wrote George Brown, "but I did not see who could take the Public Works."[17] Giving Cartwright Finance became logical because of the nature of Canadian cabinets and because of the men available for cabinet posts. Although Ontario was to have six ministers, it could have only two important portfolios. Of the six ministers, Christie and Scott were in the Senate and Blake refused an important post. Donald Macdonald was not trusted with a major portfolio.[18] Mackenzie himself took Public Works. The reversion of Finance to Cartwright was thus logical within the context of November 1873.

Once sworn as ministers, the members of the new cabinet were required to seek re-election to Parliament. Alone amongst the Ontario ministers Cartwright was opposed, an understandable enough situation. Cartwright, as a renegade Tory, must have caused extreme annoyance to Conservatives. Also he represented a threat to the Conservatives in their eastern Ontario stronghold. Defeating him would have been both gratifying and useful. Cartwright easily won re-election in Lennox, but the by-election was hard fought and very bitter, with an abundance of personal charges hurled by both sides. It was probably this by-election that caused the personal estrangement between Macdonald and Cartwright that made them bitter personal enemies.[19] After 1873, Cartwright could still call himself an "Independent Conservative" but all the value of 'independence' had vanished. He was in the Liberal Party. There was no place else to go.

IV

THUS IT WAS NOT '1869' but '1873' that made the Conservative Party an impossible political home for Richard Cartwright. As much is indicated by chronology. Until 1869 he was a Conservative backbencher, albeit an important one. From 1869 to 1873, he was a dissatisfied Conservative, but a man with numerous political and business ties with leading members of the Conservative Party. As late as 04 February 1873 he carefully protected his independence, although he was in contact with Mackenzie, a contact almost certainly initiated by the Liberal leader. He heard about the impending scandal charges by 21 February at the latest. Revealed publicly in April, these charges made logical his move from independence to opposition. Again he had reason to doubt Macdonald's leadership, but unlike the previous occasion he had no hope of exerting pressure within the party. The Pacific Scandal, then, was decisive in putting him out of the Conservative Party. The events of 1873 forced him into the Liberal Party. During 1873, he rose rapidly as an opposition leader, and by October was, as Blake said, one of those "who do the headwork." His membership in the Liberal cabinet, the Lennox by-election, and his rise to real prominence in the government determined his identification as a Liberal, and he remained an influential Liberal until his death in 1912.

Schuyler Shibley

THE UNDERSIDE OF VICTORIAN ONTARIO

At least one riding (and a rural one at that) was as tolerant of gross personal misconduct as many ridings were of financial impropriety. The place of children in Ontario society merits careful study, as does the whole question of public and private morality.

NOBODY WHO reads Professor Peter Waite's article, "Sir Oliver Mowat's Canada: Reflections on an Un-Victorian society," can accept the assumption that late nineteenth-century Canada was Victorian in any normally accepted sense of that word.[1] Waite argues that the adjective 'Victorian', as applied to Canada (or for that matter even to England) in the latter half of the nineteenth century, in terms of the stereotype usually associated with the word, is not only devoid of significant meaning, but incorrect."[2] He goes on to comment: "Ontario comes as near to the definition of 'Victorian' as any part of Canada, and even in that land of supposedly unfrivolous dedication to work and purity, much evidence is on the other side."[3] A study of the career of Schuyler Shibley, a late nineteenth-century Ontario politician, indicates that, if anything, Waite has understated his case.

One of several biographical articles written by Professor Swainson in the 1970s, this profile of a problematic politician appeared in *Ontario History*, Vol. 65, No. 1 (1973).

Portrait of Schuyler Shibley (Library and Archives Canada).

SCHUYLER SHIBLEY was born in 1820 in Portland Township, Frontenac County, and he lived in Murvale, a village in southern Portland, a few miles north-west of Kingston. In 1854, he married the daughter of a "prominent merchant of Kingston."[4] Shibley was educated at the Waterloo Academy in the Kingston area. In 1851-52, he rounded out his education with a tour of Europe "and returned to his native township one of the best informed farmers of the province."[5] Of German origin, Shibley was a member of the Methodist Church.[6] On both sides of his family, he was descended from United Empire Loyalists. Jacob Shibley, an uncle, sat for Frontenac in the Legislative Assembly of Upper Canada.

Shibley was a farmer-businessman. He farmed in Portland and pursued a variety of business interests. With David Roblin (a Lennox and Addington politician)[7] "he speculated extensively in U.E.L. scrip, became possessed of very large tracts of real estate, good bad and indifferent, and was at times reputed to be very wealthy."[8] During the 1870s, he was a director of the Kingston & Pembroke Railway. This activity brought him into business association with such local political luminaries as Alexander Campbell (Conservative), Richard Cartwright (Liberal by late 1873), George Kirkpatrick (Conservative), James O'Reilly (Conservative), C.F. Gildersleeve (Liberal), and D.D. Calvin (Conservative).

Schuyler Shibley, "a rather fast gent,"[9] acquired province-wide notoriety in 1866. It transpired that, in addition to his prestigious and prosperous wife, Shibley kept a "paramour"[10] – "a rather good looking person"[11] named Kate Davis, who lived near Sarnia. From time to time, Shibley went west to Lambton County to visit his mistress, and the result was a natural child named Kate Shibley. The details of his private life became public late in 1866 when Schuyler Shibley was arrested on the charge of murdering his natural daughter.[12] The circumstances of Kate Shibley's death, a couple of days before Schuyler's arrest, warranted the arrest of both parents.

Shibley was not in Lambton when the three and a half year old child died, but his actions and instructions (apparently motivated by his religious convictions) helped lead to the grim result.[13] The mother testified at the coroner's inquest that "the child's father, Mr. Shibley, had been there some ten days before [Kate Shibley died] and had given the child a most unmerciful beating for not saying its prayers, and ordered her to do the same whenever it refused, and that it was the carrying out of this command that had killed the child."[14] Another witness described how Shibley dealt with this little girl: "I came there on the night Shibley whipped the child, on Friday evening; on Saturday morning I saw him whip it again; this was on the 25th day of August [1866] ... [There] were several bruises on the body of the child, after Shibley whipped it with his hand, while it sat on his knee ..."[15] In addition to suffering from physical abuse, the child also suffered from malnutrition. At the coroner's inquest it was suggested that "the entire absence of food had also something to do with the result."[16]

Kate Davis, a docile young woman, followed Schuyler's instructions and example with regard to the child's religious training. On September 3 when the child again failed to say its prayers, Kate "whipped it with rawhide," trying all the while "to get the child to say its prayers."[17] During the course of the night, the child died. Shibley was obviously not involved in the final tragedy in a direct and immediate way and the charges against him were dropped. Nonetheless, he did receive general notoriety throughout the province. Kate Davis was subsequently prosecuted on a reduced charge of manslaughter and acquitted. The outraged judge "could not refrain from giving strong expression to his surprise and disappointment at the verdict."[18] The effects of these incidents on Shibley's subsequent political career, however, would remain to be seen.

John A. Macdonald knew Shibley, and was familiar with Sarnia. During the 1850s, he speculated extensively in Sarnia real estate,[19] and he was evidently on good terms with Thomas W. Johnston, once Mayor of Sarnia and in 1866 the prison doctor.[20] Johnston, who doubtless owed his patronage post to the Attorney-General West, kept Macdonald informed concerning Shibley and his plight. He told Macdonald, for example, that Shibley had learned a lesson: "He seems to have been infatuated with the girl Davis and actually had his wife write her a letter of Condolence. [His] eyes poor fellow are now open. [If] he tries another, it will not be Miss Davis."[21] The enormity of the situation seemed to cause little concern. Presumably it was enough that Shibley had learned that he would have to choose his "paramours" with more care – a good lesson to have learned by the age of 46!

Shibley did not confine his peccadilloes to child beating, or confine his less than upright activities to western Ontario. He also struck near home. While lodged in the Sarnia jail, he was sued in Kingston by one Kennedy, on two grounds. He had purchased some land from Kennedy and then paid for the property with a deed to another lot that he had also deeded away. He had also failed to pay for some farm stock that he had purchased from Kennedy. Shibley lost and was required to pay $26 to Kennedy. That was a nominal sum, but it was a heavy fine compared to the penalty incurred because of his Sarnia escapade. The death of his daughter had not cost him a penny.

II

SCHUYLER SHIBLEY had a successful public career. He served in the Frontenac County Council and for three terms (1868-69 and 1872) and was Warden of Frontenac.[22] In 1867, he contested Addington federally but lost. Needless to say, his private life was an issue in 1867. A fellow citizen of Portland attacked him:

> The Mormon prophet is the only individual, in modern times, of whom we have any recollection …, who had the honours and emoluments of office conferred upon him, as the reward for a debauched and profligate course of life. It appears, however, that even his depraved and licentious career, has not deprived Brigham of every attribute of human nature, for he is yet possessed of sufficient humanity, neither to punish with death nor severe chastisement, the innocent offspring(s) of his guilt, should they happen to neglect their devotional duties. A multitude of wives or an illegitimate offspring may be congenial to the peculiar instincts of the saints in Salt Lake Valley, but these abominations of Mormonism cannot be popular in a respectable and intelligent Canadian constituency.[23]

The "abominations of Mormonism" might not have been "popular" in Lennox and Addington, but they were not sufficiently unpopular to seriously harm Shibley's career. He polled 991 votes in 1867 to 1,120 for the victor. In the next year, he first secured the wardenship of Frontenac. After two additional terms in that office, he won three elections in Addington – in the general elections of 1872 and 1874, and in a by-election in November 1874. The by-election was occasioned by the voiding of his victory in the general election of 1874 Supporters, including his 15-year-old son Henry, had been caught bribing voters![24] These various victories were substantial:

General Election of 1872
| Shibley 1,495 | Lapum | 849 |

General Election of 1874
| Shibley 1,275 | Waggoner | 982 |

By-Election of 1874
| Shibley 1,263 | Waggoner | 920 |

In Macdonald's sweep of 1878, he garnered only 1,244 votes against 1,656 for John McRory, the Conservative candidate. The *Globe* had confidently predicted that his "prospects of re-election are of the most favourable character."[25] Shibley never contested the riding again.

III

A STUDY OF Schuyler Shibley's political affiliation reveals much about his political motivation and the complexities of the nineteenth-century party system. In 1867, James Lapum, a Conservative endorsed by such senior area party leaders as John A. Macdonald and Alexander Campbell, defeated Shibley, who, as has been pointed out, ran again in 1872. Shibley was not a Liberal, in spite of assertions in the *Globe* that he was an "Opposition candidate" and "a Reformer."[26] (The Ottawa *Citizen* contended, however, that he was a government supporter.)[27] Shibley made known his electoral intentions well before the election of 1872 and, strangely enough, his position with respect to the Conservative party was strengthened by the Liberal provincial victory of 1871.

In January 1872, Alexander Campbell's trusted political confidant, E.W. Rathbun, doubted that Lapum could again defeat Shibley and introduced the complication of provincial politics: "*Deroche* must be kept working with us if we can accomplish it + he *must* go for *Shibley*."[28] Rathbun's calculations here are obscure. Hamel Deroche, a Liberal and a Napanee lawyer, was the MPP for Addington, 1871-83.[29] His reasons for supporting Shibley are unknown. Rathbun was a Deseronto lumberman whose concern to keep Deroche "working with us" probably involved the protection of his extensive lumbering concerns from a hostile Liberal administration in Toronto. Rathbun must have come to some arrangement with Deroche after Deroche's 1871 provincial victory in Addington. Reluctance to antagonizing Deroche therefore militated against support for James Lapum, who was Shibley's enemy. Like numerous other Ontarians during the immediate post-Confederation years, Rathbun believed that political allegiance could differ at the federal and provincial levels.

Lapum made clear his desire to contest Addington in 1872, and he wanted the support of the powerful Kingstonians who dominated the party in eastern Ontario. Alexander Campbell's support was indispensable, and Lapum asked Campbell to obtain for him the influence of Bishop E.J. Horan of Kingston.[30] For the remainder of the 1872 campaign, Addington was a difficult and complex problem. Campbell saw Bishop Horan about support in general, but Addington was a special case. Campbell reported to Macdonald: "The only hitch is in Addington where O'Reilly[31] (in retaliation for Lapums [sic] old opposition to his being made a judge) has asked the Bishop not to help Lapum saying that Shibley is as good a friend of the Government as Lapum. I have asked O'Reilly by telegraph whether he has got or can get a letter from Shibley agreeing to support us or can advise him to write one. I will then see what is best to be done and may persuade Lapum to retire."[32] A couple of days later, Campbell wrote again to Macdonald. He had talked to O'Reilly and was soon to see Lapum, but was anxious to know if Macdonald had received (as O'Reilly claimed) a written commitment from Shibley.[33] Campbell was anxious to settle the Addington candidacy, even if it meant succumbing to the pressure to sacrifice Lapum. That pressure was strong: Rathbun was an important Conservative; O'Reilly was close to Horan and had recently secured the Conservative nomination in South Renfrew. The problem could be easily solved if Shibley would pledge loyalty to the Conservative Party and Lapum would withdraw. Shibley did make some sort of commitment, but Lapum refused to give way.

During the campaign, Lapum was given support, but Shibley was not driven into the Liberal camp. Lapum, however, argued that Shibley was a Liberal – or soon would be: "I had a meeting last night at Erins-ville in Sheffield. Shibley and Deroche the local member were there. Shibley spoke as an "Independent" member followed by Mr. Deroche who in his speech condemned the Government … Every rabid Grit in the County supports Shibley … No County requires help more than this County."[34] Lapum's associates applied pressure to Campbell to assist the sitting member, especially with Bishop Horan and the Catholic vote.[35] Lapum wanted official endorsement. Hence, he was anxious that either Campbell or Macdonald appear with him at his nomination.[36] He finally received help. Rathbun wrote Campbell: "I am acting for Lapum – + will at once do more. I am very busy with work – neglected in my E. Hastings affair – but I cheerfully acquiese [sic] in your desire – per telegram today + although I cannot individually go to the County I will send good men and write my friends."[37] Rathbun had initially opposed Lapum, but was brought to this energetic support by Campbell. Only a few days earlier John White had taken East Hastings, as a Conservative, against another Conservative who had the backing of Rathbun and the Conservative Party. Campbell, as a result, may have opted not to devote too much energy to faction fights. In any event, Lapum was given assistance – but apparently on nothing like the scale given to such favoured (if unsuccessful) neighbouring candidates as Wellington Frizzell and James McCuaig. This last minute support did not save Lapum, who was very bitter: "My defeat is caused firstly by Mr. O'Reillys [sic] influence through the priests throughout the riding, the Catholics almost to a man voting against me [.] Then the Land Valuators employed by the "Local" all appeared in the back Townships after Mr. Shibleys [sic] visit to Toronto." He went on to blame the Grits and their money. It was even possible, suggested Lapum, that Shibley was disqualified by "being under bonds with the Gov …" Lapum was certain that Shibley was pledged to the opposition, regardless of any statements to the contrary.[38] He, therefore, attempted to retain control of Addington's patronage.[39]

Campbell's concern, of course, was not Lapum, but Conservative strength in the Commons. Shibley was, therefore, accepted as a Conservative once he had satisfied Campbell about his loyalty: "Shibley has been with me this morning – he says that you may count on him – that he proposes to be a good supporter and to carry out all that he has from time to time said he would – this is satisfactory – he came *to me* apparently on purpose to say this to me."[40] Campbell, consequently, was willing to support Shibley. Early in September he wrote Macdonald: "I am endeavoring to get Lapum [illegible] to leave it to you to decide whether they shall petition against Shibley's return or not."[41] Macdonald doubtless decided that there was to be no petition.

Schuyler Shibley was able to go to Ottawa as a self-described supporter of the regime: "A Conservative, and 'will give the present Govt. a fair support as he considers that their legislation on the whole has been advantageous to the country'."[42] Shibley won the faction fight and controlled Addington's patronage. Hence this letter from Campbell to Macdonald:

> I return the letter from Mr. Thos. Watt, late Postmaster at "Fenroy" [?], County of Addington. There was a Petition numerously signed sent to me complaining of his bad habits and the irregularities consequent upon them. It was made out that he was frequently drunk, and when in that state retained letters from one mail to another … He was dismissed in consequence of the recommendation of Mr. Shibley on the 4th Feby last and a Mr. Rogers was appointed.[43]

Shibley had concerned himself with patronage matters during the first Parliament, but without any apparent success.[44]

Shibley's anomalous position within the Conservative Party prompted Liberal leaders to test his party loyalty. Before Lucius Seth Huntington made his famous charges that led to the revelations of the Pacific Scandal and the consequent parliamentary struggle for power in 1873, Mackenzie contacted Shibley and obtained some sort of promise of support – which Mackenzie did not take seriously.[45] In a Liberal Party memorandum of about the same date, however, Shibley was considered a likely convert: "Shibley promised to go with Reformers very soon but feels bound at present (having committed himself at time of election) to give 'fair play' [.] [He] promised Mr. Mackenzie yesterday to vote on Election motions."[46]

For men of marginal loyalty, the Huntington charges were important: loyalty to the Conservatives became less and less attractive. At the electoral level, loyalty might even be dangerous, and if the government fell, the Liberals would have the patronage power. Shibley had before him the example of R.J. Cartwright, his county colleague, who was rapidly moving into the opposition high command and who could doubtless apply considerable pressure with Lennox and Addington. Shibley began to waver. The Conservative managers understood the problem and worked to retain the support of men like Shibley. Patronage remained an important consideration, and as late as 22 September 1873, Shibley asked from Macdonald a favour for a relative.[47] A couple of weeks later Mackenzie reported: "The government are now engaged in desperate manipulations of M.P.s. In Ontario Glass [,] Shibley [,] Kirkpatrick + Lewis are plied incessantly."[48]

The opposition also "plied incessantly." Richard Cartwright was inevitably drawn into the drive to obtain the support of his neighbouring members. In October, he reported to Edward Blake: "H. [olton] came to see me partly as to S[hibley] … My information … is satisfactory + as it comes from distinct sources from yours is all the better. At the same time there is some danger from O.R.s [O'Reilly's] influence + I think it would do no harm to detail a special to look after him when he gets to O.[ttawa]."[49] Blake agreed to have someone keep an eye on Shibley.[50] Mackenzie, too, was interested. He was informed that Campbell had consulted both Shibley and his supporter James O'Reilly. Consequently, he wrote Hamel Deroche: "Will you have the kindness to let me know if Mr. Shibley mentioned Campbells [sic] mission, or if you have any fear that he had any success".[51] Deroche was probably another source of Liberal pressure.

Shibley was, in fact, obtained and became a Liberal late in 1873. Campbell admitted as much in a discussion of the fall of the government late in November 1873.[52] His defection seems to have caused demoralization and disunity within Conservative ranks in Addington. During the 1874 general election campaign, for example, a Mr. Ham was first declared to be Shibley's opponent.[53] He apparently withdrew within a week, to be replaced by D.J. Waggoner, who was defeated in due course.[54] For the remainder of his undistinguished career in Parliament,[55] Shibley was a straight Liberal and in 1878 was defeated by a Conservative.[56] He died in 1890.[57]

IV

SCHUYLER SHIBLEY is an incredible figure – a strange combination of depravity, venality, and impeccable credentials. Through business and successful careers in local and federal politics, he associated with a number of powerful and prestigious men in both Kingston and the Frontenac-Lennox and Addington area. His well-publicized private life did not prevent business and political co-operation with these leaders of the local elite. It is clear that *both* parties could easily accommodate what the electorate could tolerate.

The story of Shibley's political affiliation is interesting, and is probably closely related to his dubious morals. His private life, especially that of 1866, was well known. Nonetheless, in 1867 he polled 991 votes to Lapum's 1,120 in the federal riding of Addington. Reputation notwithstanding, he went from strength to strength. In 1868, he secured the wardenship of Frontenac and in 1872 he easily won Addington, 1,495 to 849 votes. In this election, he was supported by the local Liberal MPP as well as by many Conservatives. As soon as he was elected, he was claimed by the Toronto *Globe* as a Liberal and by the Ottawa *Citizen* as a Conservative. During 1873, he was courted by the national leaders of both parties and sat on a railway board with several powerful figures. Schuyler had come a long way from the Sarnia jail!

He was not a loyal party man. Initially, Shibley was a Conservative, willing to indulge in factionalism. In 1872, he was not the Liberal candidate but, with the active aid of Hamel Deroche, seems to have been the Liberals' candidate. Nonetheless, he retained the support of such Tory insiders as E.B. Rathbun and James O'Reilly.

After his first victory, Shibley satisfied Campbell that he was a Conservative. The Liberals thought him a possible convert, and tested his affiliation shortly after his election. He defected late in 1873, doubtless because of the likelihood of the Liberals coming to power. His career as a Conservative MP was consequently very short, but his control over Addington's patronage was not endangered by a change of governments.

The Pacific Scandal was a great affair. It occasioned the fall of the only government in Canadian history to be brought down during the life of a Parliament without the intervention of a third party. The righteous indignation of the Liberal leaders flamed so hot that it seared its way into our historical imagination. It is still not uncommon to encounter persons who see the 1870s as a struggle between the upright but inept Grits and the decadent but wily Tories. Within such a framework, one might think that the great parliamentary battle of 1873 witnessed honest Tories defecting to the Opposition because of their disgust at the activities of Macdonald and his colleagues. Only a very small number of Ontario Conservatives switched to the Liberals in 1873[58] and one of them was Schuyler Shibley. He did not desert the government because of a personal commitment to moral purity; he was simply drawn to the honey pot of patronage. Motivations of similar expediency explain the bulk of the other Ontario defections.[59]

Shortly after Macdonald resigned office, Mackenzie saw Governor General Dufferin. Mackenzie then reported to George Brown that Dufferin "offered an immediate dissolution if wanted and intimated his own opinion that the opinion of a House 'tainted as it must be with the use of Allan's money could not be respected.'"[60] The House was clearly tainted with Allan's money, but other forms of corruption also existed and were being drawn into the Liberal Party. It would be difficult to quantify corruption, but by any test it is clear that the Pacific Scandal produced for the Liberal Party a net gain of that staple component of nineteenth-century Canadian public life.

It should also be emphasized that Shibley was not a "loose-fish." His position as a Conservative factionalist was not uncommon for an ambitious man who functioned within what was essentially a one party district. Once elected, however, he became a regular party member. Because of his background of factionalism it was fairly easy for him to extricate himself when his party entered a period of crisis. Of course, he could not reverse the process in 1878. By then his political career was bound to the Liberal Party, and with it he was defeated. That defeat ended his political career; he never again ran for Parliament.

Further study will be required before one can decide whether Schuyler Shibley was a symptom or an aberration. Some conclusions do present themselves, however. At least one riding (and a rural one at that) was as tolerant of gross personal misconduct as many ridings were of financial impropriety. The Liberal Party was willing to absorb anything that would vote the right way in Parliament. The place of children in Ontario society merits careful study, as does the whole question of public and private morality.

George Airey Kirkpatrick

POLITICAL PATRICIAN

*Kingston was a major centre for both nineteenth-century political par-
ties. The politicians of that era constitute an amazing group. Merely
listing a number of them indicates the calibre of leadership found in
this city, and the place Kingston occupied in Upper Canadian, Union,
federal, and provincial politics.*

KINGSTON WAS A major centre for both nineteenth-century political
parties. [1] The politicians of that era constitute an amazing group.
Merely listing a number of them indicates the calibre of leadership
found in this city, and the place Kingston occupied in Upper Canadian, Union, federal, and provincial politics: Richard Cartwright, Christopher Hagerman, Thomas Kirkpatrick, John Counter, John A. Macdonald, Alexander Campbell, Sir Richard Cartwright, D.D. Calvin,
James O'Reilly, C.F. Gildersleeve, G.A. Kirkpatrick, Alexander Gunn,
and Hiram Calvin. In addition, Alexander Mackenzie, Oliver Mowat,
George Dormer, and John Hillyard Cameron all lived in Kingston for
a time. A number of these men have been studied, some intensively;
all deserve attention.

At one point during the 1870s, Sir John Macdonald was Prime
Minister, and another Kingstonian, Senator Alexander Campbell, was
one of his senior colleagues. Men from the Kingston district held five
seats in the House of Commons: Kingston City, Frontenac, Lennox,
Addington, and South Renfrew. This represented an enormous aggre-
gate of political power, and Kingstonians were well aware of their

Published in *Historic Kingston*, Vol. 19 (1971), this article continues Professor Swainson's decade-long preoccupation with nineteenth-century political
personalities in Kingston.

Portrait of George Airey Kirkpatrick (Library and Archives Canada).

influence. When the fifth Kingston politician was successful during the general election of 1872, the *Daily News* gloated:

> We heartily congratulate Mr. O'Reilly upon the result of the election. Apart from the gain to the conservative party ... it is a gain to the city to have another of our talented sons in the great council of the Dominion, ready to throw in his influence for the city and this section of the country. Toronto has prospered in a great measure by the number of members which she has all over the country ready to stand up for her interests on all occasions, and thus adding to her strength.[2]

The *Daily News* was correct. The Kingston politician, regardless of which seat he held, was ready to use his "influence for the city." George Airey Kirkpatrick represented Frontenac, but was very much a Kingstonian. In 1891, while discussing a matter pertinent to his native city, he explained to Parliament that Kingston was "the city whence I come, where I was born and brought up, and where I have lived all my life. It is therefore needless for me to say that I take a great interest in it."[3]

I

GEORGE AIREY KIRKPATRICK, a fourth son, was born in Kingston on 13 September 1841 and was an Anglican of Irish descent.[4] His mother was Helen Fisher and his father was Thomas Kirkpatrick, who originally came from Coolmine, County Dublin, Ireland.[5] Thomas Kirkpatrick was an important man, a long-time resident of Kingston who studied law with one of the city's most famous and important Conservatives, Christopher Hagerman.[6] He became a successful and wealthy lawyer, with an abiding interest in the city's Irish immigrants.[7] When Kingston was incorporated as a town in March 1838, Thomas Kirkpatrick was selected by his fellow aldermen as the town's first mayor.[8] The elder Kirkpatrick later served as Mayor of the City of Kingston. His decision to wage war on stray dogs inspired the famous jingle:

> *There goes St. Patrick who killed all the frogs,*
> *And here comes Kirkpatrick who killed all the dogs.*[9]

George Kirkpatrick was a wealthy and well-connected young man. From his father he inherited "large private means" and many useful contacts. [10] Thomas Kirkpatrick was a prominent Kingstonian, active in politics. From 1867-70, when he was succeeded by his son, he was MP for Frontenac. He associated with leading men of Kingston, including Hagerman, with whom he studied law, and John A. Macdonald, a family friend. [11]

In 1865, George married Frances Jane Macaulay of Kingston. She was the daughter of John Macaulay (1792-1857), who was appointed to Upper Canada's Legislative Council in 1836 and to the Legislative Council of the province of Canada in 1841. In 1841-42, John Macaulay served as Receiver-General for Upper Canada. George and Frances Jane had four sons and one daughter. The first Mrs. Kirkpatrick died in 1877,[12] and George remarried six years later. His second wife was Isabel Louise, daughter of Sir David Lewis Macpherson and a maternal grand-daughter of William Molson. Although relatively unknown, David Macpherson was an important nineteenth-century businessman-politician. He was a wealthy railroad contractor who was elected to the Legislative Council in 1864. Appointed to the Senate in 1867, he served as Macdonald's Minister of the Interior, 1883-85. Kirkpatrick and his second wife had one son.[13] George Kirkpatrick was thus related through marriage to the Macaulays, Molsons, and Macphersons.

G.A. Kirkpatrick himself formed many useful and interesting ties apart from his in-laws. He became a lifelong friend of Edward Blake,[14] and worked with Macdonald and other Kingston area politicians. In spite of political differences, he co-operated in business with Richard Cartwright and C.F. Gildersleeve, as well as with Tories like Senator Campbell, the Calvins, and J. O'Reilly. Kirkpatrick was also a militia leader. During the Trent crisis, he joined as a private and was in active service at Cornwall during a Fenian scare. Eventually, he rose to the rank of lieutenant-colonel.[15] During the nineteenth century, this kind of involvement in the militia was quite normal, and was regarded as a prestigious form of local leadership.

George Kirkpatrick received an unusually good and broad education.[16] After attending the Kingston Grammar School, he was sent to the High School at St. Johns, Quebec. From St. Johns he went to Trinity College, Dublin, where he graduated in 1861 with the degrees A.B.

and L.L.B. At Trinity, he distinguished himself by graduating as moderator and silver medalist in Law, Literature, and Political Economy. It is interesting to note that other pre-Confederation Ontarians were educated at Trinity. William Hume Blake graduated in 1830, before his move to Canada,[17] and Kirkpatrick's older and more famous contemporary, Richard Cartwright, was a student at Trinity from 1851-56. Cartwright, however, did not take a degree (for reasons which are unknown).[18] This was obviously a type of education available only to wealthy Canadians.

II

AFTER RETURNING to Canada, Kirkpatrick studied law in his father's office and was called to the bar in 1865. Thereafter, he practiced law in Kingston and was made a Queen's Counsel in 1880. In addition to practicing law, Kirkpatrick was active in a variety of business endeavours.[19] D.B. Read, the historian of Ontario's Lieutenant-Governors, commented: "As a private citizen of Kingston, during his parliamentary career and before his appointment to the Lieutenant-Governorship, he took a prominent part in establishing some of the more important industrial and commercial institutions of the Limestone City."[20] These concerns included the Kingston Water Works, of which he was president, the Canadian Locomotive Works, of which he was also president, and the Kingston & Pembroke Railway, of which he was a director.

The Kingston & Pembroke Railway is worthy of careful study, as it illustrates the kind of nineteenth-century business that was both private enterprise and a community endeavour.[21] Known locally as the "Kick and Push," the Kingston & Pembroke got under way in 1871. The object was to run a line north from Kingston to Pembroke, in order to enlarge Kingston's hinterland. This would enable the bringing of lumber to Kingston for shipment to either the United States or Atlantic ports. It was also hoped that Kingston would obtain a share of the profits of various mines and quarries along the route. In addition, the Kingston & Pembroke would connect Kingston with the main line of the projected Canadian Pacific Railway. The line was speedily constructed, and as one historian has commented, it "served the lumbering, quarrying and mining interests along its route for 40 years, to the benefit of Kingston."[22] Ultimately, the railroad was purchased by the C.P.R.

During its construction period, the line was very popular in Kingston. Local leaders like Macdonald, Kirkpatrick, Campbell, O'Reilly, Gildersleeve, and D.D. Calvin were all involved in the operation. Many had much to gain, but civic patriotism was obviously a prime motive of the line's supporters because the city, as an entity, had much to gain. Virtually every business and professional man in Kingston gave some sort of support to the railroad.

During the 1880s, Kirkpatrick became a director of the Canadian Pacific Railway, and a bit later a director of the British Columbia Southern Railway. He was also at various times connected with finance, and served, during the 1890s, as a director of the Canada Life Assurance Company and Vice-President of the Imperial Loan and Investment Company. A telegram of 1871 illustrates the ties between Kirkpatrick and other Kingstonians and the ties between business and all levels of government. In 1871, a group of Kingstonians petitioned John A. Macdonald by telegram: "Have sent alderman Price to Toronto to induce premier to introduce a bill into the assembly to grant bonus to railways without special charter [.] [M]ost important to us. Write or telegraph to induce Sandfield [Macdonald] to help us."[23] Amongst the petitioners were R.J. Cartwright, James O'Reilly, G.A. Kirkpatrick, and C.F. Gildersleeve. Cartwright in 1871 was an independent Conservative, and Gildersleeve, a major businessman, was one of Kingston's most important Liberals.[24] This telegram is especially interesting because of its involvement of all levels of government, local, provincial, and federal.

The extent of Kirkpatrick's business operations is indicated by a letter of 1872 to Alexander Campbell, attempting to interest him in a Marine Insurance Company. Kirkpatrick commented: "Carruthers and Calvin + Breck each take $25,000 to start – and there is no doubt that we can raise $200,000 here."[25] In Parliament, he acted as spokesman for a variety of businesses, especially in the fields of finance and transport. Hardly a session passed without Kirkpatrick introducing several private bills of interest to these firms.

III

K IRKPATRICK HAD no career in local politics, perhaps because he entered Parliament at the age of 29. As we have seen, he was extensively involved in business at the local level. He was also active in educational affairs, and served as Chairman and then Secretary of the Board of Trustees of Kingston Collegiate Institute.[26] In spite of his Anglican affiliation, he spoke several times in the House of Commons on behalf of Queen's University. He was obviously warmly attached to the university and on one occasion gave a spirited defence of Queen's as a national institution: "Queen's College at Kingston is, I contend, not a college of a provincial nature; its influence extends over the whole Dominion. It is an institution in connection with the Presbyterian Church of Canada, which extends from one end of the Dominion to the other, and its subscribers and supporters are found in every part of the Dominion."[27] Kirkpatrick was also deeply attached to the Royal Military College.[28] Over the years he interested himself in many of the college's problems and activities, and educated at least two of his sons there.[29] One of them, Sir George Macaulay Kirkpatrick, served as a general in the British Army.

Like his father, who was concerned with the welfare of Irish immigrants, George Kirkpatrick was involved with some of Kingston's social problems – particularly those concerning sailors. D.B. Read commented: "His connection with a lake city caused him to take special interest in sailors, and their interests were well watched by him while in the House. He was the means of having incorporated in the Maritime Court Act, introduced by Mr. Blake, that portion which aims at securing a lien for seamen's wages on vessels plying on inland waters."[30] The Kirkpatricks were men motivated by at least a degree of *noblesse oblige.*

III

G EORGE KIRKPATRICK's federal career began in April 1870, when he was elected to Parliament for Frontenac in place of his father, who held the riding from 1867 until his death in 1870. At this time, Frontenac was a small riding, including only the townships bordering on Lake Ontario. The remainder of the county was lumped together with Addington. George held the riding until 1892, when he resigned from the House of Commons. In the 1870 by-election, he defeated J.S. Cartwright with ease, winning 869 to 517. Two years later, in the general election of 1872, he received an acclamation, at least in part because of a disorganized opposition.[31] Despite the general Conservative rout in the election of 1874, Kirkpatrick again won an easy victory over J.S. Cartwright (1172-696). During the Conservative sweep of 1878, he polled 958 votes to a humiliating 148 for one J.V. Ferris, and managed to win a second acclamation in 1882. His majority in 1887 was 416, but in the hard fought election of 1891, he came close to losing, and scraped to victory by only 205 votes (1427 to 1222). When Kirkpatrick resigned in 1892, however, Hiram Calvin was able to win the by-election by acclamation and thus keep Frontenac Conservative.

As a politician, George Kirkpatrick was a minor success. Major success would have been extremely difficult (and probably impossible) because of the presence of both John A. Macdonald and Alexander Campbell in the cabinet from 1867-73 and 1878-87. Political opportunities for Kingston Conservatives were radically circumscribed. Nonetheless, Kirkpatrick obtained important offices. He was chairman of the Standing Committee of Public Accounts, and from 1883 to 1887 Speaker of the House of Commons. After leaving the speakership, the same year that Alexander Campbell became Lieutenant-Governor of Ontario, he attempted, unsuccessfully, to obtain a cabinet post.

Macdonald's opinion of Kirkpatrick's performance as speaker was far from flattering. In 1888, Sir John rejected his fellow Kingstonian's request for promotion to the cabinet with the comment: "You are not strong enough in the House, when you were Speaker of the Commons you were afraid of Blake, and decided Parliamentary questions against your Conservative friends."[32] In 1892, Kirkpatrick succeeded Campbell as Lieutenant-Governor and served in this capacity until 1897. In addition to his Q.C., he enjoyed two other honorific posts, membership in the Privy Council in 1891 and a K.C.M.G. in 1897. He refused to enter Sir Mackenzie Bowell's cabinet in 1896.[33]

As a parliamentarian, Kirkpatrick was active and able. On only very rare occasions did he deliver long-detailed speeches, but he intervened with short comments hundred of times. He was especially concerned with business problems and often spoke on banking or transportation legislation. Marine transport was also a special interest.

Local affairs, law reform, the tariff, the militia, parliamentary procedure, and land policy attracted his attention. Important Kingston
institutions like the Kingston & Pembroke Railway, the Royal Military
College, and Queen's regularly prompted his interventions. He often
defended Sir John Macdonald from opposition attacks, and occasionally spoke on behalf of Senator Campbell.

Before his election as Speaker in 1883, George Kirkpatrick's parliamentary manner was eager and aggressive. He was obviously enthusiastic about his political career and anxious to make his mark. After
he left the Speaker's chair his manner changed. He seems to have lost
interest in public life, perhaps because of his failure to obtain a cabinet post. From 1887-92, he was relatively inactive. Many of his interventions involved private bills, and they were often associated with
his own business affairs. His temper became shorter, and his interests
even more restricted. In 1891, he got into a heated argument over
whether the Bay of Quinte was a separate body of water or a part of
Lake Ontario![34] At the end of his parliamentary career, this question
interested him as much as did any other! In 1892, he doubtless wel-
comed promotion to the lieutenant-governorship of Ontario.

In Parliament, George Kirkpatrick was very much the dignified,
cultivated, and gracious gentleman. Occasionally, his touch was light,
as when he commented on the subject of his friend Edward Blake:
"When I heard him addressing the House yesterday ... I could not
[but] think how applicable to him were these lines:

> Here lies our good Edward whose genius was such,
> We scarcely can praise or blame it too much;
> Who born for the universe, narrowed his mind,
> And to party gave up what was meant for mankind."[35]

He could also be cutting, as was indicated when he attacked opposition spokesmen for their criticisms of the Great Gerrymander of
1882: "Yes," said Kirkpatrick, "I shall say it over again that the people
will tell them it is all wind, all gas, all nonsense, what they have been
uttering."[36]

Many of his ideas were standard among nineteenth-century Canadian Conservatives. He supported the deepening of the Welland
Canal because he believed in the old St. Lawrence trading system: "If

we could once get the trade of the West into Lake Ontario, there was no doubt it would go down the St. Lawrence and make Montreal a still greater city than it was."[37] Kirkpatrick supported protection, at least in part because of his attitude toward the United States: "The abstract principle of free-trade," he commented in 1876, "was incontrovertible, but it was inapplicable to Canada in its present peculiar position; give us free-trade on both sides and he would support it; and until we could really obtain it we should fight the Americans with their own weapons."[38] His view of the post of Lieutenant-Governor was, at least initially, that of his leader. In 1879, he argued: "Lieutenant-Governors occupied the same position, as representatives of the Government, as the Colonial representatives did in respect to the Crown. Lieutenant-Governors were responsible to this House, and it was only in this House that their conduct could be discussed. Otherwise, there was no tribunal to which they were responsible."[39] Kirkpatrick doubtless modified this view when he himself became Lieutenant-Governor of Ontario!

Although a sound party man, George Kirkpatrick occasionally took public swipes at his own leaders, and supported non-party policies. Strangely enough, for example, he advocated a limited form of proportional representation. When commenting on the Redistribution of 1882 (which was one of the most outrageous Gerrymanders in Canadian history), he added: "I believe another principle might have been very properly introduced, and that is the principle of grouping together some of the constituencies into districts, so as to give representation to the minority in those districts. I believe that the Parliament of this country should be the mirror of the nation, that it should represent faithfully, all shades of thought in the country, and that the minority in every district should be represented here."[40]

A rather interesting point emerges from a study of the House of Commons *Debates*. During Kirkpatrick's years in the House of Commons, there were always two other Kingstonians present (Macdonald and Cartwright) and usually more. Often, they had private debates about their native city. The bitterness which existed between Macdonald and Cartwright is well known. Kirkpatrick and Cartwright also quarreled, sometimes with considerable heat. Cartwright, for example, claimed that Kirkpatrick plagiarized his views of proportional representation from Edward Blake: "In his present speech," he said, "there was not one original idea; the only idea uttered was one stolen from the Aurora speech of the hon. member for West Durham [Edward Blake] – that Parliament should be a mirror of the feelings of the people."[41] Kirkpatrick's view of Cartwright was no more charitable. He criticized an attack Cartwright made on J.C. Rykert, the corrupt Conservative MP for Lincoln: "he was, I think, induced to wander off into the more familiar fields of political controversy and to make a political harangue full of party rancour and malice, and all uncharitable."[42]

During the long, acrimonious debate on the Canadian Pacific Railway charter, Richard Cartwright, who at the time sat for Centre Huron, and George Kirkpatrick got into a hot dispute over public opinion in Kingston. Cartwright claimed that Kingston, which was represented by his fellow Liberal Alexander Gunn, opposed the charter. Kirkpatrick was just as confident that his fellow citizens supported the charter and challenged Cartwright: "If he [Cartwright] will resign his seat for Centre Huron I will resign mine for Frontenac, and I will run against the hon. and gallant knight in Kingston, and we will test the opinion of that constituency. I will go to the city of Kingston, where the hon. Gentleman has lived all his life and where he is best known, and I will contest with him the question whether this contract should be endorsed. If he does not accept the challenge let him never state again that the people of Kingston are against this contract."[43] During the entire session, Alexander Gunn, MP for Kingston, spoke only once – when he gave a short speech on the sugar tariff![44] He was obviously not needed to represent Kingston views, with Macdonald, Cartwright and Kirkpatrick in the House! Nineteenth- century Kingston was a small city of about 13,000 in 1880. One wonders how these rivalries influenced local society and life.

V

OUTSIDE OF Parliament, but within his party, Kirkpatrick was a Conservative with a mind of his own, especially if he was personally involved in a problem. His family was important to him. During the 1873 parliamentary crisis caused by the Pacific Scandal, he was regarded by some as a man who might desert the Conservatives in disgust and support the Opposition. His activities during his early years

as an MP are therefore of unusual interest and merit special attention.
Early in 1873, he wrote Macdonald thus:

According to your request I *again* beg to remind you of the application of my brother Thomas for employment. Not only does he ask it on his own merits and qualifications, but also as the son of an old and faithful follower of yours. Surely if you were earnest in trying to get or give an appointment to the son of your old friend Thomas Kirkpatrick you could do so in twenty four hours time!

My mother has asked you and I have asked you repeatedly to carry out repeated promises to my Father and I now ask again but for the *last time*. I shall not repeat it. If you cannot find a place for him at once ... you will have to find a candidate for Frontenac as I shall not remain a "service" follower.

I suggested to you the position of Paymaster of the North West Mounted Police. I consider that no one has *better claims* than my father's son.[45]

Kirkpatrick was willing to write a stern and abrupt letter in spite of his age (he was only 32) and political inexperience. Patronage was clearly important to him, and so were his family loyalties. His independence was doubtless increased by wealth and popularity; as we have seen he was strong in his riding, and Cartwright affirmed his popularity in the district.[46]

During 1873, Cartwright felt that Kirkpatrick, as well as other Kingston-area politicians, could be persuaded away from the Conservative Party. Every vote counted during the bitter parliamentary struggle of 1873, which Macdonald and the Conservatives finally lost. Kirkpatrick was a man of considerable independence, and Cartwright might have felt that that fact, plus the Pacific Scandal, would suffice to produce another oppositionist. A very interesting exchange of correspondence between Cartwright and the leaders of the Liberal Party resulted. On 18 August 1873, Cartwright wrote Blake:

I wish to consult you on a matter of some del[icacy] . I have had a gr.[eat] many cons. [conversations] with K.[irkpatrick] and am inclined to think that with a little man.[agement] he can be induced to take a decided stand as to the late action of Gov't. To speak plainly if you or Mak[enzie] would promise to use your influence with your friends here not to oppose him hereafter, I think he can be secured. [Cartwright went on to suggest that several other area members might also be secured but that such men] "will wish to understand in the event of a re-construction if the basis will be made wide enough to warrant them in supporting it without being fairly chargeable with desertion of their own principles. Can you give any assurance on these points or will it be necessary to conv.[erse] with McK[enzie]?[47]

Blake found Cartwright's views congenial: "I have always regretted that G. Kirkpatrick did not take a more independent course in Parliament; my personal friendship and esteem for him being great, and I should regard his taking a new departure which should bring us into a general *harmony* on the depending questions as a very great thing …" Blake agreed to use his influence in Frontenac on behalf of Kirkpatrick and agreed with Cartwright that a number of men in the latter's area could work with the Liberal Party. Only a name, he argued, prevented this desirable cooperation. The new administration must be based upon the "utmost liberality" and the "broadest basis for action." He argued, however, that men in support of a government must share "common views on the questions of the day."[48] Blake thus reduced party affiliation to the lowest possible common denominator.

In a discussion of Kirkpatrick with Mackenzie, Cartwright reiterated his views in very succinct terms: "To speak plainly," wrote Cartwright, "there is now very little except the mere name to prevent him and several conservative members from co-operating to establish any honest Gov't. in place of the present one – unless indeed you proclaimed your intention of running the machine on strict party lines in which case you would place them in an awkward predicament."[49] On the question of "party," Mackenzie was in basic agreement with Blake and Cartwright, and possibly even more flexible. He wrote Cartwright:

I have only adopted party organization as a means to an end, that end being a change of policy in the government and on many grounds a change of administration. I am not particular whether the changes sought is [sic] obtained by a pure party vote or not, and nothing would give me greater pleasure than to co-operate with others calling themselves conservatives to ensure success and to give these gentlemen all my assistance at any election afterwards.[50]

Not even Sir John Macdonald could be more flexible (or cynical) than that!

Kirkpatrick, however, was not persuaded. He and others were alienated by the activities of the Quebec Liberals,[51] who indulged in complex and unsavoury actions to obtain evidence of Tory corruption. The government applied considerable pressure on all wavering members, pressure which must have been intense in the case of a man like Kirkpatrick who lived in the Conservative centre of Kingston.[52] As Cartwright commented when he criticized the Quebec Liberals, such activities would have a harmful effect on waverers, especially people like Kirkpatrick "who have pressure enough to contend with."[53] From the point of view of political careerism, conversion to Liberalism could not in 1873 have been attractive to Kirkpatrick. Richard Cartwright was obviously emerging as an important national Liberal leader. In a new government, he would be a leading member, and would make impossible the appointment to the cabinet of a second Kingstonian. Political advancement for George Kirkpatrick was highly unlikely, regardless of which party governed.

Although still a possible convert, Kirkpatrick was not considered a very good possibility by 10 October 1873.[54] In August, Blake had referred to Kirkpatrick in positive terms – "my personal friendship and esteem for [Kirkpatrick] being great …"[55] By October when Kirkpatrick's vote was still important but had slipped away, Blake was considerably less positive: "As to K.[irkpatrick] he is essentially a weak vessel. If we could get him and Lewis of whom we have very good accounts, we ought to be able to run the Ministry within a very few votes …"[56] The Liberals of course were successful and destroyed Macdonald's first Confederation government in 1873, but Kirkpatrick remained a loyal Conservative for the rest of his life.

One final point merits comment, and that is Kirkpatrick's local position within the Conservative Party. R.A. Preston, in his excellent book *Canada's RMC*, refers to Kirkpatrick as "the local party leader" and as "the local Conservative party boss."[57] Kirkpatrick was a key local

Conservative, and was always heavily involved in dispensing patronage. He was not averse to using RMC as a patronage pot. Professor Preston describes one example: "Kirkpatrick ... recommended the Rev. K.L. Jones to succeed Ferguson as professor of English by the statement that he was from 'one of our oldest Conservative families' – and he got the job."[58] To describe Kirkpatrick as the local leader or boss is, however, an exaggeration. To quote Preston again: "But Kingston was Macdonald's riding. Although he lost his seat there in 1878 to a Liberal Reformer, Alexander Gunn, the Prime Minister retained a very lively interest in the administration of its patronage and sometimes personally intervened."[59] This, of course, was the case. Macdonald and Campbell were intimately involved in political management in Kingston. Kirkpatrick was a very important local Conservative leader, but as long as Campbell or Macdonald was on the scene, he could not be regarded as *the* leader. Sir John was active until his death in 1891. Kirkpatrick left active politics a year later.

VI

GEORGE AIREY KIRKPATRICK was the aristocrat in politics, wealthy, popular, educated, connected, haughty, and Anglican. He was possessed of an adequate degree of *noblesse oblige*, and like his father, represented in Parliament the farmers of Frontenac who differed radically from him in virtually every respect. As his political neighbour George Taylor, MP for South Leeds, pointed out, "I do not think the hon. member for Frontenac [Mr. Kirkpatrick] is a practical farmer, or has ever done much in that line."[60] Kirkpatrick was very similar to his slightly older contemporary, Richard Cartwright.

Sir George Kirkpatrick was better educated and wealthier than most of his fellow Ontario Conservative MPs. But he was not really atypical. Most of his colleagues were businessmen or professionals who lived in the larger centres, regardless of which seats they represented. Most were far better educated than those they represented, and Conservative MPs tended to be wealthy. The federal caucus included few farmers. This homogeneity of type almost certainly had a limiting influence on the politicians. They were intellectually restricted by their backgrounds, colleagues, and opponents.

This limiting factor helps to explain much about policy formation in nineteenth-century Canada, why Canada developed as she did, and why the political process was not responsive to the needs of some of Canada's classes and regions. Professor John Porter explains this in an astute comment:

> From the point of view of political power what is more impor-
> tant than interest representation is the range of social perspec-
> tives which are brought to bear on public issues. If we accept
> Mannheim's persuasive argument that a person's beliefs about
> social reality are shaped by the social milieu to which he has
> been exposed, we can see that the definitions of reality which
> provide the framework for making political decisions depend
> much on the social background and life experiences of politi-
> cians. The predominance of some occupational groups and
> people of one class background means that limited perspectives
> are brought to bear on public issues.[61]

Sir George Airey Kirkpatrick, the political patrician, died prematurely in 1899. He was only 58.

Dileno Dexter Calvin

GARDEN ISLAND PATRIARCH

The history of the Garden Island community dates from the arrival of the lumber trade in the late 1830s. To study that aspect of Island history, we must turn to the man who transformed Garden Island into a lumber community.

GARDEN ISLAND IS like a large and somewhat chaotic museum. An American who visited Garden Island in 1878 described it as "the most fascinating spot I ever visited. It had an individuality ... seemed saturated in traditions and memories." Our visitor spoke of "the quaint village street" and of the litter of ancient engines, chain, anchors, small boats, masts, and spars. He found "everything testifying to many continuous years of hard work, rough experience, wrecks handled, vast quantities of timber cut, shipped and rafted down the river ... by a man of rugged character and strong-reliance." He spoke of "the simple well-ordered village where employers and workmen dwelt together and in the government of which they co-operated in harmony."[1]

The island has changed during the past hundred years. Some things, however, do not change. Garden Island continues to charm and fascinate its visitors; and vast quantities of material have survived from lumbering days. The Island is littered with square spikes, boat

---

Professor Swainson had an enduring fascination with Garden Island, where he kept a summer home. This paper was presented to the Kingston Historical Society and the Kingston Marine Museum and became the foundation of the pamphlet *Garden Island and The Calvin Company*, published by the Kingston Marine Museum, Museum Publication No. 3.

Portrait of Dileno Dexter Calvin (Library and Archives Canada).

parts, winches, anchors, loading equipment, mooring rings, decaying docks, wrecked boats, nineteenth-century household artifacts, and all sorts of machine parts. When the water level is low, the ribs of sunken ships can be seen to the south-east. Divers retrieve incredible quantities of clay pipes, bottles, boat parts, crocks, chains, and lamps. Small boys forage around and find keys and nineteenth-century coins among other "treasures." Most of the buildings on the Island date from the lumbering period. Some have been very nicely restored.

The artifacts are impressive, but the most important single source for the study of the Calvins and their company remains the *Calvin Company Papers*. This collection, which was housed in a warehouse on Garden Island until the 1970s, was donated to Queen's University by the Calvin family. It is a large collection that includes some 300 volumes and boxes of manuscript material. This is a huge collection, but it is not a comprehensive record of the company's activities. Much has been lost, and as a result several runs of records contain serious gaps.

The *Calvin Company Papers* are supplemented by some very valuable sources. First, a variety of extremely useful materials, including several fascinating scrapbooks, remains in family hands. This material was loaned to the author. Second, several manuscript collections that relate to Kingston and Kingstonians include numerous references. Third, Kingston newspapers and directories are invaluable. Fourth, members of the Calvin family have written several articles and books.[2] One of these, *A Saga of the St. Lawrence*, by D.D. Calvin the younger, is of particular value to the historian. Fifth, the recent availability of the *Calvin Company Papers* has generated some research on Island and company history. Three students at Queen's University have made particularly impressive contributions: Beverley Doherty, Chris Norman, and Sarah Edinborough.[3] A final source must be mentioned. Hundred of photographs that illustrate aspects of the lumbering period of Garden Island have survived. These can be supplemented with more recent photographs of artifacts, documents, buildings, restorations, the Garden Island museum and so on.

As an introduction to the history of Garden Island, four topics are discussed:

1. The Island before the lumbering period. Here we have no systematic history – only occasional glimpses of interesting people and unusual circumstances.
2. Dileno Dexter Calvin, who founded the firm, and dominated it until his death in 1884.
3. The business itself.
4. The unique community that evolved on Garden Island.

I

Lady simcoe, the wife of our first Lieutenant-Governor, noted what might well have been the first European social held on the Island.[4] The date was Monday, 16 July 1792, and the distinguished guest commented, "We sailed ½ a league this evening in a pretty boat of Mr. Clarke's, attended by music to Garden Island."[5] Social activity continued. A description of a gala event staged on 3 July 1826 has survived:

On Tuesday last the inhabitants of Kingston were much gratified with the sight of a race between the pleasure boats of Lieutenant Jones of the Royal Navy and Lieutenant O'Brien of the Royal Artillery. The boats were moored off the Commissioners Wharf, and at 10 o'clock, on a signal gun being fired from Point Frederick, proceeded round Garden Island and back again ...

During the contest, the bay and river in front of the town exhibited a spectacle unequalled in brilliancy by anything that has occurred here for many years – that beautiful sheet of water being nearly covered with pleasure boats, containing groups of the fair fashionables of the place.

At 4 o'clock the Boat Race Club entertained a party of from 80 to 90 on Garden Island. The Dinner was sumptuous, and in the general arrangements, elegance was happily blended with the most substantial comforts. The sounds of the bugles of the 68th Light Infantry, proceeding from the aboriginal forests in rear of the temporary encampment – combined with the noble view which is presented to the eye from Garden Island – of the town of Kingston – the Military defences of Fort Henry – the dismantled Hulls of the Royal Ships in the Navy Yard – and above all, the confluence of the Cataroque [*sic*], and the Majestic Saint Lawrence, with her thousand Isles – heightened exceedingly the interest of the scene.

In the cool of the evening a few quadrilles were danced, and between 8 and 9 the party embarked for Kingston, seemingly much pleased with the amusements of the day.[6]

A few years later, a somewhat bizarre incident was recorded in the *Chronicle and Gazette*. The story, titled "Amphibious Cow," is as follows: "A week ago … a milch cow swam from within a few yards of Garden Island, to the shore near Fort Henry, a distance of three miles. After being in the water nearly five hours, the 'milky mother' was helped ashore by some men of the 66th Regt. apparently but little the worse for the aquatic excursion."[7]

In 1835, the Montreal *Gazette* published a fine and unusually revealing traveller's description of Garden Island. "The neighbourhood of Kingston abounds in many delightful walks," reported our early tourist and he goes on:

> No place, however, near Kingston, and very few in Canada, can vie with Garden Island, for the advantages it possesses, in point of beautiful scenery, and healthy recreation … The soil is, generally speaking, rich and highly productive. Towards the upper extremity, it consists of a black vegetable loam; about the middle, it is stiff, adhesive brown clay, from which bricks of excellent quality are now being made … Where the land has not been cleared and put under crop, we meet with a great variety of the most beautiful and aromatic plants … [and wild fruits] … Garden Island should be the favourite resort of the numerous boating parties which, during the pleasant months of summer, may be daily seen pushing off from the wharves at Kingston and Point Henry.

The author then said something about the history of Garden Island:

> I understand that this island was granted several years ago, by Sir John Colborne, to a Sergeant of the 79th Regiment … The gift, unlike many others, appears to have been well bestowed

and duly appreciated. The proprietor has already about forty acres under crop, and has erected a large and commodious house, with barns and numerous other outhouses: he has besides constructed a wharf, which projects a considerable distance into the deep water of the Lake, and affords the most perfect protection to the numerous pleasure-boats and small vessels, which from time to time, visit the Island. The improvements which have been effected, have, I am credibly informed, cost upwards of £700 ...

The proprietor, for reasons that have not survived, could not make adequate use of "large and commodious house"; rather, it was "let by its proprietor as a hotel ..." We then discover that the tenant, W.J. Ellsworth, was an early tourist operator who employed techniques not often associated with the early nineteenth century. The traveller's account continues:

From the centre of the house which has been erected on the island, a sort of tower rises up to the height of nearly fifty feet. On the top of this tower there is a commodious platform, from which we enjoy a most delightful view of the surrounding country. We stand in the centre of a circle ... Kingston present[s] a much more favourable aspect to the spectator, than when viewed from any other quarter.[8]

Mr. Ellsworth was an enterprising person, and advertised his attractive-sounding facility regularly during the summer and fall of 1835:

GARDEN ISLAND RETREAT.

W.J. Ellsworth having rented these premises, begs leave to inform the Ladies and Gentlemen of Kingston, that he has appropriated part of the house for

PUBLIC ACCOMMODATION.

The Natural advantages of the situation for Parties out fishing, or merely enjoying the air, are proverbial; in addition to

Dileno Dexter Calvin   213

which the largest vessel navigating Lake Ontario might moor in safety.

Although the fare kept at this solitary situation cannot, as yet, be equal in variety to what is found in the city, the advertiser trusts that few who call there shall be disappointed, and that his improvements shall keep pace with the increase of patronage.

Kingston, June 3, 1835.[9]

These vignettes about Garden Island between 1792 and 1835 amount to substantially less than a systematic history of an organized community. They make clear, however, that Garden Island was more than a bit of picturesque terrain to the south of Kingston; it possessed a farm, a very small brick works, and an embryonic tourist industry. We do not know very much about these enterprises, but they do not seem to have been particularly successful.

The history of the Garden Island community dates from the arrival of the lumber trade in the late 1830s. To study that aspect of Island history, we must turn to the man who transformed Garden Island into a lumber community.

II

DILENO DEXTER CALVIN was a remarkable entrepreneur. Like many of his lumbering contemporaries, he was an American. Calvin was born in Vermont, 15 May 1798. His father was Sandford Jenks Calvin; his mother, Abigail Chipman. D.D. Calvin was the fourth of five children.[10] The family had claims to elite status. According to family belief, Sandford Calvin was a descendent of Richard Warren, a Mayflower pilgrim. Sandford, however, offered little assistance to his children; he was "an unsuccessful lawyer who ... turned farmer." Sandford died when D.D. was only eight; D.D. Calvin started life with little in the way of education or inheritance.[11]

The young Calvin left Vermont in 1818. First, he went to Rodman, New York, "where he worked for three years as a labourer."[12] Calvin was clearly ambitious and sought advancement. He pioneered near Lafargeville, close to Clayton, New York; he cleared his land, and in the process became *both* a farmer and a lumberman. In 1825, he undertook his first serious lumbering operation. With an American partner he made some square timber, rafted it on the St. Lawrence, and took it to Quebec City for sale.[13]

A.R.M. Lower has argued that farming and rafting were incompatible in Upper Canada. Drawing his evidence from the Ottawa valley he comments, "The farmer-lumberer was by no means unknown upon the Ottawa but he never became the typical figure of the industry. Where he existed he generally ruined himself as he did in New Brunswick."[14] Calvin discovered that it was notoriously difficult to mix the two vocations; after attempting the mix for several years he chose lumbering, and in 1835 moved to Clayton, New York, which is on the St. Lawrence-Lake Ontario line south and a little east of Kingston. There, "for nearly a decade," according to a Clayton newspaper, "[he] was a most prominent citizen and a large lumber dealer."[15]

Calvin's personal and family history is both interesting and important. The Clayton connection was never lost. In 1831, D.D. Calvin married Harriet Webb. They had six children, five of whom were born while the family lived in Clayton. Another crucial aspect of his life dates from the Clayton years. During the winter of 1842-43, the town witnessed a religious revival led by the Baptist and Methodist Episcopal churches. Calvin was converted, but was not baptized as a Baptist until after his wife died on 4 July 1843. For the remainder of his life Calvin was a devout and active member of the Baptist church.[16]

D.D. Calvin remarried twice. In 1844, he married Marion Breck, who died in 1861; they had six children. His third wife, whom he married in 1861, was Catherine Wilkinson. They had two children. Calvin's fourteen children were born over a span of 34 years (1832-66).[17] Tragedy haunted Calvin and his family; only six of his children survived to adulthood. We have a graphic description of the death of the thirteenth child. Calvin's partner and former brother-in-law explained to a business associate: "It is with great sorrow that I have to inform you of a sad affliction which has fallen on Mr. and Mrs. Calvin – poor Willie their son 4 years old is no more [.] he was missed from home yesterday P.M. about 6 o'clock and after diligent search his Body was found floating in the water [-] 'drowned' just between our house and the wharf back of Mr. Calvin's house – where or how he fell in is uncertain but probably from the pier back of Mrs. Calvin's kitchen as the last that was seen of the little fellow alive was between

4 & 5 o'clock ... It is another heavy stroke of affliction on poor Mr. Calvin and must bring vividly to his memory the loss of poor Dexter some ten years since.[18]

<h2 style="text-align:center">III</h2>

D.D. CALVIN WAS a dynamic personality who dominated an important Canadian lumbering operation for almost 50 years. The core of Calvin's business was rafting timber and delivering it to the timber coves at Quebec City, where it was transshipped to British markets. For reasons that remain unrecorded, Calvin concluded that Clayton was not an adequate base for his operations. Consequently, he relocated on rented land on the eastern end of Garden Island, which is 65 acres in extent and located two miles south of Kingston. From Garden Island, Calvin was able to operate within the British trading system. Physically, the Island is delightful; geographically the choice was brilliant.[19] The southeast configuration of the Island, with Wolfe Island to the south, provides a sheltered bay, prosaically called "the back bay," that is ideal for disembarking timber, holding it, and building rafts. Initially, Calvin was dependent on sail, and Garden Island gave easier access to sailing craft than either Kingston or Clayton. Finally, the Island is located at the foot of the Great Lakes navigation system. Timber could be transported throughout the Great Lakes by ship. It could not conveniently nor economically, however, be transported down the St. Lawrence in any form but the timber raft. Thus, while canals and railways contributed to Kingston's loss by Confederation of what geographers call the "break-in-bulk-function," the timber raft remained an indispensable part of the timber trade.[20] While Kingston lost its key economic function as a transshipment point, Garden Island, situated where lake becomes river, remained an important transshipment point until the decline of the forest in the twentieth century.[21] This single crucial fact was the economic justification of the extensive operations of D.D. Calvin.

Calvin became active in the Kingston district long before he left Clayton. In 1836, he promoted the Kingston Steam Forwarding Company,[22] which evolved into his first Canadian-based timber partnership with John Counter, a prominent Kingstonian, and Hiram Cook, an American business associate. They were active on rented land at the foot of Garden Island from 1836, although Calvin himself did not move to the Island until 1844. Until his death, D.D. Calvin controlled his firm, but was always associated with at least one partner.[23]

The essence of Calvin's timber operation was simple. He maintained a fleet of lake vessels that transported square timber and staves, chiefly oak and pine, to Garden Island. There, the timber was unloaded and built into rafts. This was a considerable operation.[24] The basic component of a raft was a "dram," which consisted of a series of "cribs." A crib was a floating framework, made without bolts or nails, that measured 60 by 42 feet. Four or five cribs were fastened together to make a dram, which was 250 to 300 feet long. Sticks of timber were then arranged on the cribs and firmly fastened with withes, which were saplings rendered pliable by being twisted or crushed.

Withes can be used to illustrate an important point about the Calvin Company: its ability to be technologically innovative. Initially, the tens of thousands of required withes were made in a tedious labour-intensive fashion. D.D. Calvin, the grandson, explains that prior to 1854, "the withes had been softened for use by manpower, by rolling them up on drums between pairs of six-foot wheels such as were used for steering the river steamers."[25] Another method might also have been used. It is described by Keefer: withes "are formed by taking young birchen trees about the size of ship stalks and fastening their butts firmly, by means of wedges, into an auger hole bored into a stump, then commencing at the points and twisting them ... until the whole of the fibre is separated and the twig becomes as pliant as a rope."[26] In 1854, a horse-powered withering machine was developed, which replaced 12 men. About 1880 a company employee produced an even better machine, powered by steam. A man who observed it in operation commented: "It would be difficult to describe this steam withe-machine in any detail, elaborate drawings would be needed. Suffice it to say that the machine did three things simultaneously – it gripped the withe at the butt, twisted it (to break open the fibre) and wound it around a revolving drum, which at the same time moved toward the revolving jaws which held the butt. When the steam was cut off, the withe, as it unrolled, whipped violently back in an attempt to regain its original straight line."[27] Apparently, this mechanical marvel exerted an hypnotic force on the persons who gathered to watch it perform. The history of the Calvin Company is replete with examples of engineering innovation on an impressive scale. This topic merits a separate study.

Let us go back to our raft. With the aid of withes, the drams were constructed. A dozen or more drams made a raft that could be well over half a mile long and include 165,000 cubic feet of timber. The St. Lawrence timber raft even included cooking and sleeping shanties for the raftsmen who would accompany it all the way to Quebec City. The raft was broken into its component drams when it passed through rapids. Many considered a raft journey to be an enjoyable adventure. Friends and relatives took the trip from time to time and reported on their exhilarating experiences.[28]

Although Calvin purchased timber for resale and on occasion financed independent timber makers, the bulk of the timber delivered to Quebec belonged not to D.D. Calvin, but to various timber makers in the Great Lakes basin.[29] It was carried 350 miles to Quebec City for a fee. Calvin was therefore shielded from some market vicissitudes because he charged his fee regardless of his customers' profit margins.[30]

While the essence of Calvin's operations was simple, the logistics and organization were not; the scope of the operations was vast.[31] Until 1854, a branch of the company operated in Hamilton; there was always a branch in Quebec City and agencies were established in a variety of places including Liverpool, Glasgow, Sault St. Marie, Defiance (Ohio) and Marquette (Michigan). Twelve to fifteen ships were maintained to deliver timber to Garden Island from as far afield as Michigan and Minnesota. Permanent employees lived on Garden Island; additional persons were employed on the Island in the summer and on the rafts as they passed through difficult portions of the upper St. Lawrence. Initially, the rafts moved only with the aid of current and sail; eventually they were towed. As many as 700 men were on the payroll at peak periods. Although heavily dependent on credit, the firm was, as we have seen, largely self-sufficient in the technological sphere.[32]

In order to maximize the utility of his investment and maintain a permanent work force, Calvin sought business opportunities apart from rafting. The result was a substantial diversity in the firm's operations: Calvin and his partners operated as general merchants, manufacturers, forwarders, common carriers, wharfingers, warehousemen, ship owners, lumber merchants, wreckers, and rafters. They rented sheds for the storage of flour, salt, and rails, bought and sold salt, and freighted rails. The company's ship-building enterprise was large; the company's policy was to build a ship a year.[33] The partnership also operated a lucrative government-subsidized tug boat service on the St. Lawrence above Montreal, 1858-74.[34]

The growth and prosperity of the firm are indicated by its assets, which increased from $216,000 in 1854 to $460,000 in 1871. Interestingly enough, the employees shared in this growth and prosperity. Between the 1850s and 1880s, real wages increased 11%. In 1880, the company had $75,000 invested in its towing and wrecking business alone.[35] Most of Calvin's business activity was carried out through his firm. He did, however, purchase and retain large quantities of land in the United States; he also served as a director and second vice-president of the Kingston & Pembroke Railway.[36] In 1865 and other years, Calvin's was the largest timber operation at the coves of Quebec City; it was also one of the half dozen largest timber firms in Canada.[37] When he died in 1884, D.D. Calvin owned ninety-two per cent of Calvin and Son, and left an estate conservatively valued at $324,242.[38]

IV

CALVIN'S BUSINESS was a major enterprise in nineteenth-century Canada, and richly merits study. Perhaps more interesting and important, however, was Calvin's role as a benevolent patriarch. This must be studied along with the nature of the society that evolved on Garden Island.

Initially, Calvin and his partners rented land at the foot of Garden Island. Calvin and Cook purchased 15 acres of that land in 1848. By 1862, the partnership owned the entire island, and in 1880 Calvin personally purchased the property.[39] Referred to by his employees as "the Governor," Calvin dominated the little society that developed on Garden Island. During 1860-85, the height of the company's prosperity,[40] as many as 750 people lived and worked on the Island. Their occupations included master mariner, shipwright, teamster, raftsman, engineer, merchant, sailor, carpenter, sailmaker, customs officer, blacksmith, clerk, boatman, farmer, cook, agent, bookkeeper, lawyer, boiler-maker, labourer, foreman, joiner, sparmaker, rigger, painter, saddler, baker, butcher, and teacher.[41] All but the school teachers, farmers, and customs officers were directly employed by the company; the farmer cultivated land owned by the firm; everybody lived in company-owned houses.

The small farm provided dairy products; a company-owned general store sold household necessities at competitive prices.[42] The store extended credit, sold items for cash, and exchanged goods for company issued scrip. Eight pieces of Garden Island scrip have recently been discovered. They came in a variety of denominations: 5c, 10c, 25c, 50c, $2. Each piece in circulation carried an accession number, and bore the signature of a company officer. These bills were made from engraved plates; each included a promissory statement: "Good to the Bearer for the sum of Ten Cents [or somesuch] in Goods." The eight bills that I have seen indicated that at least two series were issued – 1864 and 1869.[43]

Fuel was plentiful because of large amounts of scrap from raftmaking and shipbuilding. The lake was rich in fish. An elementary school, generously subsidized by the firm, operated at a higher standard than did neighbouring schools.[44] The islanders possessed one of the finest Mechanics' Institutes in Canada, with a library of 1,600 volumes by 1884[45] and sustained several fraternal societies: a Masonic lodge, an Orange lodge, a chapter of the Order of Chosen Friends and a Temperance Society. These various associations used the "hall" built by the company.[46] After 1868, the Island even had its own post-office.[47]

Garden Island was rigidly prohibitionist. The labouring population, which was surprisingly stable, included French Canadians, Scots, Irishmen, Americans, Indians from Caughnawaga, and Englishmen, but ethnic and religious conflict was largely avoided (or suppressed.)[48] The French language was extensively used both on the Island and in company correspondence.[49] Until at least Confederation, Garden Island was functionally bilingual.

Island society was pleasant and unique. An American visitor, who went to Garden Island in 1878, spoke of "the simple well-ordered village where employers and workmen dwelt together and in the government of which they co-operated in harmony." Professor Michael Cross, a leading student of the lumber community, comments: "The lumber community, wherever it touched other segments of society, was a socially disturbing factor, both in the behaviour of its employees, and in the fatal lure of its glamour … The lumber community does not present an attractive picture. It was avaricious, uncultured, foolhardy, vicious. It was a society organized for only one purposes – material gain."[50] Cross was concerned for the most part with the Ottawa valley, but *his* approach might cause one to question the idyllic picture painted of Garden Island society (by both the American visitor and the present writer) and the extent to which Dileno Dexter Calvin was benevolent. Yet three careful studies confirm this attractive picture.[51]

Beverly Doherty, in her thesis, *Real Wage Changes as Revealed in the Manuscripts of the Shipyard of the Calvin Company, Selected Years:* 1848-1884, concludes "that the Calvin Company was a paternalistic firm whose decisions were based on the welfare of its employees rather than on rational employment decision-making." Chris Norman's paper, "Garden Island: A Social Study at Mid-Century, An Introductory Survey of an Early Company Community," argues: "The Garden Island Community was initially a product of the company's demands for manpower in a labour intensive industry. Yet, we can detect a subtle transformation in the company/employee relationship whereby the welfare of the Islanders assumes an increasingly important role … [A]s the Islanders became a part of a growing and distinctive community … Garden Island evolved from a company community to a community-based company." After analyzing the Island's educational facility, Sarah Edinborough commented, "It is evident from the surviving records that Calvin had the best of intentions for the children of his men, and he worked hard for their educational interests."[52]

Calvin's paternalism is illustrated by his approach to the crisis caused by the panic of 1873. Doherty describes the scene as well as anybody: "He called his senior employees into his office and said that wages would have to be cut but if they all stuck together they could weather the storm. He had the *Garden Island*, an ocean going vessel, built to keep his employees working, an effort which proved very costly."[53] In short, the largest shipbuilding operation ever undertaken on Garden Island was designed to keep the workforce and the Island community together during a period of economic crisis, D.D. Calvin was motivated by community, not entrepreneurial considerations.

Strong opposition to organized labour was perfectly consistent,

Calvin's paternalistic role. In the late 1870s, the Seamen's Union organized the sailors on Calvin's Lake Ontario vessels. The union's issue was wages: "Mr. Calvin was never known to pay a fair day's pay unless he was forced to do," claimed C.W. Crowley, the union president. At issue for D.D. Calvin was his authority: "One or the other must go down," he declared.[54] The sailors proved stubborn, so Calvin fired all union members and replaced them with sailors imported from Glasgow. These imports had not been told that they were strikebreakers; they were also probably intimidated by local members of the Seamen's Union. In any event, the Scots joined the union, and soon left the country. Ultimately, Calvin won. He turned his schooners into barges and towed them on Lake Ontario. This enabled him to dispose of most of the sailors in his employ. The *D.D. Calvin*, which was built at a cost of $75,000, was laid down in 1881 specifically to meet this towing need. She was launched in 1883.[55]

This is an interesting incident. It is hardly fashionable these days to do anything but denigrate the motives of those who systematically break unions. But the evidence indicates that Calvin was not motivated by avarice. He was, of course, a proud man, and could not sit idly by while union organizers took over his firm. C.W. Crowley had said, and in print, that "Some of the seamen know just as much as Mr. Calvin."[56] Calvin no doubt took such remarks as direct challenges to the authority that he was convinced he derived from ownership. This was no doubt a factor that influenced his judgment.[57]

There was more. The evidence indicates that Calvin acted in the best interests of his community, as he saw those interests, even when such action violated his own self-interest. Had Calvin given in to the Seamen's Union he could have destroyed the harmony and unity of his island community. He could also have diminished the wage flexibility that enabled him to adjust wages as economic conditions changed. That flexibility permitted his society to survive depressed periods. Calvin was not, however, averse to sharing his prosperity with the stable portion of his workforce. That is why he raised wages when he could, and allowed senior workers to purchase small portions of the business.[58]

V

D.D. CALVIN'S LEADERSHIP role also had its public side. He became a British subject in 1845 and a monarchist. [59] In 1860, Calvin joined John A. Macdonald and the Prince of Wales aboard the *Kingston* a few miles down river from Garden Island. Anthony Malone, the company's bookkeeper, described the meeting: "Calvin was taken aboard the *Kingston* and John A. Macdonald introduced him to H.R.H. as 'an old Vermont Yankee.' In good humour Calvin replied, 'Why do you call me a Yankee I can *holler* for the Queen as loud as you can.' At this retort the prince laughed heartily."[60]

Calvin was commissioned a magistrate in 1845. By 1865, he was Reeve of Wolfe Island, of which Garden was a part, and served as first Warden of Frontenac County after it was separated from Lennox and Addington. In 1866, Garden Island was incorporated as a village.[61] This presented Calvin with an unusual situation: he owned his entire constituency and employed virtually all the voters. A grandson of D.D. Calvin noted that "the men ... wisely voted ... Conservative. A Liberal vote in the island ballot-box meant that there was a newcomer in the village who had not yet fully learned our traditions."[62] For the remainder of his life, he was routinely acclaimed as Reeve; he was also a perennial member of the Frontenac County Council and served as Warden four times.[63]

In 1870, Sir John A. Macdonald appointed Calvin, along with such luminaries as Hugh Allan (chairman), Casimir Stanislaus Gzowski, George Laidlaw, Pierre Garneau, William James Stairs, Alexander Jardine, Samuel Leonard Shannon, and Samuel Keefer (secretary), to the *Royal Commission to Inquire Into the Best Means for the Improvement of the Water Communications of the Dominion and the Development of the Trade With the North-Eastern Portion of North America.* This was only our fourth federal royal commission. The commissioners urged the improvement of various canals on the St. Lawrence, but Calvin opposed making the river navigable for ocean shipping; he did not want Chicago turned into a deep sea port.[64]

In 1868, Calvin entered provincial politics. With the reluctant support of Sir John A. Macdonald, he became the Conservative candidate to replace the deceased Sir Henry Smith as MPP for Frontenac.

Macdonald's concern about Calvin's reliability was based on a letter written by R.J. (later Sir Richard) Cartwright on 24 September 1868. Cartwright hoped "Britton [a local businessman] will pluck up heart to oppose Calvin and get well thrashed, which will effectively dispose of him in future" Cartwright then went on to say: "By the way I should like to know can you rely on Calvin himself any longer than he holds his contract from the Dominion? I have seen something of him since I have been living on the Island and I have my reasons for asking. He is perhaps our best available man and I like him very well myself, but in spite of his good service in 1863 I have some doubts how far he is to be relied on."[65] Cartwright's cynicism need not be taken very seriously. He might well have been projecting his own disloyalty; only a few months later he began his own slide into the Liberal Party.[66] What is interesting is the suggestion that R.J. Cartwright lived for a time on Garden Island and knew a great deal about Calvin and his business.

In any event, Calvin was the Conservative candidate in the by-election of 1868 and did thrash B.M. Britton. In 1871, he was elected by acclamation, but, in 1875, he lost the Frontenac County nomination.[67] Calvin reentered provincial politics when the sitting Conservative died in 1877. Again he won an easy victory and repeated his success in the general election of 1879. Calvin was not a candidate in the general election of 1883, when he was 85.

D.D. Calvin was not a major provincial politician, although he was active and presented his views with vigor. Like most nineteenth-century politicians, he worked hard to obtain patronage for his constituents.[68] He passionately favoured tax reform, arguing that "it was unjust to tax personal property and allow a person who held mortgages, bearing, perhaps, 8 per cent, to go free." In his opinion a man's personal property should be exempt to the amount of his indebtedness.[69] He also argued that all property, including stocks and wild lands, should be assessed. Curiously enough, Calvin sided with agriculture against lumber when their interests clashed. He favoured "a scheme under which the settlers should be custodians of the lumber. He was opposed to the granting of the great lumber limits, on the ground that it retarded settlement. Calvin was anxious to promote settlement, arguing that if "we encourage the colonization of the back regions, the country would get as much good from each settler as it would from $1,000 additional capital."[70]

Calvin's opposition to "the great lumber limits" and desire that "we encourage the colonization of the back regions" is evidence of the extent of his individuality. Most lumbermen regarded frontier settlement as a totally unacceptable blight. The lumber barons argued that such settlers stole timber, ruined timber districts, and caused extremely expensive forest fires. Professor H.V. Nelles, in a discussion of a later period, comments, "the lumbermen accused settlers and governments as the two outstanding agents of destruction ... 'The greatest engine of destruction that the forests of Canada have suffered from,' Senator [W.C.] Edwards claimed, was 'illegitimate settlement.' It was not enough to maintain fire-ranging systems to put out fires, he added, 'the man who most frequently starts the fires, the pretended settler, must be eliminated.'"[71] Senator Edwards, a lumberman himself, spoke in the early years of the twentieth century, but his views were common and representative of Calvin's period. J.R. Booth, for example, who was a powerful lumber baron from the mid-nineteenth century until well into the twentieth century, was equally adamant. "In the public interest," he declared, "spruce or other trees valuable for timber and lumber should be withheld from settlement and made a permanent forest reservation."[72] Men like Edwards and Booth represented the views of lumbermen on this issue; D.D. Calvin was the maverick. Calvin's business contemporaries must have shaken their heads in disbelief when they heard a major lumberman advocate frontier settlement at the expense of lumbering.

D.D. Calvin also favoured minor reforms in the electoral and judicial systems. Prohibition was a lifelong passion, and he spoke regularly on that subject.[73]

Calvin was 70 years old when he entered provincial politics. A colourful figure, he was described as "One of the eccentrics of the early days of the Ontario Parliament."[74]

VI

DILENO DEXTER CALVIN never lost his affection for his American home. He never sold the "Calvin Homestead" at Lafargeville, and after he died at Garden Island on 18 May 1884, he was buried at Clayton beside his mother and first wife.[75] His funeral suited the man who founded "the Garden Island monarchy."[76] D.D. Calvin was taken from Garden Island to Clayton aboard the *Maud*, accompanied by 200 mourners – including Kingston's City Council. The *Chieftain* followed with most of the Garden Islanders. Calvin's pallbearers included Prime Minister Sir John A. Macdonald, G.A. Kirkpatrick, MP for Frontenac and Speaker of the House of Commons, and Alexander Gunn, MP for Kingston.[77]

D.D. Calvin's death ended neither the Calvin Company nor the rafting business. His son, Hiram Augustus, took over the firm, which was known as "the pioneer rafting and forwarding company"[78] as late as 1895. But the great days of the timber trade were over. The rafts became fewer and fewer; the business did not diversify. The Calvin Company went out of business at the outset of World War I.

D.D. Calvin and his firm are important subjects. They merit study, if only to help complete our knowledge of a neglected side of lumber industry. More important perhaps is the opportunity provided for a micro study of a fascinating community. We are enabled in this way to test various hypotheses, and to pose questions:

- How do we fit a peaceful, prohibitionist, co-operative and family-oriented society into the general frame-work that most of use have concerning lumber society and company-dominated towns?
- Many of our social historians assume the inevitability of class conflict. If it cannot be found, how was it ameliorated? Should not this assumption be examined on a case study basis? Did benevolent patriarchs represent a last (and possibly better) alternative?
- To what extent was nineteenth-century capitalism non-avaricious? Is the hostility of liberals and intellectuals to business so marked, that most professional scholars will not even ask the correct questions?

James Richardson

FOUNDER OF THE FIRM

James Richardson built a major business between 1857 and 1892. It was strong enough to become the base for one of twentieth-century Canada's most dynamic corporate instruments. James Richardson is the most important businessman produced by Kingston.

Most reasonably well-informed Canadians are at least aware of the firm of James Richardson and Sons, a giant operation that has been with us since the middle of the nineteenth century. Its headquarters is in Winnipeg – in the city's tallest structure, the Richardson Building, at the corner of Portage and Main. [1] The company is a private firm – its shares are not publicly traded; all the shares are owned by four Richardson siblings. Since 1857, a century and a third, it has been headed by only six Richardsons:

James Richardson, President, 1857-1892.
George A. Richardson, President, 1892-1906.
Henry W. Richardson, President, 1906-1918.
James A. Richardson, President, 1919-1939.
Muriel Sprague Richardson (widow of James A.), President, 1939-1966.
George T. Richardson (with James A. Richardson as chairman and chief executive officer 1966-1968), President since 1966.

Published in *Historic Kingston*, Vol. 38, 1990, this article grew out of research Professor Swainson did in the Richardson business archives while writing *Kingston: Building on the Past*. It is the last biography he wrote in his Kingston personalities series.

JAMES RICHARDSON
1819 — 1892

Portrait of James Richardson (Library and Archives Canada).

It is not the purpose of this paper to present a history of James Richardson and Sons Ltd., which has been described as "the best known corporation in the West, run by the least known group of celebrities in Canada."[2] However, it is useful to know a little about "the firm,"[3] as it is usually called by those associated with it.

I

THE RICHARDSON firm is now a prairie operation centred in Winnipeg with extensive interests throughout the prairie region. It also operates some Canada-wide enterprises. The firm started to buy Manitoba wheat in the 1880s. It located its executive offices in Winnipeg in 1922, and made its full formal move to the Manitoba metropolis in 1939.

The primary interest of James Richardson and Sons is grain. In the twentieth century, it became the biggest grain trader in the Commonwealth. In 1913, it formed the Pioneer Grain Company that became central to its trading activities. Pioneer eventually operated some 450 grain elevators and was the only important private elevator company to survive the competition of the wheat pools. The Richardson operation also owns the Richardson terminal at Thunder Bay, a facility that has an 11.5-million-bushel capacity.

The company has always had an interest in diversity. Hence in 1911 the Richardson Stock Farms came into existence. In the 1920s, the firm acquired a number of radio stations, most of which were sold in 1940. Also in the 1920s, Richardson Securities of Canada (now Richardson Greenshields of Canada Ltd.) was added to the company's empire. Western Canada Airways Ltd. was founded in 1926. After undergoing re-organization it was sold to Canadian Pacific. And in 1969, the company's office tower was built on western Canada's most famous corner, Portage and Main in Winnipeg. Obviously, Richardson enterprises – and only a sketchy introduction is given to them here – are huge, extremely important to prairie economic activity and very powerful. Richardson Greenshields, for example, employs 1,830 people and has offices throughout the country.[4]

Recently, George T. Richardson, President of James Richardson and Sons Ltd., announced that he planned to sell the huge Richardson Greenshields brokerage firm. The plan was ultimately abandoned, but in the interim our "national newspaper," the *Globe and Mail*, published an article on Richardson Greenshields, in which it discussed the ownership of the firm. The *Globe and Mail* reported: "It is owned 25 per cent by senior employees and 75 per cent by descendants of grain merchant James Richardson, who founded the family's extensive business empire in Winnipeg in 1857."[5] Once again, a prominent Toronto institution, and is there any more obvious such institution than the *Globe and Mail*, has belittled that city's historic rival at the east end of the lake, and in this case, Kingston suffers for a Winnipeg that did not even exist in 1857. We all know that James Richardson was a Kingstonian and that his famous firm was founded here and operated from Kingston for a good two generations. James Richardson, the "Founder" of the "Firm" is the subject of this paper.

II

ACCORDING TO HIS obituary, James Richardson was born at Aughnacloy, County Tyrone, Ireland, in 1819.[6-7] His grave marker in Cataraqui Cemetery states that he was born in Dungannon, County Tyrone, on 16 July 1820.[8] He died of paralysis at Kingston, 15 November 1892.[9] His father was Daniel Richardson; his mother was Janet Armstrong.[10] He was a member of Sydenham Street Methodist (now United) Church, where he taught Sunday School. Richardson "was greatly interested in the first building on the present site of his church home, and a very liberal contributor to the remodeled and beautiful church of today."[11] James Richardson married twice. In 1845, he married Roxanna Day,[12] who was known as "Roxie Ann."[13] They had two children, Sydney James (who died in infancy) and Mary.[14] Roxanna died on 20 November 1848,[15] and in 1850, Richardson married Susannah Wartman, a niece of his late wife. The second marriage produced two sons. George Armstrong Richardson and Henry Wartman Richardson became major businessmen.[16] Susannah Wartman Richardson survived her husband.

The origins of James Richardson were hardly auspicious. His father had been married twice; the first marriage produced four children, one of whom died in infancy. The second marriage produced Martha and James. Janet Armstrong, the second wife, died shortly after the birth of James, and Daniel married for a third time. In 1822 (or 1823), Daniel emigrated to Ontario with James, his sister Martha, and his half-sister Elizabeth (known as Eliza). [17] They settled in the Adolphustown district, where Daniel died in 1826. [18] Eliza, a teenaged girl, was left in charge of her two younger siblings. By 1829, she had moved the family to Kingston, where James lived for the rest of his life. [19] He was brought up by a sister of Daniel. [20]

James Richardson had a limited formal education. He sold newspapers and was apprenticed to a tailor, John Dawson, who had a shop on Brock Street. [21] The Dawson connection was an important one. Mrs. Dawson was a member of the Wartman family, as were both of Richardson's wives.

III

RICHARDSON WAS in business by 1841, in which year "James Richardson and William Sanderson were fined the sum of 5 pounds each, for hawking and peddling without a license, contrary to the form of the Statute." [22] For a brief time he was in a tailoring partnership with one Little and by 1844 was in business on his own. His advertisement read:

> *James Richardson,*
> *(late of the firm Little + Richardson)*
>
> MERCHANT TAILOR
> BROCK STREET
>
> *At the Shop lately occupied by Mr. Thomas Bilton,*
> *Second door from "Head Quarters."*
>
> NOTICE
>
> *The Subscriber begs leave to recommend Mr. James Richardson, Merchant Tailor, at the Stand lately occupied by the Subscriber, to the patronage of his friends and the public.*
>
> THOS. BILTON
>
> *Kingston, 20 July 1844.* [23]

Richardson continued to advertise his wares in the local press and clearly was prospering and expanding:

"J. Richardson, Merchant tailor . . . Begs to acquaint his customers and the inhabitants of Kingston generally, that he has received direct from Montreal and New York, his Fall and Winter Goods, comprising a large assortment of broadcloth, cassimes, tweeds, doeskins, vestings, etc., in great variety. Naval and Military clothes of all descriptions; blue, black, and brown beavers of different qualities, all of which he is prepared to make up to order, and in the very best manner as regards style, Fit and workmanship and at unusually low prices. J.R. would also beg to intimate, that he is always in receipt of the latest fashions, and as he employs only first-rate workmen is confident of giving satisfaction to all who may favour him with their patronage."[24]

He noted that he also offered a wide "assortment of Fashionable Buttons, Trimmings, etc. etc. " In 1848, Richardson's operation " REMOVED to the third house below his former residence, where he will be happy to execute all orders in his line with PROMPT DESPATCH and on REASONABLE TERMS."[25]

Richardson owned the property occupied by his firm on Brock Street, between King and Wellington. He lived above his shop and had several merchant tenants.[26] In 1848, James Richardson was 29 years of age. He had developed into an enterprising and successful young businessman.

IV

I N THE MID-1850s, an important event occurred in the life of James Richardson. He had become a prominent and active Kingstonian. At the same time his fellow townsman, John A. Macdonald, had become a leading figure in the government. The Kingston business community pressured Macdonald and the government to provide construction activity in the city. The government succumbed and in 1856 called tenders for a major public building in downtown Kingston. Originally, a single building was to be built at the corner of Clarence and Wellington Street to house the Post Office and Custom House.[28]

The contract went to Thomas C. Pidgeon, who was required to "supply the names of guarantors for enterprises such as the construction of new buildings authorized by the government of the day."[29] Pidgeon's guarantors were Samuel Smyth (a tavern keeper), James O'Reilly (an influential Roman Catholic Tory and a lawyer),[30] and James Richardson. Pidgeon was in difficulties from the beginning. There was delay, and it was decided to erect separate buildings for the Post Office and the Custom House, and the site of the Custom House was changed. It was to be built on the corner of Clarence and King Street, a site that would require a more expensive form of excavation. Pidgeon was unable to proceed; Smyth and O'Reilly reneged on their commitment.[31] In the end, Richardson completed the work by September 1858.

According to G. Newlands, "Had it not been for Mr. Richardson, the work could not have been completed ... [H]e lost over 1700 pounds on the deal."[32] Richardson was most unhappy with the outcome, as he explained to the Board of Works:

> "I venture to say every person examining it will pronounce it to be a building on which the greatest possible outlay has been entailed for the purpose of producing the least possible good. Certainly, if the superintendent of the Board of Works caused an outlay of upward of £10,000, where a little more than one fourth of the sum would have constructed a building serving equally as well any purpose that usefulness or ornament could require, it is no cause why I should not be paid. My outlay, permit me to say, has been much greater than my limited means can sustain under the present depressed state of trade and the impossibility of obtaining money unless at a great sacrifice."[33]

The completion of the Custom House is important in two ways. First, it can be seen as the beginning of the large number of major benefactions that various Richardsons have showered on Kingston and Queen's University. The Custom House is one of Kingston's finest public buildings, and it is instrumental in defining the streetscape of the old part of the city. In 1971, the Historic Sites and Monuments Board of Canada declared it a building of national significance. Its architectural importance was explained thus: "The style of building is of British derivation, and is quite unlike the public buildings of the United States which at that time were often in the Greek Revival style. The buildings [the Custom House and the nearby Post Office] are very fine examples of mid-nineteenth century architecture ... [and] show great sensitivity in the handling of stonework."[34] Second, in his letter to the Board of Works, Richardson complained about the financial burden imposed on him by the construction of the Custom House and referred to "the impossibility of obtaining money unless at a great sacrifice." It would seem that his financial difficulties forced him to become more heavily involved in the grain trade than had hitherto been the case.

On 31 December 1856, Richardson mortgaged his Brock Street property to his half-sister since 1832, Eliza Hart, for £750.[35] A company historian notes: "This was undoubtedly the spur that turned him to serious grain trading in order to carry on in the face of great difficulty ... In effect," argued the company historian, "James Richardson's experience as the guarantor ... propelled him into serious grain trading, which is the reason the founding of the family grain firm dates to 1857."[36] James Richardson had dabbled in grain for some years because his customers occasionally paid him with grain,[37] and he certainly did not abandon his tailoring business until the 1860s.

Some sense of this transition from tailor to grain merchant can be gained from entries in the directories of Kingston's business community during this period. In 1855, James Richardson is referred to as "merchant tailor, 21 Brock St.," but the 1857-1858 entry is as "merchant tailor and draper, and contractor for the New Custom House." Five years later, in 1862, he is still "tailor, 21 Brock," but reference is now made to a house on King Street. It is not until 1865 that he is first referred to as "grain dealer h., King nr. Gordon." The 1873-1874 directory refers to several members of the family, including "Richardson, George, Stuart St.," "Richardson, James Senr. Res. Stuart St.," "Richardson, James, Jr., res. Stuart St." The same directory also includes a major commercial entry for "RICHARDSON & SONS, Grain Dealers, Commercial Wharf, foot of Princess St." By 1875, the entry is for "grain merchant, h. 61 Stuart St.," the address being changed by 1881 to "grain merchant, 100 Stuart St."[38]

Despite this patchy and perhaps misleading evidence, it would appear that Richardson's serious preoccupation with grain dates from the 1857 founding of James Richardson and Sons,[39] an informal arrangement as long as the firm's founder was alive. James was joined by his sons George A. and Henry W. Richardson, who became full partners. Initially, the company's office was on Richardson's Brock Street property. In 1882, it moved into a building next to the Princess Street elevator.[40] In the twentieth century, the firm became a prairie-centered firm, but its nominal head office remained in Kingston until 1939.

That the Customs House was not Richardson's only foray into building and speculation is evidenced by a comment recorded in one of Dr. Barker's annual "Spring walks" of 7 March 1864:

> Mr. James Richardson, having recently purchased the Phair Property in Princess St, means to build up a row of three large stone houses, with shops and offices, on that locality. They will be put up this summer and be ready for occupation in the fall.[41]

Clearly, Richardson was making his mark on the Kingston scene.

V

RICHARDSON'S GROWING interest in grain coincided with the boom in Bay of Quinte barley.[42] This barley was of high quality and was purchased in great quantity and at premium prices by American manufacturers. It remained an important export commodity until the trade was ruined by the McKinley tariff (1890) and the Dingley Act (1897).

Richardson used rented and company-owned sloops and schooners able to carry from 1,000 to 20,000 bushels. The Richardson lake fleet consisted of such vessels as the *Richardson, Navajo, B.W. Folger, Hanlon, White Oak* , and *Lyman Davis*. The famous local "mosquito fleet" consisted of such privately owned vessels as the *Echo, Granger, Ariadne, Highland Beauty, Two Brothers, Minnie P, Madcap, Monarch, Katie Eccles, Pilot*, and *Queen of the Lakes*. With these varied vessels, Richardson's fleet collected barley (and other grains) at various places in the Bay of Quinte area, including Bath, Sandhurst, Conway, Glenora, Belleville, and Wolfe Island. Some of this grain was then shipped directly to American ports, particularly Oswego and Cape Vincent. These were the carriers of the Richardson commercial empire, including "the small hookers ... which worked along the river and bay shore and the Rideau."[43]

.Some grain went directly from a collection place to an American port. Much, however, was collected at Richardson's Kingston dock or, later, stored in Richardson's grain elevator – which became the heart of his grain business – for transshipment to American or European destinations. In 1868, James Richardson purchased a waterfront property at the foot of Princess Street and built an elevator there. The *Daily British Whig* described the plans for the site:

> ... the old Commercial Wharf, so long the depot of the Royal Mail Line of steamers, having been purchased by Mr. James Richardson, that gentleman is putting it in a thorough state of repair, with a view to future occupation by the Kingston grain buyer. It has been greatly extended into the harbour, and will make one of the most commodious wharves in the town.[44]

Later, this became the site of the first Richardson grain elevator. "Richardson No. 1" was built in 1882[45] with a capacity for 60,000 bushels[46] and could load 2,000 bushels per hour.[47] James Richardson's elevator outlived him by five years. It succumbed to fire in 1897. An observer thought it quite a marvelous sight:

> While the conflagration was in progress it presented a beautiful spectacle. The city was brilliantly illuminated, and millions of sparks emanating from the blaze, floated over the city, standing out like myriads of sparkling stars against the somber blue-black clouds of the wintry night. It was a grand sight viewed from a spectacular standpoint, but one maddening to behold when considering the loss entailed.[48]

In 1897, a new elevator of 250,000 bushel capacity replaced the one that had burned.[49]

VI

THE PRAIRIE REGION was not a major grain producer during the lifetime of James Richardson, but it did produce grain, and Richardson realized that the West was potentially important. Until the twentieth century, Western business was under the care of Edward O'Reilly, a Wolfe Islander who moved to Manitoba during the early 1880s.[50] He quickly gave up agriculture for the grain trade, with an office first in Neepawa and then at Portage la Prairie.[51] In the mid-1890s, he followed the leading grain merchants to Winnipeg, where he bought produce for the Richardson firm.[52] O'Reilly operated as a private businessman in Winnipeg; the Richardson name was not used there in the nineteenth century.[53]

The Richardson company was proud of its early involvement on the prairies. James A. Richardson, grandson of James and president of the firm 1919-1939, noted to A.R. Bingham, a Liverpool businessman: "The first Western Canadian Wheat shipped out of Fort William was in the fall of '83, and ... this wheat, which was the first Western Canadian wheat shipped from this continent was shipped by our house to the Atlantic Seaboard in the winter of '84 and consigned to your house in Liverpool."[54]

James Richardson was extremely active in the export business. Apart from the United States trade, he dealt with grain firms in Holland, Britain, Switzerland, France, Ireland, England, Scotland, Norway, and Argentina. Barley and wheat were important to James Richardson, but he traded in numerous other commodities, including potash, oats, hay, corn, furs, apples, coal, lye, maple syrup, and feldspar.[55] He diversified his interests beyond commodity trading.[56] Richardson acquired substantial amounts of property in the Kingston region. He invested in the Kingston & Pembroke Railway, the Street Railway Company, and the locomotive works. In 1881, Richardson, as the largest shareholder, became president of the Kingston Cotton Manufacturing Company. He also invested in the town's woolen mill, the Kingston Hosiery Company, and the Kingston Oil and Enamel Cloth Company.

Other investments initiated a Richardson interest in local mineral development that was to continue well into the twentieth century. In the last decades of the nineteenth century, there was much interest in the possible development of such minerals as mica, phosphates, feldspar, iron, and graphite throughout the southern shield region behind Kingston. In particular, there was much activity along the line of the Rideau Canal and also of several railways. The Kingston & Pembroke Railway entered the back-country in 1876, extended to Sharbot Lake by 1877, and to the rear of Frontenac in the 1880s; the Toronto-Ottawa branch of the CP in 1884; the Toronto-Montreal branch of the CP arrived in 1912. Another factor facilitating speculation in mineral prospects was the abundance of experienced miners in the south-shield area because of the prevalence of mica, phosphate, and other small-scale mine operations that depended upon similar operational skills as phosphate works: "The operation of a feldspar quarry required some knowledge of mining, and hand sorting of spar and waste in the pit required some knowledge of feldspar in order to distinguish potash spar from soda spar."[57] Because of these local factors, together with an increasing interest in industrial development in general, the mineral economy boomed, and Kingston, together with Perth and Ottawa, became an active, albeit short-lived, centre of mineral investment, processing, and transshipment. The Richardson family became involved in all aspects of this.

Perhaps the most productive, and certainly the most prominent, Richardson local mineral enterprise was the Bedford Township feldspar mine. The "Richardson Mine" of the Kingston Feldspar Mining Company was acquired in the 1880s and commenced operation in 1900.[58] Located on Con. 11 Lot 1, Bedford Township, the Richardson Quarry was the largest producer of feldspar in Canada in its time (90% Ontario production),[59] employing an average work force of some 45 men. The ore was loaded onto trams that ran down an inclined tramway to Thirteen Island Lake; there the cars were loaded onto scows and ferried across the lake by small tug; the trams were then wheeled off the scows and run across a narrow neck of land to Thirty Island Lake where they were loaded onto scows for the journey to the railway at Glendower.[60]

Feldspar was chiefly used in the manufacturing of many types of ceramics and also in washing compounds and cleansers. The principal markets for high-grade feldspar were throughout the eastern United States, where several ceramic works were located. Because of high U.S. tariffs on processed feldspar, it was shipped to New Jersey and Ohio potteries in its raw state, or as "ground spar" from a grinding plant at Genesee, near Charlotte, N.Y. Because of the expense of shipping the unprocessed feldspar, mining in Canada was limited by "the demand for the product within a profitable shipping range of the quarries."[61]

By the date of the 1889 Royal Commission on Minerals, George Richardson could declare that "I have seen nearly all the mines in the Frontenac section and have handled the product of pretty much all the phosphate mines in this part of the country.[62] According to a 1967 study: "From 1900 to 1920, almost the entire Canadian production came from the Verona area with the Richardson mine being the major producer. During this period feldspar production ranged from 10,000 to 20,000 tons a year.[63]

In 1902, Mr. H. Richardson, "one of the owners," spoke of plans "to erect a crushing plant at Kingston and ship the fine feldspar in bags, thus reducing the loss of material en route, avoiding contamination, and obtaining a better price."[64] This was Senator Henry W. Richardson, uncle to George Richardson, President and General Manager of KF & MC, whose feldspar holdings by this date included not only the Richardson Mines but also the Reynolds and Cord Mines.[65] Production declined during World War I because of fuel shortages but picked up again after the war. As another outgrowth of this enterprise, the Richardsons launched the Kingston Floor and Wall Tile Company in 1913 and a plant was built in the city.[66]

Other interests included the Baby Mica mine acquired in 1904 in Lanark County as a "phosphate of lime property" for $4,150. It consisted of a boiler house, mica house, boarding house, and wooden derrick structure;[67] the Baby Mica mine was worked by the Richardsons' Kingston Feldspar Mining Company until 1942.[68] Another venture was the Long Lake Mine or Richardson Zinc Mine, which was worked from 1897, but the first major find was in 1901 and some 100 tons of zinc ore were produced.[69] Other mineral properties were the Richardson mica mines at several locations throughout Loughborough Township.

Impressive as these mining activities might have been, they were never central to the economy of the overall Richardson operation. Years later, a member of the family referred to the "40 or so 'fun' mines we had around Kingston."[70]

When James Richardson died in 1892, his two sons were equal partners in the firm. Most of his one-third of the firm was left to his wife with a curious provision concerning its ultimate disposition: "after her death I give devise and bequest the same to my two sons George and Henry in such a manner that George shall have ten thousand dollars (10,000) more than Henry."[71] Both sons served as company president: George A. Richardson, 1892-1906, Henry W. Richardson, 1906-1918.

VII

WHILE NOT ONE of the city's principal political figures during the portentous years of Kingston's struggle to attain a national and regional role, James Richardson was active in some arenas of municipal life. Thus, the *Minute Book* of the Kingston Board of Trade opens with the inaugural meeting of "Merchants, Bankers, Forwarders and Traders of the City of Kingston on Friday the 22nd August 1851 at 8 O'clock P.M. for the purpose of organizing a Board of Trade."[72] James Richardson was one of the 36 "Gentlemen" present who "signified their intention to become members of the Board of Trade."[73] However, Richardson never became an important or active member of the Board. He held no prominent post and served on not a single one of the board's delegations. According to the *Minutes,* he attended a meeting of the Board of Trade on 10 March 1855 and then skipped meetings for 16 years.[74] He re-appeared on 14 January 1871 when he was elected to the Board. He duly attended another meeting in a later year, but then vanishes from the record.

On 10 January 1871, James Richardson was a member of the four man Board of Examiners for the Office of Inspector of Flour and Grain.[75] And on 6 May 1872, he was one of the authors of a report concerning harbour improvements.[76] The Report recommended that the federal government be asked to dredge the harbour and construct a breakwater extending half a mile from the shore at Murney Tower, to be 26 feet deep (i.e., six feet above water) and 36 feet wide. The cost was estimated at $40,000. While one of the authors of the report, Richardson did not join the delegation that took it to Ottawa.

In 1873, James Richardson, Alexander Gunn (who was to defeat Macdonald in Kingston in 1878), and James Swift were appointed examiners of "Wheat and other Grain."[77] Richardson did further

"Wheat and other Grain" service in 1876 and 1877. He also served as an examiner of "Pot Ashes and Pearl Ashes" in 1873, 1876, and 1877.[78] In 1886, Richardson indicated his deep interest in transport facilities by seconding a motion that declared that "additional Railways terminating in Kingston are necessary to the growth of the city."[79]

Obviously, James Richardson's involvement with the Board of Trade was peripheral. This contrasts strongly with the role of his son and successor as President. George A. Richardson was elected to the Council of the Board of Trade in 1887, became second Vice-President in 1891, first Vice-President in 1891, and on 12 April 1892, he was elected President of the Board of Trade.[80] A few months later, George A. Richardson was President of James Richardson and Sons Ltd.

James Richardson was also a municipal politician. He was Councilman for St. Lawrence Ward in 1860 and Alderman for the same ward in 1861.[81] Later, he joined City Council again as Alderman for Victoria Ward, 1870-1874.[82] His attendance at Council meetings was erratic. He attended most meetings in 1860 but only 26 of 42 meetings in 1861. During his second stint on Council, he attended 84 of 146 meetings.[83] Richardson served on a variety of standing committees; their very names help explain the recurring difficulty in obtaining high quality aldermen: Fire, Water and Gas; Printing; Police; Finance and Accounts; and Schools."[84]

For the most part, Richardson was an alderman who took little part in public debate. When he was active, the issues of interest to him normally related to harbour concerns, economy in public spending, and business. Richardson was notoriously anxious to put limits on costs. This produced mild bits of controversy on two occasions. In 1860, he was elected to the "Marine arrangements" committee, which had a role in planning the eagerly anticipated visit to Kingston of the Prince of Wales. He then seconded a motion, which was defeated, that public monies proposed to finance a gala reception for the Prince be submitted to a public meeting for approval.[85] Needless to say, those with invitations to the reception were less than amused by any suggestion that could diminish or threaten their opportunity to meet the Prince at the social event of the decade.[86]

A similar incident occurred during his second period on Council. On 9 June 1873, he seconded a motion to block the use of city funds to send a delegation of Kingstonians to the funeral of Sir George-Etienne

Cartier, John A. Macdonald's long-time co-leader of the federal Conservative Party.[87] This motion passed, but was subsequently reversed, and the Mayor represented Kingston at the funeral.[88] Richardson only seconded these motions and was clearly not a civic leader of much importance.

James Richardson was never active in provincial or federal electoral politics, although his son, Henry Wartman Richardson, was active enough to obtain a seat in the Senate in 1917. Nonetheless, James and his sons, all Tories, had political influence and played the political game in the manner typical of the nineteenth century. That is, Richardson used his influence to assist politicians and expected to receive assistance and favours in return. The evidence here is not extensive, but it is both interesting and revealing.

In 1889, the firm had difficulty getting a contract to supply wheat to Kingston Penitentiary. The head office blamed the warden and bookkeeper at KP and complained to George Taylor, Tory MP for Leeds South. Taylor was a prominent businessman with lots of influence in Ottawa. The letter concluded:

> Neither will we bother in future with elections and spend both time and money to support a party that allows its warmest supporters who neither need nor ask for any favours but simply fair play to have their tender thrown out for a few thousand Bushels of wheat that we defy any business man who knows what he is talking about to say we asked a fraction more than its market value then or what it is worth today.

The letter went on to ask Taylor to use his influence to set matters right. "We are getting slugged by either Scobell or the Warden ... I do not come for the thing as a matter of dollars and cents but it is galling to be handled by these two men in charge of the Prison this way." Taylor did intervene and the letter went to an official named Thompson, who passed it along to the Prime Minister. As was often the case, Sir John scrawled his response on the back:

Dear Thompson

The Richardsons are and always have been strong and influential friends of mine. Young Richardson [George A. or Henry W.] will probably succeed me as MP for Kingston.[89]

The prison problem was not resolved, and George Richardson wrote Taylor about the matter a couple of months later: "We find that tenders have been received for the supply of wheat for the Prison and were asked today to send one in. This we will not do as our tender in July for this contract was a fair one and we are entitled to it in that tender. We have written you fully in the matter before and hope it will not be asking too much for you to go to Ottawa and find out why we are treated in this manner." George Richardson went on, "One thing is certain[.] [U]nless we are awarded this contract The party here will find itself short the workers of this family not because we intend voting Grit but any party which allows its supporters to be snubbed in this way need not expect them to turn out and work."

Again the letter went to Thompson, who again passed it along to the Prime Minister. This time the scrawl on the back read:

My Dear Thompson

Don't get me into a scrape with the Richardsons. They are my pillars in Kingston.[90]

Various letters urge Macdonald to make particular patronage appointments and boost Kingston business. James Richardson asked Macdonald to give "Young Robinson" the place made vacant by the death of Robinson's father.[91] The firm urged Macdonald not to use an outside contractor to build a structure at the Royal Military College: "If possible place it in the hands of one of our own builders[.] [I]t would strengthen us very much at the next election."[92]

At one point, Macdonald was considering James Richardson for some patronage post or other. He consulted one E.H. Smythe, whose assessment of Richardson is of interest and which nicely summarizes the man's style of operation: "I am disposed to think he would be a very good man. He has means and has no weak points i.e. points which make him objectionable to any large portion of the community."[93]

VIII

RICHARDSON'S BUSINESS interests were symbolic of the transmutation being pursued by the Kingston of which he was part. He managed the shift from traditional commercial trading roles to investment in various manufacturing and financial enterprises associated with the new industrial age. Moreover, he had been stimulated to invest in Kingston at the height of its commercial dominance in the mid-nineteenth century.

Perhaps more important is the fact that Richardson and his firm serve as a symbol of Canada's nineteenth-century economy. His initial trading operations were local and regional; they were heavily dependent on water-based transportation and transshipment; north-south as well as east-west trading patterns were utilized. As the National Policy, with its emphasis on east-west trade, rail transportation, and Western economic growth began to flourish, the Richardsons joined in. That took them to the prairies in search of wheat and involved them massively in international wheat exports. Ultimately, the logic of the National Policy led them to take their business out of Kingston to Winnipeg, which the National Policy had transformed into Canada's grain capital.

Commentary

*Cartoon aerial view of destruction of heritage buildings at the corner of King and Princess,
now the Royal Block. Cartoon by Frank Edwards, 1988 (Whig-Standard).*

Lost Opportunities

HISTORY OF KINGSTON'S OUTER HARBOUR

We are fortunate that the essential character of our waterfront has been merely eroded, not entirely ruined. Kingston's nineteenth-century flavor, unique among the cities of Ontario and Canada, remains strong.

T HE WATERFRONT OF Kingston has, for most of the city's history, been crucial to its economic and social development. Situated at the foot of the Great Lakes, at their junction with the Rideau and St. Lawrence routes to tidewater at Montreal, Kingston was for generations an important point of transshipment for water-borne traffic. Successive classes of specialized "lakers" were unloaded on to equally specialized river-craft and "canallers," designed to negotiate the rapids and locks of the evolving system. Through Kingston's wharves and warehouses cargoes flowed east and west: furs, potash, and barrels of pork and flour from the backwoods settlements of early Upper Canada; rafts of lumber assembled off Garden Island from the extensive watersheds of the lower Great Lakes. Bulk cargoes of the new staple, wheat, were loaded from lake schooners into Kingston's elevators, then into the barges and canallers of the Rideau and St. Lawrence routes; immigrants and merchandise travelled up the system from tidewater to the interior settlements of an expanding Ontario.

All this traffic ensured that Kingston and its surrounding area became a major ship-building and ship-repair area. For much of

During the late 1980s and 1990s, Professor Swainson became engaged in protecting Kingston's heritage in the face of developers. This article, written in collaboration with Professor Brian S. Osborne in the Geography Department at Queen's University, first appeared in the Kingston *Whig-Standard Magazine*, 28 June 1986.

Aerial view of the Outer Harbour during its industrial age showing the Richardson grain elevators and the extensive locomotive yards (Queen's University Archives).

the nineteenth century, Kingston's waterfront was marked by elevators, wharves, warehouses, and a miscellany of shipping. But by the middle of the nineteenth century, another waterfront was emerging. A new mode of transport, rail, had arrived; and it too depended on access to water-borne cargoes of passengers and goods. Soon Kingston, like other nineteenth-century towns on rivers and lake systems, gladly gave over its waterfront to the new symbols of progress: railroads and rail-yards.

With the rails came industry. Warehouses and wharves along Ontario Street were replaced by Kingston's major industrial employer, the locomotive works. Ship-building and repair facilities were enhanced by an expanded drydock. A steam-powered water-supply system contributed to the smoke of progress. And the route of the railroad, following the western shore of the inner harbour, attracted such innovative ventures as textile works, mineral refineries, tanneries, and metal workshops. By the early twentieth century, the addition of industrial land-use to the earlier commercial land-use had completed the severance of Kingston's waterfront, with the exception of blocks of land nominally reserved for the military but actually used as public open spaces.

Economically, the importance of the waterfront to Kingston cannot be over-estimated. Physically, its presence dominates the townscape. And psychologically, Kingstonians live in a world dominated by the surrounding waters: Lake Ontario, the St. Lawrence, the Great Cataraqui, and the system of rivers, lakes, and locks to the north. Water views, smells, and sounds are part of our collective consciousness and of our mental inscapes of Kingston. It would be inconceivable for Kingstonians not to be preoccupied with their waterfront. For some two centuries, it has nourished them economically and esthetically.

But circumstances change, and so has the waterfront. Under the pressure of social and economic change, virtually nothing has survived from a hundred years ago. Because such change has been particularly dramatic over the last two decades, Kingston has in that time witnessed a furious debate over the future of our waterfront, a debate that is really about the very nature and future of this city. Block D is the current centre of attention, and its future is indeed important to the evolving form of the waterfront. But the ultimate disposition of that property should not be decided outside the context of developments that began in the 1960s and before.

K INGSTON ACHIEVED its early prominence as a commercial and administrative centre. Viewed from the waters of the Great Cataraqui River and Lake Ontario, its skyline – City Hall, St. George's dome, and St. Mary's spire – records this background and constitutes a unique nineteenth-century urban prospect. Across the river, the shoreline is dominated by the historic village of Barriefield, by the Royal Military College in its manicured setting on Point Frederick, and by the imposing fortification of Fort Henry across Navy Bay.

But Kingston has also been an active port. The "penny bridge" across Cataraqui River, later replaced by the La Salle Causeway, divided the waterfront into two sections: Kingston's outer harbour extends from the causeway for a mile to the south-west, fronting on to the open waters of Lake Ontario; the inner harbor consists of the extensive sheltered waters of the estuary of the Great Cataraqui. This inner harbour was made accessible to the lake by the development of the channel and lift-bridge facilities at the causeway.

A person standing on Kingston's waterfront can see much of this, together with the softer waterscape of the lake backed by Cedar, Wolfe, Garden, and Simcoe Islands. But while the nineteenth-century Kingstonians built elegant houses, fine churches, and a magnificent city hall, they paid little attention to the city's waterfront setting: this was neither an issue nor a concern. The ethic of the day assumed that the waterfront was a commercial, shipping, and industrial area: the appropriate locus for wharves, grain elevators, warehouses, and railroad sidings. During this period, the view of the lake was screened from the people by this barrier of commercial and industrial development.

Attractive open spaces were few and were rarely the product of any civic initiative. The magnificent parcels of land east of Queen's University that now constitute Macdonald Park, City Park, and the cricket field were Crown property over which the city never had full control, although public access was not restricted. The military preserved the territories on the east side of the outer harbour and adjacent to the causeway on the west side. After the military demolished the Market Battery, built in 1848 on the shoreline in front of City Hall, the town acquired the property as a public park. Ten years later, it leased these prime 2.2 acres to the Kingston & Pembroke Railway as a switching yard and passenger station. The Canadian Pacific Railway acquired the site when it absorbed the K & P in 1912.

The city's decision in this case was the diagnostic mark of Kingston's municipal planning. The private sector could have virtually anything as a gift of city fathers eager for industrial development and growth. As in urban centres elsewhere throughout North America, municipal politicians were mesmerized by the dream of a vibrant industrial economy located along an expendable waterfront.

This dream became increasingly unrealistic as the twentieth century advanced. Transshipment prosperity had become a golden-age mythology by the first decade of the century. The First World War breathed some life into shipbuilding, locomotive enterprises, and other habour-related activities, but only for a brief period. Shipping activity was minimal during the 1920s, and in the Depression years the waterfront was marked by underused elevators and row upon row of empty ships. A second world war provided another spurt of temporary activity, but in reality Kingston was finished as a port.

The figures on the collapse of shipping are dramatic. In 1966, 762,598 tons of shipping entered Kingston harbour, 467,700 in 1970, and a mere 408,169 in 1976. In comparison to Hamilton's 13 million tons, these figures make mock of *The Whig-Standard*'s latter-day boosterism, which as late as 1955 asserted that:

> Kingston has many good reasons why the Dominion Government should rehabilitate the waterfront. Kingston has excellent repair facilities, and excellent shipbuilding potentialities. It also stands at the very head of the St. Lawrence, and has been a natural transshipping point ever since Kingston became a city. It is true that the construction of the new canals [i.e. the St. Lawrence Seaway] will mean that lake boats now denied access to the sea and seaports will be able to get through. But the fact is that not many of the lake boats really want to get through. It would be much better for them to operate on the lakes as before, where they can operate more economically ... [I]t is obvious that Kingston is soon going to generate enough tonnage to merit a good harbour.

The problem of the waterfront district was compounded by ancillary factors. Development during and after the Second World War tended to be on the western side of the city. Alcan, DuPont, and CIL all located to the west of the established urban area, a trend that was dramatized by the city's annexation of lands to the west and north in 1952. Throughout the 1960s and 1970s, sustained population growth and steady suburbanization were accompanied by the development of shopping centres and other business activities in western Kingston and Kingston Township. Faced with such challenges to its historical commercial and social supremacy, the vitality of the historic waterfront-downtown district was called into question.

Its physical deterioration was an alarming and telling indicator of the transition. Docks were ramshackle and dangerous. Industrial establishments were under-used and falling into serious disrepair. Ancient hotels were dominated by sleazy drinking establishments. Substantial amounts of fire-trap slum housing emerged behind the outer harbor. Historic Sydenham Ward, in which most of the old harbour is included, contains one of the most beautiful old residential areas in Canada. Waterfront blight and commercial activity invaded this area and threatened its destruction.

By 1960, Kingston's historic balance was threatened. A dynamic area of new residences, businesses, and suburbs to the west threatened to become the city's new focus, in place of a mouldering, deteriorating, uneconomic, and occasionally dangerous waterfront-downtown district. A redevelopment report in 1964 stated the situation succinctly: "Citizens were almost wholly excluded from the more enjoyable functions of the waterside, and in a true sense, the 'city' became introverted."

II

THE 1960S OFFERED the opportunity for remarkable change. Kingston could revitalize its downtown, save the historic section of Sydenham Ward, reclaim the waterfront from its derelict state, and re-establish the beauty of the city. The opportunity did not go unnoticed. In 1964, a group of Kingstonians made a prophetic statement:

> The removal of warehousing, of coal storage, of rail freight loading, is either completed, or in the offing for much of the central

waterfront. It is imperative that the city take advantage of this rarest of opportunities, that of developing plans for the integration of downtown and waterfront, so that the potential of the site and situation of Kingston may be realized.

During the late 1950s and 1960s, economic logic and fortuitous circumstance combined to open for redevelopment virtually the entire outer-harbour shoreline. Competition from fuel oil rendered obsolete the Richardson coal yard, which occupied the waterfront between Simcoe and West Streets. A new water filtration plant, built half-a-mile to the west on the site of yet another redundant coal-yard, superseded the municipal pumping station to the east of West Street. The radical increase in the size of Great Lakes shipping vessels made the drydock-shipyard facilities owned by the Canada Steamship Lines uncompetitive, and they were closed in 1968; the demise of the shipyard reopened historic Mississauga Point for redevelopment after some 150 years of shipbuilding activities there.

Close by, the old locomotive works occupied a 400,000-square-foot site covered by old and dilapidated buildings and an industrial plant. With the closing of the plant in 1969, the city was presented with another area for imaginative waterfront development. Similarly, the construction of elevators at Little Cataraqui Bay to compete with the new facilities at Prescott may have failed, but it did make redundant Kingston's downtown elevators at the foot of Johnson and Princess Streets. Even the old Kingston & Pembroke Railway, owned by CP Rail since 1912, ceased to run regular trains to the waterfront area in 1957. This made available the property between City Hall and the water, an area occupied since 1885 by a switching yard and passenger station.

Indeed, the only vestiges of the old docks and wharves of the nineteenth and early twentieth centuries were to be found to the northeast of City Hall, where the attractive grounds of Tête du Pont Barracks survived as an island of lawns and trees surrounded by wharves and docking facilities.

It is doubtful that any other old Canadian city has ever been given such an opportunity for creative redevelopment. The entire outer harbour, with the exception of a couple of small parcels of property, was available for holistic treatment. As former *Whig-Standard* managing editor Warren Stanton, an unusually astute observer, commented when Fairbanks Morse announced its decision to close its Kingston operation: "Hurray! That land is now available. Let's make the most of it ... It can be the location of a municipal-commercial development that has almost unbelievable possibilities."

Kingston is a natural tourist centre. Its surviving military installations and impressive number of fine pre-Confederation buildings make it unusually attractive. Large numbers of boaters visit the city because of its location at the junction of Lake Ontario, the St. Lawrence and the Rideau waterway, with the splendid sailing waters of the Bay of Quinte near by. A sustained attempt to develop a water-based tourist industry would seem so logical for Kingston that an observer might assume that such would be one of the city's highest priorities. The collapse of the old commercial waterfront provided that opportunity.

But creative redevelopment was not to be. The waterfront district was not to become an attractive combination of low-rise waterside housing, mooring facilities for recreational boaters, open area, boardwalks, parks, leisure centres, stores, and hotels designed to be compatible with waterfront locations. The town's old skyline of domes and spires, a skyline which had always impressed visitors approaching Kingston from the water, was to be lost.

Two factors explain the bungling of this unique opportunity. First, it is clear that civic leaders, ignoring the excellent advice given them by several officials and committees, failed to realize that the opportunity existed. They never resolved to use the full weight of government to obtain complete planning control over the entire district. As a consequence, *ad hoc* and discrete decisions were made early in the process that rendered comprehensive and creative planning impossible. Hence, the Richardson coal yard was replaced by a high-rise apartment house of a standard North American design. Its only redeeming virtue is that it is slightly more esthetically acceptable than a 50-foot pile of bituminous coal. This decision was prophetic: it placed an entire block of shoreline in private hands.

Similarly, the Richardson property at the foot of Princess Street was alienated. It became the site of a large motor hotel complete with outdoor and indoor swimming pools and a huge parking lot. Inexplicably, though it was built on what had been a dock in a town noted for its water-borne tourism, mooring facilities were not incorporated into the design. Former *Whig-Standard* advertising director W.J. Coyle commented on the curious result:

> One important point that seems to have been overlooked in approving the plans for this waterfront hotel is that the five storey brick building will seal off completely the view of the harbor and the Royal Military College which residents and visitors now enjoy from lower princess Street. When city council sold the water rights for $8,000 it parted with a valuable asset.

A second chain hotel was built on Ontario Street diagonally opposite City Hall. It does not have a waterfront location, but it is clearly visible from the lake and helps to disfigure Kingston's skyline.

Another developer purchased the shipyard property west of the drydock and built a large apartment complex that is thoroughly undistinguished and inconsistent with the character of the old portion of the town. It is complemented by three equally unattractive apartment houses on Ontario Street that are now prominent parts of the skyline. Eric Thrift, a leading town planner, delivered the correct assessment of these buildings when he commented that one of the numerous proposed apartment houses was "out of scale" and in "direct conflict with what's next to it, whether it's one block away or six."

Not all of the decisions were foolish. The city's old pumping station was retained as a well designed and popular steam museum. The nineteenth-century stone buildings and facilities at the drydock site were opened in 1976 as the Marine Museum of the Great Lakes at Kingston; it is a fine museum with an extensive and valuable collection of documents and artifacts. But it, its neighbour, McAllister Towing and Salvage Ltd., Confederation Basin in front of City Hall, and the Kingston Yacht Club are the only waterfront properties that continue to reflect Kingston's water-based heritage.

The city had never sold the property between City Hall and the shoreline. In 1961, the CPR agreed to abandon it for a site on the north side of the town, and the city transformed it into Confederation Park, a somewhat mixed concept. In front of the park, a public marina was opened in 1967. By 1986, it had moorings for 180 boats: 60 seasonal and 120 transient. It has proved to be a major success and is heavily used during the boating season by craft from all over eastern

North America. In 1985, some 4,500 boats berthed there. Boaters enjoy the opportunity to moor within walking distance of shops, restaurants, and historic buildings. The public marina is a single demonstration of the enormous but only partially realized tourist potential of downtown and waterfront Kingston.

IV

FAILURE TO understand the existence of an opportunity to create a unique waterfront district explains much of the inept and haphazard evolution of the area during the 1970s. An equally important factor was the city's inability to accept and support creative projects evolved by others for the central portion of the outer harbour's shoreline.

In May 1970, Wyllie Unfal Weinberg and Schenkenberger, a town planning firm from Rexdale, Ontario, published a re-development scheme for Sydenham Ward. The scheme's two major concerns were the rehabilitation of the residential area in old Kingston and the transformation of the waterfront.

The main feature of the waterfront portion of the plan was the construction of a huge landfill site anchored on Carruthers Shoal. (Ironically, the shoal had always been a key impediment to the use of Kingston harbour for deep-water shipping.) This scheme would have extended Johnson Street in a westward arc until it approached the foot of Gore Street. The central part of the old outer harbour would then have fronted on the new "Kingston Laguna." Further protection was to be provided by a breakwater running west from the landfill to the Kingston Yacht Club with an entrance a little east of the foot of West Street.

This imaginative plan addressed itself directly to key and obvious concerns. Substantial new construction would have shifted the population balance to the waterfront. Needed low-cost and student housing was part of the plan, as were tasteful school, shopping, parking, hotel, and convention facilities. Above all, the plan was designed to make the revitalized harbour area a mecca for water-based leisure activity. The provision of extensive, first-rate marina and mooring facilities for boaters would have benefited townspeople and tourists alike.

The plan, while breathtaking in some respects, was not without its problems. The historic skyline and streetscape as viewed from the water would have been destroyed by modernistic and excessively tall buildings scattered along the shoreline and landfill. There was concern over the extent of the landfill proposed and over the complexity of the changes recommended for the residential area behind the harbour. For example, King Street would have been closed at West Street and the portion of the street to the westward connected with Ontario Street to create a new major thoroughfare. In any event, the "WUWS" scheme sank into oblivion with scarcely a ripple.

This lack of ripple was no accident. A mere two months prior to the publication of the WUWS plan, a much more substantial scheme was announced to the public. It was not more advanced in terms of conceptualization, but by the time it was announced its proposer had purchased most of the central waterfront district. Thus, in March 1970, Kingstonians learned that William Teron, an Ottawa developer with a first-rate reputation for high quality and tasteful housing design and construction, had purchased the Fairbanks Morse property and the Swift dock on the eastward side. This gave William Teron Associates control over 11 acres bounded by Confederation Park, Ontario Street, Gore Street, and the waterfront.

Teron's plans for the site were ambitious. He proposed to fill it with shops, theatres, office accommodation, walk-ways, restaurants, hotels, leisure facilities, housing, and an "Atlantic City-type boardwalk for use along the shoreline." Moreover, all this was to be integrated with the salvageable historic buildings in the area. Teron emphasized the need to populate the district and make it live again. "We want an alive downtown, not some place that vacates at 5:30 every night," he said. "Anyone who says this area should be made into a park is not being realistic ... However, we are interested in the ability of people of the city to participate in the waterfront area – to walk by it, sit by it and drive by it."

The Teron proposal was modified from time to time, but during the early period of its life it included 750 apartment units, 185,000 square feet of commercial space, 120,000 square feet of office space, a 250-unit hotel, and a 150-unit apartment hotel. Construction was to cost some $30 million.

But although Teron Associates owned the vast bulk of property on the "Marina City" site, they did not own it all. The missing pieces were to cause substantial complications for the project and for the city. The

Marina City project immediately became extremely controversial, and the controversy became quite byzantine. Full documentation is not yet available, and the motives and activities of the various actors cannot be definitely explained. Yet some things are clear.

Kingston's political establishment was not united in support of Marina City. J.E. Benson, Kingston's Liberal MP and Federal Minister of finance, wanted the shipyard resurrected, a proposal which would have restored a noisy heavy industry to the waterfront adjacent to a residential area.

The policy made so little sense that a senior official of Canada Steamship Lines, which owned the site, wrote to Mayor E.V. Swain: "I was most surprised ... since I cannot help feeling that any such move would be entirely opposed to the City of Kingston's best interests and would in all probability seriously affect the plans of Mr. Teron and would, in our opinion, prejudice the best development of those areas of Kingston waterfront not already covered by Mr. Teron's proposed project." But the powerful and now extremely irritated minister pursued his policy insistently and did manage to inspire a brief and final flourish of activity at the drydock in the early 1970s.

Citizen opposition to Teron was persistent and noisy but far from wide-spread. The labour council opposed the project and sought to obstruct it through the imposition of complicated terms: it asked City Council to block construction until Teron had agreed to deed the city a 50-foot strip around the project and build 2,400 parking spaces. The labour leaders also wanted a variety of other zoning and timing conditions imposed.

The local NDP, then controlled by the radical "Waffle" wing, with its core of Queen's graduate students, entered the fray for reasons that are far from clear. The NDP was flatly opposed to Teron and wanted a completely new project owned by a Crown corporation. A party spokesman argued that "the provincial government is spending $500 million to develop the Toronto waterfront and is prepared to make a similar arrangement with Kingston if City Council requests it." The unlikelihood of a miniscule group of radicals in Kingston speaking for Ontario's Conservative government was evident to even the most naïve observer, but the NDP was able to generate a fair amount of publicity and add to the growing perception that Marina City was a misguided project.

Other opposition came from a more conservative perspective. Conservationists and local historians were appalled at the suggestion that some fine pre-Confederation structures along Ontario Street might have to be destroyed. They were not reassured by the promise that destruction would be kept to a minimum and limited to structurally unsound buildings or buildings that could under no circumstances be incorporated into the project's concept. (Their worst fears were to be realized in 1973, when Plymouth Square, built in 1832 and for many years the residence and commercial establishment of John Counter, Mayor of Kingston in 1841-43, 1846, 1850, 1852-53 and 1855, was demolished.)

These critics were also concerned, and properly so, that Marina City was too large in scale and would ruin the general proportions and arrangement of the buildings that constituted much of the nineteenth-century charm and ambience of the area.

Sporadic opposition came from other sources. Some local residents wanted no extensive commercial or residential construction between their properties and the waterfront. John Meister, an NDP alderman, wanted a return of heavy industry and its concomitant employment and was opposed to hotel and leisure facilities. Various other objections were heard.

The concept of a huge waterfront park attracted some support. For others, however, such a scheme was hardly necessary in a district that already possessed substantial amounts of attractive parkland, especially when less privileged wards were crying out for better facilities. And again, Teron's housing proposals irritated those who wanted to protect their own low-density, low-rise and, by implication, high-value properties. Even the Kingston Fire Department entered the debate with a series of complaints about the fire safety provisions for Marina City.

This strident opposition clearly irritated Teron Associates – as did a protracted negotiation concerning a small piece of property owned by the Royal Canadian Horse Artillery Club. The property was neither large nor of much intrinsic value, but Teron claimed that it was an essential entranceway to the hotel proposed for the site. The veterans wanted substantial compensation; and the more they were portrayed as an obstacle to the project, the more upset and stubborn they became.

Negotiations dragged on, with Mayor Swain acting as intermediary. Finally, an agreement was reached. At this point, a downtown activist intervened by challenging the city's right to accord the needed permission to divide the RCHA property. The outcome was uncertain, and the appeal process promised to be lengthy.

William Teron took this occasion in May 1972 to cancel the entire project. His motives are not known. *The Whig-Standard* claimed that he was frustrated by the federal government's insistent attempts to revive the shipyard, the outpouring of bitterness over the clear threat to Plymouth Square, the protracted and nasty negotiations over the RCHA property, and the constant sniping from various activist groups and individual citizens. The newspaper was less than kind in its assessment: "William Teron … packed in Marina City this week because, after more than three years of having much of his own way, he ran into a group that wouldn't play by his rules."

It was no doubt a major tactical error for an outside developer to arrive in Kingston with a ready-made plan for massive redevelopment that would have changed the nature and character of the city. Such an approach was bound to generate hostility in the minds of many, with little prospect of creating a great deal of support elsewhere.

It is true that it would have changed the city's skyline and produced relatively high-density residential areas. This was to happen in any event. But it was imaginative and sensitive to many aspects of the community. It made provision for public access to the waterfront and for a healthy variety and diversity of land uses. Above all, it would have brought permanent dwellers to a well-landscaped waterfront amply provided with facilities for residents and visitors alike. This was far preferable to schemes whereby developers simply plunked standard North American high-rises wherever possible, filled them with people and left the new residents and the area to make whatever accommodation they could.

William Teron built nothing in Kingston, but he demolished much, including the entire Fairbanks Morse property. Kingstonians were left with a huge area of cleared and desolate waterfront and a grudging fear that neither politician nor activist knew what he was doing.

In 1973, Teron became chairman of the Central Mortgage and Housing Corporation. His various holdings, including all his Kingston lands, were placed in trust under Urbanetics Ltd. This property remained empty and ugly until the end of the decade, when the Teron interests were liquidated, and another group of developers and realtors entered the scene. Their plans called for two high-rise condominiums and yet another chain hotel on the eastern portion of the property. These projects were unimaginative in every respect.

Some citizens opposed the project, but City Council, which seemed capable only of responding to proposals put to it rather than initiating its own concepts, was hungry for any downtown development and let the developers have their way. As Mayor Ken Keyes put it, when he supported one proposal, "It is time for Council to make up its mind whether to get on with it or watch weeds grow there for another seven years."

The result is a contemporary motel of standard proportions and undistinguished design, flanked by two monolithic condominiums that represent all that was feared by the opponents of earlier proposals. None of the developments incorporated the waterside location into their concepts in any meaningful way. They rise fortress-like above the adjacent parts of old Kingston, especially when viewed from the lakeside or the eastern approach along King Street. Such architectural pearls as St. George's Cathedral and City Hall are dwarfed and overshadowed by structures that would be as much at home in Calgary or Dallas or Ottawa.

Kingston entered the 1970s with an unparalleled opportunity to develop a truly beautiful and profitable waterfront-downtown district. The decade was spent dissipating that opportunity as the old policy (more properly, the old *habit*) of isolated, *ad hoc* decisions prevailed.

Ten years later, as the town faced the 1980s, the damage had been done. The mile of Lake Ontario shoreline from the Kingston Yacht Club to the La Salle Causeway had suffered new and permanent disfigurement. The district had been chopped up and dotted with buildings that clashed with the neighborhood, ruined the skyline, and possessed little if any architectural merit. Three chain hotels complemented the half-dozen apartment and condominium buildings, while a central part of the waterfront that had been cleared by Teron's bulldozers remained as empty and unattractive as it had been 10 years earlier.

There were some redeeming features to the transformation of the 1970s. In 1974, city planning officer Kent Mumm diagnosed the waterfront as "dormant," "decaying," and "a cancerous growth," concluding that

> The urban development of the city and its growth in other directions for other reasons, finds today's Kingston not facing the lake but actually having turned its back to it ... But the waterfront is still there – part of it dormant, some parts lingering and few prospering. The way the land is used is affecting the adjacent areas, in some parts adversely and in others favorably. This to me is the most important of all urban problems in the city ... William Teron was all too correct when in 1970 he said, "Anything we do here will be better than what you have now."

By the 1980s, much of the "cancerous growth" was gone and the downtown-waterfront district had been revitalized. The three chain hotels provided 432 units for visitors and close to 500 peak-season downtown jobs for Kingstonians. Some 478 units of apartments and 305 units of condominium housing were built on or near the waterfront during the 1960s, 1970s, and 1980s in a district bounded by Simcoe Apartments to the west and Frontenac Village to the east. Two old and decrepit hotels were restored to provide needed restaurant space and additional rooms for tourists. In 1982, the Macdonald-Cartier Building, an office building for the Ontario Hospital Insurance Plan and other provincial agencies, was constructed a little north of the river harbour, bringing 750 workers into the downtown area.

Many fine nineteenth-century structures were saved from mouldering decay and renovated into restaurants, bars, bookstores, and boutiques. Virtually all the sub-standard housing in the downtown area was demolished, and substantial improvements have taken place in the residential areas of Sydenham Ward, now a thriving and attractive place. In spite of the doubts of many local politicians, the downtown shopping area has been rehabilitated without the alleged benefit of a shopping mall or major department store and is crowded with people throughout the year.

Waterfront construction, combined with some singularly unfortunate structures built by, or in alliance with, Queen's University, have wrecked the city's nineteenth-century skyline, but for Kingstonians who frequent the downtown, the esthetic situation has improved markedly. Confederation Park is an attractive foreground for City Hall. The public marina and the emergence of Kingston as a world-class sailing centre (a feat engineered by the leadership of the Kingston Yacht Club) keep the harbour area filled with colorful sailing craft of all sizes and descriptions. The opening of several street-ends has returned to Kingstonians the prospects across the bay to RMC and the islands.

Above all, the balance of the city has been corrected. During the years after 1945, there was a real danger that growing suburbs and new shopping centres on the west side of the city and in Kingston Township would become the dynamic centres of the area in place of the historic downtown. The suburbs, shopping malls, and general community development throughout the adjacent townships of Pittsburgh, Kingston and Ernestown continue to extend the Kingston urban area to the east and west. But these developments are now accompanied by a complementary growth at the centre: a downtown infusion of workers, permanent residents and new commercial activity.

VI

B ut though Kingston's downtown has been revitalized, the esthetic cost to the waterfront area has been unacceptably high. Opportunity for recapturing a unique section of Kingston's heritage, enhancing the lived-in environment for Kingston's residents and developing a valuable resource for the tourist industry, has been lost. Block D represents a final large-scale opportunity to rectify the balance between development for its own sake and development that combines public interests with aesthetics and good business. These concerns are not irreconcilable.

Several considerations should govern the use to which Block D should be put. Clearly, it must not be allowed to be yet another "high-rise" structure blocking off the city from its waterfront and destroying the sensitive proportions of its skyline. Neither should it be so massive that the street-end vistas of the lake are interrupted. Block D represents an opportunity to return to earlier concepts calling for an appropriate mélange of water-based parks and marina facilities, commercial premises and unobtrusive and tasteful residential accommodations. In this way, Ontario Street and downtown in general will continue to grow into a dynamic district accessible to all – not an enclave of condominiums, apartment houses, and chain hotels.

What was done in the 1970s was unpardonable. The damage already wreaked on the waterfront cannot be undone; it must not be compounded. We are fortunate that the essential character of our waterfront has been merely eroded, not entirely ruined. Kingston's nineteenth-century flavour, unique among the cities of Ontario and Canada, remains strong. Let us hope that our present City Council will not complete the ruination that its predecessor – through little but luck – managed to avoid.

Kingston's
Eroding Heritage

*Our civic leaders, collectively, have not the slightest concept of the
nature or importance of an old Canadian city. They have no vision
of what Kingston was, is, or should be.*

A RECENT VISIT to St. Andrew's, New Brunswick, was at once revealing and disheartening. At the corner of Water and Edward
Streets stands an ancient, two-storey frame home, in superb restored
condition. The house is tastefully painted in an oyster-beige tone and
trimmed in a slightly lighter shade of the same color. It has two gables
on the second storey and a pleasing gabled porch.

St. Andrew's is a coastal town on the Atlantic. Water Street, which
the house faces, runs parallel to the ocean, which at low tide reveals
extensive and beautiful tidal flats. The house commands a view of
these flats as well as of the many-colored sail craft moored there.

The house in St. Andrew's carries a plaque designation put in place
by the St. Andrew's Civic Trust Inc. It reads: "First Two-Storey Building
in Town. Erected by John Dunn, prominent Loyalist, in 1784. Frames
Shipped From New York."

Upon inquiry, it was discovered that the building now consists of
four apartments for senior citizens. It was converted and restored "several years ago" and is owned by a public housing authority.

We have a similar house in Kingston. It stands on the corner of
Ontario and Earl Streets. It is frame, but only one storey. It dates from
the eighteenth century, probably from the 1780s, and might well have

---

A year later Professor Swainson's vision of enlightened preservation of historic Kingston grew dimmer as indicated in this commentary column in the
Whig-Standard, 15 September 1987.

Photographs of the Lines House at the corner of Ontario and Earl Street being moved to North Street on the Inner Harbour where vandals set it on fire, 1987-1988 (Whig-Standard).

been moved to its present location when the British transferred their base from Carleton Island to Kingston after the close of the American revolutionary wars. Our house might well be the oldest surviving structure in the province of Ontario.

Ontario Street, Kingston, like Water Street, St. Andrew's, is an old street that runs parallel to the water. Our house, like the house in St. Andrew's, enjoys an excellent view of the lake and its colorful sailing boats. Unlike the house in St. Andrew's, our house is in peril. Unlike the house in St. Andrew's, our house has never been restored. To use the parlance of the city's property standards people, it "is in need of paint." Until recently, our house bore a little sign that read, "Nuclear Weapons Free Ontario." Otherwise it has had no plaque and nothing to indicate that it is one of the oldest – perhaps the oldest – house in Ontario. Unlike the house in St. Andrew's, our house is not designated. Why not?

There is another difference between the Water Street house and the house on Ontario Street. The St. Andrew's house is a living component of the ambiance of a beautiful historic town. The Kingston house is to be ripped down. It is to be torn away from the location it has occupied for over two centuries. Our house is not to be a living component of anything. If the necessary funds are raised it will be rebuilt, inappropriately, in some park or other, and become Ontario's oldest reconstructed house. In its place will be erected some townhouses that will have to be totally undistinguished if they are to meld into the architectural wasteland that Ontario Street, for the most part, has become.

What does all of this reveal about the politics of historic cities? This writer knows very little about the politics of St. Andrew's, although he is able to appreciate a superbly preserved and maintained old town that has not been made ugly by high-rise condominia, inappropriate waterfront hotels, unattractive apartment houses, and the wanton destruction of wonderful old structures like Plymouth Square and the Mowat round-cornered building.

At the same time this writer knows all too much about the politics of Kingston. Our civic leaders, collectively, have not the slightest concept of the nature or importance of an old Canadian city. They have no vision of what Kingston was, is, or should be. They fail totally to understand that the old city is loved and admired because of its historic quality and that that quality is undermined and diminished every time an historic building is destroyed and replaced with some non-descript structure ill-suited to the locale. Because our civic leaders have no vision, they have no plan. As a result they merely react to an endless series of propositions from private-sector operators who cannot be expected to have any interest other than immediate profit. The result is an on-going erosion of an important national heritage.

There are ironies involved that stagger the mind. If a group of teenaged thugs vandalize a school or a pavilion that can be repaired or replaced, they are charged and punished. If a respectable private-sector operator demolishes 200 years of history, he can have the acquiescence, and more likely the active support, of the city fathers, and in the process, turn a buck or two. One thing is clear: we need a new legal definition of urban vandalism.

And all the while, what of the persons who govern our city? Most continue to make their counterproductive contribution to the evolution of Kingston and stubbornly insist on marching to the beat of an outdated concept of municipal development and "progress."

The Big Question

WHO'S IN CHARGE HERE?

A VERY BASIC question confronts every Kingstonian: who is in charge of this city?

Yesterday a chunk of lower Princess Street was destroyed by a nonresident developer. Great Northern Developments, advised of their illegal actions, destroyed heritage buildings that belong to Kingstonians and to all Canadians. In a flagrant violation of civility and the law, they wrecked several buildings under circumstances that were totally unconscionable.

Witnesses who objected to actions that were clearly illegal were abused verbally and threatened by the group of thugs that had been employed to destroy heritage properties. The Kingston Police, convinced that intervention in civil matters is improper, aided the vandals. The police cordoned off Princess Street to assist the wreckers in their work. It is doubtful that our municipal police force has ever managed to do itself a more major disservice.

The city acted – or tried to – and the destruction crews were served with orders to halt their clearly illegal activity. That was ignored.

Rubble and destruction littered Princess Street, all, of course, protected by the barricade of the police department.

So, what do we do? The buildings have been destroyed. Anger and frustration will not bring them back.

The logic of municipal government is to say, "my goodness – Lower Princess Street has been ruined – let us have the developer proceed with his silly and totally unacceptable mall that violates every canon

---

This editorial appeared in the Kingston *Whig-Standard*, 3 June 1988.

of taste and urban sense." This has been done in the past and we have allowed major outrages like the destruction of the Mowat round-cornered building on the corner of Princess and Bagot.

Yesterday's antics were different. If the city allows the destruction at the foot of Princess Street to pass, the city has ceased to govern Kingston.

In symbolic terms, and this point is made irrespective of one's views of heritage and old buildings, if the illegality that was perpetrated yesterday is to be tolerated, Kingston as a community is out of business. We will become the creatures of out-of-town developmental urban vandals and those local "professionals" who choose to make their livings as their spokesmen and representatives.

The City of Kingston has no choice. It has a moral and broader duty to govern the town. That means that the wanton and disgusting violation of the law that was carried out yesterday in full public view must not be tolerated. City Council must do its duty. The developer, whose minions demolished heritage structures, must be charged under the law as must all of the shovel-threatening employees who systematically ruined fine buildings. More, the developer must never receive a permit to build anything on Princess Street. And, if the Corporation of the City of Kingston has even the remotest intelligence or interest in the welfare of Kingston, it will use its power of expropriation to take the vandalized land and, after adequate studies, use it properly for the benefit of the people of this city. Nobody is suggesting that anything illegal or improper has been done by local politicians. What is suggested is that they have done little at all, and have, over time, behaved stupidly. It is time that our local politicians wake up to the fact that they preside over the finest single architectural mass in English-speaking Canada. Their job is to protect this heritage – not to aid and abet its wanton and vicious destruction.

This writer cannot imagine a situation that should make Kingstonians more appalled and sickened than yesterday's activities on Lower Princess Street.

Preserving Kingston's Personality

It makes no sense to destroy what attracts loyalty from within and admiration from without.

U RBAN LIVING and urban society have come to be the diagnostic mark of North American society. Yet, many of our cities are plagued with problems that affect the quality of life they provide. Some are too big, forcing many citizens to spend an unreasonable proportion of their time traveling to and from work or trying to flee the cities for recreation. Slums and ghettos have come to dominate too many downtown areas, while the central business districts have often been transformed into collections of corporate architecture that are depopulated at night except for security guards and janitors. Polluted air and water are widespread. In such environments, attaining comfortable, satisfying and truly "urbane" lifestyles requires strategies and investments that are only accessible to the affluent, a situation which furthers the breakdown of cities into separate districts that are physically and socially isolated.

At the same time, North America possesses some towns and cities that remain safe, comfortable, and pleasant for citizens of most economic levels. Moreover, they retain an essential distinctiveness that differentiates them from other cities. Kingston is such a place.

With the cooperation of Brian S. Osborne, Professor Swainson continued to champion the forces attempting to preserve the old stones of Kingston, as seen in this article, published in the Kingston *Whig-Standard Magazine*, 18 June 1988.

Model of the "Marina City" development proposed for the Outer Harbour and Sydenham Ward. (Courtesy of George Muirhead).

It has achieved this status because of a combination of characteristics that make the town unique and blend together to produce Kingston's quintessential ambience and form. Four of these characteristics may be isolated.

I

FIRST, THERE IS age. Kingston is an old town by Canadian – especially English-Canadian – standards. The French established a post here in 1673, and that site has been continuously occupied since it was established as the principal reception centre for the displaced Loyalists in 1783-84. Kingston's formal origins, therefore, can be traced back 315 years.

Second, there is location. The British returned to the site of the French fort because they recognized its potential as a town site to administer the settlement of the Loyalists. The military favored its development as a naval base and garrison because of its proximity to the "line" separating British and American influences and because of its sheltered and defensible coves. For the men of commerce, Kingston's location at the junction of the St. Lawrence River and Lake Ontario made it the ideal place for the transshipment of goods from river to lake carriers and lake to river carriers. And for subsequent generations of inhabitants, a major attraction has been the esthetics of the site. Fronting onto the Great Cataraqui River and Lake Ontario, with vistas of the islands and open lake to the south and west, Kingston's waterfront beauty is unrivalled.

Third, there is the military presence. Kingston has always been an important military town. The French built Fort Frontenac. From 1783 until 1870, Kingston housed a British garrison. In the 1870s, Royal Military College was established. After the departure of the British, the Canadian military took over some of the facilities at Kingston, and there is still a large military establishment here. The military has had an enormous impact on Kingston. Over the past two centuries, it has poured money into our community. It has combined with the Loyalist tradition to exert a conservative influence on social and political life and to add pomp, ceremony, and color to the community.

But perhaps the most obvious contribution of the military to the character of Kingston is visual. The parcel of land composed of the

Cricket Field, City Park, and Macdonald Park was originally British Ordnance property. It was purchased by the military for government use when Kingston was the capital of the province of Canada. The capital was moved, but the lands remained under control of the Imperial authorities. Eventually the property was ceded to Kingston with the wise proviso that it never be severed for commercial purposes. Hence the city has never been able to lease, sell, or give it to developers or manufacturers.

Then there are the ubiquitous military structures inherited by the city. For many, Kingston's Martello towers are the principal symbols of the town's uniqueness. Again, the east side of the Great Cataraqui River is dominated by RMC and Fort Henry. One can fairly ask what would have happened had the Crown not acquired and the military developed and retained its huge properties throughout the Kingston area. Would these lands also have been turned over to wharves, grain elevators, and rail yards? Would these now be developed into the "Murney Tower Condominium," "Point Frederick Village and Marina" or "Point Henry Shopping Mall?"

Fourth, modern Kingston is the product of the lack of economic success in the conventional sense. Like city fathers elsewhere, Kingston's early leaders pursued wealth and greatness. They did a superb job of exploiting military spending and the transshipment possibilities of the site. Kingston flourished. Until the 1840s, it was the largest town in the province. From 1841 to 1844, it was the capital of the union of Ontario and Quebec. Greatness seemed to be guaranteed.

But then came devastation. The capital was carted off to Montreal, and Kingstonians suffered grave psychological damage. The transshipment function was eroded and ultimately wrecked by canals, waterways, and finally the St. Lawrence Seaway. Not only did Toronto surpass Kingston in size, so did Hamilton, Ottawa, and London. Not only did Kingston fail to keep up with these successful competitors, on several occasions throughout the nineteenth and early twentieth centuries the town actually decreased in size.

The city's leadership fought desperately to avoid the consequences of these grievous developments. Attempts were made to divert rail and water traffic to New York's waterfronts and markets, with Kingston as the transshipment point for this north-south traffic. A railway to the north was subsidized in an attempt to make Kingston a mining and lumbering centre. Avid attempts were made to attract industry. Kingston fought to be recognized as the eastern terminal for the huge vessels that penetrated the lower lakes following improvements in the canals at Welland.

These various initiatives met with little success. Kingston was not to be a Pittsburgh or a Buffalo and could not compete with Toronto. But while the city fathers pursued rail yards, textile mills, canning factories, and metal smelters, other decisions were taken incrementally that nobody seemed to notice. From the beginning, Kingston had a major public sector institution: the military. As the nineteenth and twentieth centuries progressed, this public sector involvement – supplemented by other major institutional presences – came to dominate Kingston's economic and social life.

The massive prison system that exists in this area began with the construction of Kingston Penitentiary in 1834. A major psychiatric hospital was built here as an offshoot of the penitentiary. Kingston became the diocesan seat for both Catholics and Anglicans. The Presbyterians founded Queen's University. The Catholics built their own Regiopolis. The Liberals gave Kingston RMC. Later in the twentieth century, Kingston acquired a restored Fort Henry and a battery of other municipally, provincially, and federally funded historic sites. To these were added a panoply of government agencies and departments, dominated by the relocation here in recent years of the Ontario Health Insurance Plan (OHIP) headquarters. The military, correctional, medical, government, and education facilities continued to grow as Kingston's few textile, metallurgical, and shipping enterprises declined. Kingston emerged as a public sector town.

II

THE INTERTWINING of these characteristics has given us the modern City of Kingston. Each characteristic is a crucial part of the whole.

Because we are an old community, we possess a diverse architectural stock. We have, in fact, the largest collection of heritage buildings outside of Quebec. More important than mere numbers alone, these buildings still largely retain their original relationship with one another. What is produced, therefore, is no mere fortunate survival of interesting structures but, rather, an assemblage which retains much of the original streetscape of the nineteenth-century town.

Because of site and its corollary, transshipment, Kingston had a cohort of very wealthy merchants in the nineteenth century. It is their homes that figure large in Kingston's extensive inventory of heritage structures. Often well-executed architectural statements of their owners' wealth and influence, they occasionally aspire to stately and magnificent structures as are exemplified in the Gildersleeve house, Roselawn, and Rockwood Villa.

Kingston's early economic success, combined with the military presence, explains the selection of Kingston as capital in 1841. George Browne was the government architect, and during his short stay here, he built City Hall, the manse at St. Andrew's Church, Hales Cottages, and the buildings that once housed the S&R Department Store and the Victoria and Grey Trust Company. These structures constitute another key element of our historical heritage.

The military, of course, is absolutely central, having contributed Fort Henry, the various heritage buildings at RMC, the Martello towers, and Fort Frontenac (formerly the Tête-du-Pont Barracks). Of no less importance was the military's role in reserving to itself waterfront land which otherwise would have been severed for commerce, industry, and transport. These now remain as preserves of greenery to set off the heritage structures with which they are associated.

The institutional presence combined with the fact that Kingston has normally been a centre of substantial political influence accounts for buildings like the Custom House, old Post Office, Grant Hall, and Kingston Hall. The Roman Catholic diocese built St. Mary's Cathedral and the Anglican congregation produced in St. George's a structure grand enough to serve not only as a church for the community but also as a cathedral for the diocese in the 1860s.

A final category of heritage structures – often neglected in our preoccupation with the mercantile and institutional structures of Sydenham Ward – are the clusters of domestic and commercial architecture to be found in the nineteenth-century suburbs and villages that were later absorbed into Kingston's built-up area. The old communities of Williamsville, Chathamville, Charlesville, and Picardville are marked by substantial structures together with unique assemblages of nineteenth-century domestic architecture throughout Frontenac,

Cataraqui, and St. Lawrence wards. The distinctive integrity of the villages of Barriefield, Cataraqui, and Portsmouth also add to the collage of nineteenth-century domestic, commercial, and institutional architecture throughout the Kingston area.

The preservation of all these historic buildings has been aided by Kingston's relative lack of economic success in the conventional sense. Had our civic leaders been successful in making Kingston into a large commercial-industrial centre, that would have led inevitably to a massive destruction of nineteenth-century building stock in order to make space for a bigger downtown, factories, warehouses, railway yards, and various other "essential" prerequisites for a growing city. The character and tone of the city today are a result of the failures of generations of civic leaders to realize their economic goals. Those who find Kingston a beautiful and livable city should be forever grateful to the ineptitude of former city fathers. Certainly, they did not plan it. Their sins of omission *and* commission ensured that modern Kingstonians would inherit the architectural fabric of a pre-industrial city.

Further, the fact that Kingston is relatively small and its stock of heritage buildings relatively large means that our legacy from the past can have a defining impact that would be impossible in a much larger city. Conventional economic failure has made it possible for Kingston to survive with a unique nineteenth-century character. Moreover, the juxtaposition of these historical artifacts with the potentially magnificent waterfront and its vistas renders Kingston's heritage, esthetics, and ambience into a new resource to be protected. Indeed, it is this which makes our architectural collection more than of simple local significance: it transcends the city's responsibility and constitutes a provincial and a national treasure.

IV

IT IS BECAUSE Kingston has a visible heritage, small-town social networks, and attractive water-based recreational amenities that the city is emerging as a major retirement and tourist centre. Kingston is an interesting, beautiful, personal community, well served by cultural and social facilities. Ironically, it is this very success which is prompting a new wave of growth and new challenges to the very character that has made Kingston attractive. It makes no sense to destroy what attracts loyalty from within and admiration from without. It is hardly wise to demolish what people want to see in order to provide facilities for those who want to see what was demolished.

The rhetoric of those who boast about the charms of "Historic Kingston" is not backed up by sound decision making. In the absence of imaginative and comprehensive planning, incremental decisions have been made based upon dangerous assumptions: one more building demolished will not ruin the nineteenth-century flavor of Kingston; some buildings are "more historical" than others; there are plenty of others still standing. Kingstonians must challenge such thinking. The citizens of this city must collectively confront the issue of Kingston's heritage and physical fabric, which are central to the logic and integrity of the community and its history.

At one level, the municipal government has done this. The city's Official Plan states that "it shall be the policy of Council to encourage the preservation of buildings and sites having historical or architectural value." In 1970, City Council established a "committee of architectural review" to allow Council "to take action to preserve buildings of architectural and historical merit." In 1975, the Local Architectural Conservation Advisory Committee was established under the terms of The Ontario Heritage Act of the previous year. These committees have produced several volumes of *Buildings of Historic and Architectural Significance*. In each of the six volumes running from 1971 through 1985, the mayor of the day has pledged support for the notion that this vital portion of our legacy must be preserved.

V

BUT MUCH OF the legacy had already gone, and even during this period of increased awareness, more was threatened. Plymouth Square is gone; the Ontario Trust Building is no longer with us; the Notre Dame Convent has been taken away; the Mowat round-cornered building was demolished. At the same time, there have been some successes: the Royal Canadian Horse Artillery Brigade Association protected its quarters on Ontario Street from being blended into the questionable Marina City project; the "Kick and Push" and Grand Trunk stations survive; the Kingston Library integrated Bishop

Alexander Macdonnell's house into its new building. The Victoria and Grey Trust, W.H. Smith's book store, the Empire Life Building, Montreal Trust, the Prince George Hotel, the Kingston Brewing Company, Chez Piggy, and the several proprietors fronting on Market Square have all demonstrated that it is possible to combine taste, civic responsibility, and practicality in refurbishing their premises.

Nonetheless, in recent months three other buildings of major value have been demolished, and these illegally. On the outskirts of Portsmouth Village, a designated building was destroyed by Kingston Psychiatric Hospital – an agency of the provincial government. No permit was sought; no effective action resulted from what was clearly an illegal act. Next, the Lines houses were removed from Ontario Street to an isolated and unsupervised spot at the foot of North Street; it was destroyed by arson. Finally, in broad daylight and on Princess Street in the very heart of downtown Kingston, two designated buildings were destroyed by developer Tracy Christie, who had not been issued the necessary demolition permit. Watched by a crowd, the demolition proceeded while protesters were restrained by members of the Kingston City Police Force.

Various aldermen and municipal officials have suggested that if citizens knew that arson or illegal demolition were imminent, they should have spoken up and informed the appropriate authorities. This seems to be a little naïve. The pattern of illegal destruction is clear enough: Kingston's heritage resource – a totally unrenewable resource – is at clear risk, and that is plain for all to see. And, of course, the legal destruction of heritage properties is, if anything, more serious. All that Tracy Christie needed was 180 days of patience and he could have demolished all of his heritage properties with a city demolition permit in his pocket.

If the City of Kingston is serious about retaining its heritage as a dominant component of its character, it must take deliberate steps to ensure that the attrition of heritage stops. Certainly, attention must be directed to the inventorying and protection of individual buildings, but more is necessary. All of these buildings must be considered as interacting elements of an entity. Demolishing two structures at the corner of King and Princess is not only an incremental loss of two units, but it also does much to destroy the nineteenth-century tone of that portion of the city. The removal of the Lines houses and their replacement by three little townhouses massively decreased our stock of eighteenth-century woodframe houses, but also eroded the emerging heritage-laden character of parts of Ontario Street.

VI

THREE PREVENTIVE steps should be taken immediately. First, City Council must seek tougher provincial legislation to give it adequate power to prevent unwarranted demolition that is now legal. Second, the sanctions against illegal demolition must be made substantially tougher; several European centres already have such legislation in place, and advice should be sought of heritage experts with experience elsewhere. Third, the city should provide itself with some economic clout in this area.

Clearly, conservation and management of heritage costs money. Buildings can only be acquired, saved, and restored if there are resources available to do so. The Lines houses are a good example: the city should have purchased them, rehabilitated them on the site, and put them to municipal use. Reliance upon the generosity and responsibility of such citizens' groups as the Frontenac Heritage Foundation (which has provided sterling service in this area) and others is not the way to conduct an integrated campaign of planned heritage conservation. A Kingston Heritage Fund is desperately needed.

As noted recently by former Mayor E.V. Swain, such a fund could be generated by appropriating an agreed-upon portion of the municipal assessment and applying it to these purposes. The municipality of Vaughan (north Toronto) has had such a system in place since 1979. In the current year, some $325,000 has been generated by designating .25 of a mill to funding "Heritage Vaughan." The town now holds title to nine heritage-designated buildings and is currently engaged in a $700,000 refurbishing of the original Township Hall and a restoration of the Vallore Schoolhouse. Other Toronto area municipalities are exploring this initiative too.

Vaughan Township is not a major heritage centre, but it is preserving and husbanding what it has. Kingston, with its valuable legacy from the past, has an even greater duty to see that its heritage stock is not further eroded by irresponsible and wanton patterns of destruction.

V

THE MAYOR, Council, and the civic leadership in general have a clear duty. Developer Tracy Christie's action has mobilized a degree of public awareness and activism not seen in Kingston since the early 1970s. Moreover, this round of concern has a broader base of popular support than that of any other time. Kingstonians want the tone and character of their city retained, and they want this for commercial as well as aesthetic reasons. It is not some simple-minded opposition to growth and change that is being advocated. Rather, the call is for planned and rational growth that ensures Kingston will continue as both a *living* and *livable* community.

The Kingston area architectural conservation committees (LACACs) are doing a superb job of listing, designating, and describing the several hundred important buildings in Kingston. That activity must continue. They have also led the way in considering such integrated assemblages as the villages of Barriefield and Portsmouth and Kingston's Market Square. We must go even further. Recent events demonstrate that City Council must recognize the need for a heritage plan that demonstrates a vision for the whole of the city. Such planning must involve St. Lawrence, Cataraqui and Frontenac wards as well as Sydenham Ward.

What Ontario Street has experienced in the 1970s and 1980s, the area fronting on the Inner Harbour will experience in the 1990s. While attention will be focused on the benefits of replacing old industrial plants and derelict lots with yet more condominiums and increased tax base, isolated developments will again threaten the essential character of those neighbourhoods.

Urban growth and development is more than increases in numbers of building permits, housing stock, and population. The quality of life also needs to be protected and even enhanced. It would be a tragedy if we were able to permit the incremental destruction of the finest architectural legacy in Ontario. We are about to enter the twenty-first century. Surely, some of the eighteenth and nineteenth centuries should be allowed to go with us?

Endnotes

NOTE ON ENDNOTES: Not every article included in this volume is accompanied by endnotes. Professor Swainson followed a basic decorum: academic publications were supported by formal endnotes; more popular pieces were not burdened with these academic conventions. With or without endnotes, Professor Swainson's research was impeccable and often quite original. The endnotes to "Why Examine Local History? and "Chronicling Kingston" are arguably still the most comprehensive bibliographies of books and articles on Kingston available and continue to inspire further research.

Introduction: Why Examine Local History?
The Canadian Case

1. These streets are named after prominent public men who lived in Kingston for at least a time. Charles Poulett Thomson (1799-1841), first Baron Sydenham of Kent, was the Governor General of Canada, 1839-41. He was thus the first Governor General of the Province of Canada, of which Kingston was the capital. Sydenham's successor as Governor General was Sir Charles Bagot (1781-1843), who represented the Crown in Canada, 1841-43. Both Sydenham and Bagot died in Kingston. Norman McLeod Rogers (1894-1940) was a professor of political science at Queen's University, who was elected Liberal MP for Kingston in 1935. He served as Minister of Labour (1935-39) and Minister of Defence (1939-40) in Mackenzie King's third government.
2. These five short streets in the Queen's University-Kingston General Hospital district were named after George Okill Stuart (1776-1862), who became archdeacon of Kingston in 1827.
3. The title of Arthur Lower's textbook, *Colony to Nation* (Toronto,1946), represents the same theme, even though it was published 20 years later.
4. Sub-titled, *A Study of Civic Education in Canada*, this is volume 5 in the *Curriculum Series*, published by the Ontario Institute for Studies in Education. The study is described as "The Report of the National History Project, a privately sponsored study initiated by the members of the Governing Body of Trinity College School, Port Hope, Ontario."
5. *A Study of Civic Education in Canada*, 74.
6. Symons, THB. *To Know Ourselves: The Report of the Commission on Canadian Studies*, Vols. I and II, Ottawa, ON: Association of Universities and Colleges of Canada, 1975.

7. Symons, I, 27.
8. J. Richard Finlay, "The Strange, Skeptical Mood of the Campus: A Poll Uncovers Surprising Attitudes – And Heroes – Among Students." *Saturday Night*, October, 1979.
9. Finlay, 37.
10. Finlay, 36.

Chronicling Kingston: An Interpretation

1. Cited in Richard A. Preston and Leopold Lamontagne, *Royal Fort Frontenac* (The Champlain Society, Toronto, 1958), 40.
2. See Leopold Lamontagne, "Kingston's French Heritage," *Historic Kingston*, No. 2 (1953), 27-39; and Neil A. Patterson, "The Mystery of Picardville and the French Church," *Families*, Vol. 19, No. 4 (1980), 211-22.
3. Preston, Richard A, *Kingston Before the War of 1812* (Toronto, 1959), 1.
4. Cited in J. MacKay Hitsman, "Kingston and the War of 1812," *Historic Kingston*, No. 15 (1967), 50.
5. Strachan, James, *A Visit to the Province of Upper Canada in 1819* (Aberdeen, Scotland, 1820).
6. C.P. Stacey makes clear the fact that the border was far from undefended and the lakes only partially demilitarized. See his *The Undefended Border: The Myth and the Reality*, Canadian Historical Association, Historical Booklet No. 1, especially 10-11: "Evading the Rush-Bagot Agreement."
7. Bouchette, Joseph, *The British Dominions in North America*, 2 vols. (London, 1831) I, 77.
8. Robert Baldwin to this father, August 4, 1843, cited in Violet Margaret Nelson, *The Orange Order in Canadian Politics*, M.A. thesis, Queen's University, 1950, 83 and 83, note 12.
9. Cited in David B. Knight, *Choosing Canada's Capital: Jealousy and Friction in the Nineteenth Century* (Toronto, 1977), 65.
10. Cited in Helen Nicholson, "Kingston and the Capital Question," unpublished research paper, Department of History, Queen's University, 1979.
11. Cited in David B. Knight, *A Capital for Canada: Conflict and Compromise in the Nineteenth Century* (Chicago, 1977), 86-87.
12. From the Chronicle and Gazette, cited in James A. Roy, *Kingston: The King's Town*, (Toronto, 1952), 231.
13. John A. Macdonald to his mother, March 17, 1856, in J.K. Johnson, ed., *The Papers of the Prime Ministers*, Vol. I, *The Letters of Sir John A. Macdonald, 1836-1857* (Ottawa, 1968), 356.
14. Max Magill, "The Failure of the Commercial Bank," in Gerald Tulchinsky, ed., *To Preserve and Defend: Essays on Kingston in the Nineteenth Century* (Montreal, 1976), 169.
15. John D. Wilson, *The Economic History of the Kingston Port, 1853-1900*, Honours thesis, Department of Economics, Queen's University, 1977, 69, 46.
16. Wilson, 76.
17. Kingston *Chronicle and Gazette*, October 25, 1845.
18. Robert Gourlay, *Statistical Account of Upper Canada* (London, 1822), I, 128.
19. Arthur R.M. Lower, "The Character of Kingston," in Tulchinsky, 21.
20. J. Edmison, "The History of Kingston Penitentiary," *Historic Kingston*, No. 3 (1954), 34.

21. John A. Macdonald to Henry Smith, January 27, 1855, in Johnson, I, 228-29.

22. J.B. Bury, *The Idea of Progress: An Inquiry into its Origin and Growth* (New York, 1955), 25.

23. H. Butterfield, *The Whig Interpretation of History*, (New York, 1965, f.p., 1931), 101. One is occasionally given a brutal reminder of the pervasiveness of this concept. In a review of David Jay Bercuson and Phillip A. Buckner, eds., *Eastern and Western Perspectives*, Rosemary Ommer dismisses a thoroughly respectable article by J. Murray Beck as an "unfortunate inclusion in this otherwise progressive collection of essays." *Canadian Forum*, April, 1982, 32.

24. Marvin McInnis, *Kingston in the Canadian Economy of the Late Nineteenth Century*, Institute for Economic Research, Queen's University, Discussion Paper No. 132, 1.

25. Some examples are R.A. Preston, "The History of the Port of Kingston," *Historic Kingston*, No. 3 (1954), 3-25; John D. Wilson, *The Economic History of the Kingston Port, 1853-1900*, Economics Honours thesis, Queen's, 1977; D.D. Calvin, *A Saga of the St. Lawrence: Timber and Shipping Through Three Generation*, (Toronto, 1945); Donald Swainson, *Garden Island: A Shipping Empire/L'Empire Maritime de Garden Island* (Kingston, 1983).

26. For the army and navy, see Ronald L. Way, "Kingston and the British Army," *Historic Kingston*, No. 1 (1952), 28-39; George F.G. Stanley, "Kingston and the Defence of British North America," in Tulchinsky, 83-101; William Patterson, "Fort Henry: Military Mistake or Defiant Deterrent?" *Historic Kingston*, No. 29 (1981), 30-41; John W. Spurr, "The Royal Navy's Presence in Kingston, Part I: 1813-1836, *Historic Kingston*, No. 25 (1977), 63-77, "The Royal Navy's Presence in Kingston, Part II: 1813-1853," *Historic Kingston*, No. 26 (1978), 81-94, "The Kingston Gazette", the War of 1812, and "Fortress Kingston," *Historic Kingston*, No. 17 (1969), 16-29, "Sir Robert Hall (1778-1818)," *Historic Kingston*, No. 29 (1981), 3-15, "Sir James Yeo, A Hero on the Lakes," *Historic Kingston,*, No. 30 (1982), 30-45, and "Garrison and Community, 1815-1870," Tulchinsky, 103-18.

27. Some key works of general interest on the years 1783-1830 are Richard A. Preston, *Kingston Before the War of 1812*; Hitsman; A.H. Young, *The Parish Register of Kingston, Upper Canada 1785-1811* (Kingston, 1921); S.F. Wise, "Tory Factionalism: Kingston Elections and Upper Canadian Politics, 1820-1836," *Ontario History*, Vol. LVII, No. 4 (1965), 205-25. The major narrative accounts all focus on the early period: *C.W. Cooper, Frontenac, Lennox and Addington: An Essay* (Kingston, 1856); Agnes Maule Machar, *The Story of Old Kingston* (Toronto, 1908); Edwin Horsey, *Cataraqui, Fort Frontenac, Kingston*, Manuscript, 1937, Queen's University Archives; James A. Roy, *Kingston: The King's Town* (Toronto, 1952). The finest study of early Kingston, which includes an excellent overview of the period from 1785-1830 plus a truly innovative section that uses data from 272 biographical sketches to arrive at computer-based conclusions is Kathryn M. Bindon, *Kingston: A Social History, 1785-1830*, unpublished Ph.D. thesis, Queen's 1979.

28. Biographical material concerning Kingstonians and those associated with the town during the pre-Confederation period is extensive and is made

even more so by the current interest in loyalism and Loyalists. Some interesting examples are: C.E. Cartwright, *Life and Letters of the Honourable Richard Cartwright* (Toronto, 1876); Donald C. MacDonald, *Honourable Richard Cartwright, 1759-1815* (Toronto, 1961); James Robertson Carruthers, *The Little Gentleman: The Reverend Doctor John Stuart and the Inconvenience of Revolution*, M.A. thesis, Queen's, 1975; A.H. Young, "The Rev'd George Okill Stuart, M.A. LL.D," Ontario Historical Society, *Papers and Records*, 1927; Peter Baskerville, "Donald Bethunc," *Dictionary of Canadian Biography*, IX; S.F. Wise, "The Rise of Christopher Hagerman," *Historic Kingston*, No. 14 (1966), 12-23, and, "John Macaulay: Tory for All Seasons," Tulchinsky, 185-202; H. Pearson Gundy, "The Business Career of Hugh C. Thomson of Kingston," *Historic Kingston*, No. 21 (1973), 62-75, and "Hugh C. Tomson: Editor, Publisher, and Politician, 1791-1834," Tulchinsky, 203-22; Richard A. Pierce, "Nils von Schoultz – the Man they had to Hang," *Historic Kingston*, No. 19 (1971), 56-65; Margaret Angus, "John Counter," *Historic Kingston*, No. 27 (1979), 16-25; J. Douglas and Mary Stewart, "John Solomon Cartwright: Upper Canadian Gentleman and Regency 'Man of Taste," *Historic Kingston* No. 27 (1979), 61-77; John W. Spurr, "Edward John Barker, M.D., Editor and Citizen," *Historic Kingston*, No. 27 (1979), 113-126; H. Pearson Gundy, "Thomas Liddell: Queen's First Principal," *Historic Kingston*, No. 19 (1971), 17-27; George Metcalf, "Samuel Bealy Harrison: Forgotten Reformer," *Ontario History*, Vol. L, No. 3 (1958), 117-31; William R. Teatero, "A Dead and Alive Way Never Does:" *The Pre-Political Professional World of John A. Macdonald*, M.A. thesis, Queen's, 1978; Donald Creighton, *John A. Macdonald: The Young Politician* (Toronto, 1952); Mary Winnett Fraser, "William Coverdale, Kingston Architect 1801?-1865," *Historic Kingston*, No. 26 (1978), 70-80. For some post-Confederation material see Donald Swainson, "Kingstonians in the Second Parliament: Portrait of an Elite Group," Tulchinsky, 261-77.

29. For example, Marilyn G. Miller, *The Political Ideas of the Honourable Richard Cartwright 1759-1815*, M.A. thesis, Queen's, 1975; Jane Errington, *A Developing Upper Canadian Identity: Kingstonians' View of the United States and Britain 1810-1815*, M.A. thesis, Queen's, 1980.

30. Political aspects have been much discussed: Fred Cook, *The Struggle for the Capital of Canada* (Ottawa, n.d.); James A. Gibson, "Sir Edmund Head's Memorandum on the Choice of Ottawa as the Seat of Government of Canada," *Canadian Historical Review*, Vol. XVI (1935), 411-17, and "The Choosing of the Capital of Canada," *The British Columbia Historical Quarterly*, Vol. XVII (1935), 75-85; D.J. Pierce and J.P. Pritchett, "The Choice of Kingston as the Capital of Canada, 1839-1841," Canadian Historical Association, *Annual Report*, 1929, 57-63; Edwin E. Horsey, *Kingston A Century Ago* (Kingston, 1938); J.E. Hodgetts, "The Civil Service When Kingston was the Capital of Canada," *Historic Kingston*, No. 5 (1956), 13-24; George F.G. Stanley, "Kingston, and the Choice of Canada's Capital," *Historic Kingston*, No. 24 (1976), 18-37; David B. Knight, *A Capital for Canada, and Choosing Canada's Capital*. G.A. Neville provides some interesting material on an earlier seat of government issue in "Kingston and the Capitals of Upper Canada – An Early Instance of Civil Service Reaction," *Families*, Vol. 19, No. 4 (1980), 277-82. Other aspects of the capital period

have also received attention. See Machar, Chapter XIII: "Kingston as the Capital of Canada;" Margaret Angus, "Lord Sydenham's One Hundred and Fifteen Days in Kingston," *Historic Kingston*, No. 15 (1967), 36-39; J. Douglas Stewart, "Architecture for a Boom Town: The Primitive and the Neo-Baroque in George Browne's Kingston Buildings," Tulchinsky, 37-61. The impact of the presence of the seat of government on one industry, printing, is made clear by an analysis of the listings in A.R. Hazelgrove, *A Checklist of Kingston Imprints to 1867* (Kingston, 1978).

31. Some key works are R.A. Preston, "The History of the Port of Kingston;" Wilson; McInnis; Duncan L. McDowall, *Kingston, 1846-1854: A Study of Economic Change in a Mid-Nineteenth Century Canadian Community*, M.A. thesis, Queen's, 1973, and "Roads and Railways: Kingston's Mid Century Search for a Hinterland 1846-1854," *Historic Kingston*, No. 23 (1975), 52-69; Brian Osborne, "The Settlement of Kingston's Hinterland," Tulchinsky, , 63-79, and "Kingston in the Nineteenth Century: A Study in Urban Decline," in J. David Wood, ed., *Perspectives on Landscape and Settlement in Nineteenth Century Ontario* (Toronto, 1978), 159-81; Walter Lewis, "The Trials and Tribulations of the 'Kick and Push': A Business History of the Kingston & Pembroke Railroad, 1871-1912," *Historic Kingston*, No. 28 (1980), 95-111. Neil A. Patterson, "Kingston's Industrial Hinterland," *Historic Kingston.*, No. 29 (1981), 109-21 tells us much about the nature of the hinterland. Industrialization and banking have received some attention: Joan MacKinnon, *Kingston Cabinetmakers, 1800-1867* (Ottawa, 1976); Ian R. Dalton, "The Kingston Brewery of Thomas Dalton," *Historic Kingston*, No. 26 (1978), 38-50; Max Magill, "James Morton of Kingston – Brewer," *Historic Kingston*, No. 21 (1973), 28-36, and "The Failure of the Commercial Bank;" George Richardson, "The Canadian Locomotive Company," Tulchinsky, 157-67; Anne MacDermaid, "Kingston in the Eighteen-Nineties: A Study of Urban-Rural Interaction and Change," *Historic Kingston*, No. 20 (1972), 35-45; *125 Years of Progress* (James Richardson & Sons Ltd., Winnipeg, 1982). The fate of the printing business can be followed in Hazelgrove.

32. There are specific studies of some of these institutions: J. Edmison, "The History of Kingston Penitentiary," W.G.C. Norman, *A Chapter of Canadian Penal History: The Early Years of the Provincial Penitentiary at Kingston, and the Commission of Inquiry Into its Management, 1835-1851*, M.A. thesis, Queen's, 1979; Margaret Angus, *Kingston General Hospital: A Social and Institutional History* (Montreal, 1973); Catherine Anne Sims, *An Institutional History of the Asylum for the Insane at Kingston, 1856-1885*, M.A. thesis, Queen's, 1981; D.D. Calvin, *Queen's University at Kingston* (Kingston, 1941); Hilda Neatby, *Queen's University, Volume I: 1841-1917* (Montreal, 1978); R.A. Preston, *Canada's RMC: A History of the Royal Military College* (Toronto, 1969); George Lothrop Starr, *Old St. George's* (Kingston, 1913); A.H. Young, *The Parish Register of Kingston, Upper Canada* (Kingston, 1921); D.M. Schurman, "John Travers Lewis and the Establishment of the Anglican Diocese," Tulchinsky, 299-310. Some are discussed in part or tangentially in J.E. Rea, *Bishop Alexander Macdonell and the Politics of Upper Canada* (Toronto, 1974); Louis J. Flynn, "Bishop Edward John Horan," *Historic Kingston*, No. 24 (1976), 43-54; P. Lloyd Northcott, "The Financial

Problems of the Reverend John Stuart," *Historic Kingston*, No. 13 (1965), 27-40; J.M. Beattie, ed., *Attitudes Towards Crime and Punishment in Upper Canada, 1830-1850: A Documentary Study* (Toronto, 1977); Kathryn M. Bindon, Queen's Men, *Canada's Men: The Military History of Queen's University, Kingston* (Kingston, 1978).

33. D.C. Masters, *The Rise of Toronto, 1850-1890* (Toronto, 1947).

34. W.L. Morton, "The Significance of Site in the Settlement of the American and Canadian Wests," in A.B. McKillop, ed., *Contexts of Canada's Past: Selected Essays of W.L. Morton* (Toronto, 1980), 87.

35. Margaret Angus in Ian E. Wilson, J. Douglas Stewart, Margaret Angus and Neil K. MacLennan, *Kingston City Hall* (Kingston, 1974), 11.

36. Cited in Knight, *Choosing Canada's Capital*, 30.

37. Sydenham to Russell, March 13, 1840, Paul Knaplund, ed., *Letters from Lord Sydenham, Governor-General of Canada 1839-1841, to Lord John Russell* (Clifton, 1973), 53.

38. Cited in J.C. Dent, *The Last Forty Years: The Union of 1841 to Confederation*, ed., Donald Swainson (Toronto, 1972), 68-69.

39. Cited in G.P. de T. Glazebrook, *Sir Charles Bagot in Canada: A Study in British Colonial Government* (Oxford, 1929), 35-36.

40. Cited in Knight, *A Capital for Canada*, 54.

41. Cited in Knight, *Choosing Canada's Capital*, 38-39.

42. Creighton, 87-88.

43. Stewart in Wilson, Stewart, Angus and MacLennan, 4.

44. For a superb account of the fire and its influence on the development of Kingston, see John W. Spurr, "The Night of the Fire," *Historic Kingston*, No. 18, 1970, 57-65. Spurr argues, persuasively, that the fire "explains why and how Kingston became "the Limestone City."

45. Wilson, Stewart, Angus, MacLennan, 6.

46. For an interesting beginning, see Lubomyr Luciuk, *Ukranians in the Making: Their Kingston Story* (Kingston, 1980). Gordon Taylor, *The Mississauga of Kingston: A Study in Ethnohistory*, M.A. thesis, Queen's, 1981 is an excellent study of an earlier period.

47. While the heritage movement as such has received little attention, the actual heritage has been magnificently documented: Margaret Angus, *The Old Stones of Kingston: Its Buildings Before 1867* (Toronto, 1966); J. Douglas Stewart and Ian E. Wilson, *Heritage Kingston* (Kingston, 1973); Dana H. Johnson and C.J. Taylor, *Reports on Selected Buildings in Kingston*, Ontario, two volumes, Manuscript Report Number 261, National Historic Parks and Sites Branch (Ottawa, 1976-77); Gerald Finley, *In Praise of Older Buildings* (Kingston, 1976); City of Kingston, *Buildings of Architectural and Historic Significance*, 5 vols. (Kingston, 1971-1980). Blake and Jennifer McKendry, *Early Photography in Kingston* (Kingston, 1979) includes some unusual and important photographs.

48. Some interesting and suggestive preliminary work has been done in this area: R.A. Preston, "The British Influence of RMC," Tulchinsky, 119-37; Bryan Palmer, "Kingston Mechanics and the Rise of the Penitentiary, 1833-1836," *Histoire Sociale/Social History*, Vol. XIII, No. 2 (1980), 7-32. Some interesting examples of social analysis are Robert Francis John Barnett, *A Study of Price Movements and the Cost of Living in Kingston Ontario for the*

Years 1865 to 1900, M.A. thesis, Queen's, 1963; Margaret Angus, "Health, Emigration and Welfare in Kingston 1820-1840," Donald Swainson, ed., *Oliver Mowat's Ontario* (Toronto, 1972), 120-35; Patricia E. Malcolmson, "The Poor in Kingston, 1815-1850," Tulchinsky, 281-97; Allan G. Green, "Immigrants in the City: Kingston as Revealed in the Census Manuscripts of 1871," Tulchinsky, 311-30; Harvey J. Graff, *The Literacy Myth: Literacy and Social Structure in the Nineteenth Century City* (New York, 1979); R. Harris, G. Levine and Brian Osborne, "Housing Tenure and Social Classes in Kingston, Ontario, 1881-1901," *Journal of Historical Geography*, 7, 3 (1981). Robertson Davies provides fascinating insights into at least some strata of Kingston society. In particular see his *Fortune, My Foe* (Toronto, 1949); *Tempest-Tost* (Toronto, 1951); and *Leaven of Malice* (Toronto, 1954).

Sir Henry Smith: The Politics of Union

1. Henry J. Morgan, *Sketches of Celebrated Canadians* (Quebec, 1862), 622, The Henry Morgan Collection, P.A.C., indicates that Morgan did careful research for his sketch of Smith. He is generally a reliable source.
2. Tablet, St. George's Cathedral, Kingston.
3. *Sir Henry Smith Papers*, P.A.O., [hereafter cited at *Smith Papers*], M. Maud to Henry Smith, July 13, 1818. This letter was addressed to Smith at Montreal; Morgan, 623.
4. *Smith Papers*, Scrapbooks, undated clipping.
5. *Smith Papers*, M. Maud to Smith, July 13, 1818.
6. Morgan, 623.
7. *The Canadian News*, April 27, 1859.
8. *The Canadian News*, April 27, 1859.
9. *Smith Papers*, Smith to his mother, September 8, 1831.
10. *The Canadian News*, April 27, 1859. Morgan, 623, gives the date as 1836. The earlier date seems more plausible. By 1834 he had been an articled student for six years. Also, his activities in 1836 and after suggest that he was by then a fairly experienced lawyer.
11. *Kingston Daily News*, September 18, 1868.
12. J.O. Cote, *Political Appointments and Elections in the Province of Canada From 1841 to 1865*, Second Edition (Ottawa, 1918), 126.
13. *Smith Papers*, Smith to Mary, November 13, 1836.
14. *Smith Papers*, Ross to Smith, July 1, 1853.
15. *Smith Papers*, "To the Free and Independent Electors of the County of Frontenac," Kingston, January 21, 1841, signed Henry Smith Jr.; See also Donald Creighton *John A. Macdonald: The Young Politician* (Toronto, 1952), 172.
16. Toronto *Globe*, January 12, 1869.
17. Creighton, 57.
18. Creighton, 56-58.
19. J.K. Johnson, *The Letters of Sir John A. Macdonald*, I (Ottawa, 1968), 21 note.
20. *The Letters of Sir John A. Macdonald*, 302.
21. *The Letters of Sir John A. Macdonald*, 228.
22. *The Letters of Sir John A. Macdonald*, 393.
23. *The Letters of Sir John A. Macdonald*, 336.

24. *The Letters of Sir John A. Macdonald*, 364-65.
25. *The Letters of Sir John A. Macdonald*, 392.
26. *Smith Papers*, Pew deed for Church of Saint George, April 23, 1852.
27. *Smith Papers*, Scrapbooks, undated clipping.
28. Margaret Angus, *The Old Stones of Kingston: Its Buildings Before 1867* (Toronto, 1966), 88.
29. *Smith Papers, Scrapbooks*, undated clipping.
30. H.P. Gundy, ed., "Kingston Collegiate Institute, By Samuel Woods, M.A. Principal 1862-1876," *Historic Kingston*, No. 9 (1960), 62 note.
31. Creighton, 80.
32. *Smith Papers*, Adjutant General's Office, D. Macdonald to Smith, June 6, 1848.
33. *Smith Papers*, Henry Smith Sr. to Henry Smith Jr., June 1, 1858.
34. *Smith Papers*, Scrapbooks, undated clipping.
35. Cote, passim.
36. Toronto *Globe*, September 19, 1868.
37. *Smith Papers*, "To the Free and Independent Electors of the County of Frontenac," Kingston, January 21, 1841, signed Henry Smith Jr.
38. Toronto *Globe*, September 19, 1868.
39. Smith's activities in the Assembly can be followed in *Canadian Mirror of Parliament, 1841: Mirror of Parliament*, 1846; *Thompson's Mirror of Parliament*, 1860; *Debates of the Legislative Assembly of United Canada*, eds. Elizabeth Nish and Elizabeth Gibbs, Vols. I-IV; *Parliamentary Debates*, Canadian Library Association, Newspaper Microfilming Project, 1846-61.
40. This could refer either to S.B. Harrison or his successor, to John A. Macdonald, or possibly to Alexander Hagerman.
41. From a statement in his own defence by Henry Smith Sr., *Macdonald Papers*, P.A.C., 135919.
42. J.M.S. Careless, *Brown of the Globe: The Voice of Upper Canada, 1818-1859* (Toronto, 1959), 79.
43. J. Edmison, "The History of Kingston Penitentiary," *Historic Kingston*, No. 3 (1954), 31.
44. Edmison, 30.
45. The penitentiary commission incident can be followed in *Macdonald Papers*, P.A.C., passim; Creighton, passim; Careless, passim; Edmison, passim; J. Edmison, "Kingston Penitentiary A Century Ago," *Canadian Welfare*, Vol. XXV, No. 5 (October 15, 1949), passim.
46. He was, for example, asked to attend a Conservative dinner in Picton in 1851. See D.B. *Stevenson Papers*, P.A.O., Smith to Henry J. Thorpe, September 30, 1851. There are also numerous references to such activities in the *Macdonald Papers*, P.A.C. See also *Smith Papers*, Macdonald to Smith, August 2, 1855 and January 22, 1857.
47. *Kingston Daily Herald*, November 29, 1851, in *Smith Papers*.
48. Cote, 6.
49. Cote, 113.
50. *Parliamentary Debates*, C.L.A., 1854-58, passim.
51. *Parliamentary Debates*, 1856, passim.
52. *Parliamentary Debates*, March 24, 1857; see also *Journals of the Legislative Assembly of the Province of Canada*, Session 1857, March 10, 1857.

53. Cote, 3.
54. *Parliamentary Debates*, C.L.A., February 25, 1858.
55. *Parliamentary Debates*, C.L.A., February 25, 1858.
56. Toronto *Globe*, February 23, 1858.
57. *Parliamentary Debates*, C.L.A., February 25, 1858.
58. *Parliamentary Debates*, C.L.A., February 25, 1858.
59. Toronto *Globe*, February 26, 1858.
60. Careless, 16.
61. Morgan, 623.
62. *Mackenzie-Lindsey Collection*, P.A.O., Smith to Charles Lindsey, February 10, 1859, February 20, 1860, March 21, 1860.
63. *Smith Papers, Scrapbooks*, clipping from unidentified newspaper, April 24, [1860].
64. *Smith Papers, Scrapbooks*, undated clipping.
65. *Daily Colonist and Atlas*, February 10, 1859, in *Parliamentary Debates*, C.L.A.
66. Perhaps the best result of Smith's speakership was a portrait of Sir Henry by the excellent Kingston artist William Sawyer. See *Macdonald Papers*, P.A.C., 359, Sawyer to Macdonald, June 23, 1879.
67. For Victoria Bridge see G.R. Stevens, *Canadian National Railways*, I (Toronto and Montreal, 1960), 265 ff.
68. *Macdonald Papers*, P.A.C., 336, Part 2, Smith to Macdonald, June 7, 1859.
69. *Galt Papers*, P.A.C., Smith to Galt, May 14, 1859.
70. Handwritten excerpt from *London Times*, June 29, 1859, in *Henry Morgan Collection*, P.A.C.
71. *Smith Papers*, undated quotation from *London Free Press*, cited in unidentified newspaper clipping.
72. *Thompson's Mirror of Parliament*, March 14, 1860.
73. *Newcastle Papers*, P.A.C., a document dated July 1859 and headed: "Gov. Head July 1859. H. Smith (Speaker) His proposed Knighthood. French Intrigues in Canada."
74. *Thompson's Mirror of Parliament*, March 14, 1860.
75. *Smith Papers, Scrapbooks*, undated clipping, but obviously from 1860.
76. From the Toronto *Globe*, cited in Henry J. Morgan, *The Tour of H.R.H. The Prince of Wales Through British America and the United States* (Montreal, 1860), 75-78.
77. Morgan, 80.
78. Morgan, 82.
79. *The Canadian News*, April 27, 1859.
80. *Mirror of Parliament*, 1846, March 27, 1846.
81. Creighton, 308.
82. This had to do with some "swampy ground in the neighbourhood of Sarnia." Macdonald and several associates had a somewhat dubious involvement with this land during the 1850s. See J.K. Johnson, "John A. Macdonald, The Young Non-Politician." *The Canadian Historical Association*, Historical Papers, 1971, 143.
83. *Brown Papers*, P.A.C., McDougall to Brown, April 1, 1861.
84. The election address is printed in the Toronto *Globe*, June 19, 1861.
85. Toronto *Globe*, June 11, 1861.
86. Toronto *Globe*, June 19, 1861.

87. Quebec *Chronicle*, cited in Toronto *Globe*, June 27, 1861.
88. Toronto *Globe*, June 27, 1861.
89. Montreal *Evening Pilot*, June 24, 1861.
90. Quebec *Chronicle*, cited in Toronto *Globe*, June 27, 1861.
91. Picton *Gazette*, July 5, 1861.
92. Picton *Gazette*, July 26, 1861.
93. Cited in Creighton, 311.
94. *Macdonald Papers*, P.A.C., 537, Smith to Stevenson, June 22, 1861. It is not known how Macdonald obtained this letter.
95. *Macdonald Papers*, 537, Smith to D'Arcy McGee, January 7, 1863.
96. *Macdonald Papers*, 537, Smith to D'Arcy McGee, January 7, 1863.
97. *Macdonald Papers*, P.A.C., 188, copy of letter, King to Smith, June 25, 1861, sent by King to Macdonald in 1873.
98. Toronto *Globe*, July 11, 1861.
99. Ferguson polled 1,372 votes to Smith's 1,222. *Canadian Parliamentary Companion*, 1864, 63.
100. *Smith Papers, Scrapbooks*, undated clipping.
101. Roderick Lewis, *A Statistical History of All the Electoral Districts of The Province of Ontario Since 1867* (Toronto, n.d.), 62.
102. Toronto *Globe*, December 28, 1867.
103. For Smith's activities in provincial politics see Toronto *Globe*, 1867-68: *Smith Papers, Scrapbooks; Macdonald Papers*, P.A.C., 341, Smith to Macdonald, February 2, 1868.
104. See for example the interesting discussion of the Contingencies Committee, Toronto *Globe*, December 30, 1867.
105. *Smith Papers*, Scrapbooks, undated clippings.
106. *Macdonald Papers*, P.A.C., 341, Smith to Macdonald, January 26, 1868.
107. *Macdonald Papers*, P.A.C., 341, Smith to Macdonald, February 2, 1868.
108. *Smith Papers, Scrapbooks*. This clipping is obviously from a Reform newspaper. It is dated January 10, 1868 and is identified only with part of the title "Advertiser."
109. Toronto *Globe*, September 19, 1868.
110. Kingston *Daily News*, September 18, 1868.
111. Toronto *Globe*, September 19, 1868.
112. Cited in Statutes of the Province of Ontario, (Toronto 1869), 331-32.
113. Statutes of the Province of Ontario 332.
114. Toronto *Globe*, January 12, 1869. For their affair see also January 15, 1869 and January 19, 1869. See also *Journals of the Legislative Assembly of the Province of Ontario*, Session 1868-9, passim.
115. Toronto *Globe*, January 12, 1869.
116. *Statutes of the Province of Ontario* (Toronto, 1869), Cap. LXXIV, "An Act to Grant Relief to Lady Smith, and to Enable her to Manage the Estate of her late husband, Sir Henry Smith."
117. For a study of this riding, see James Eadie, "The Political Career of David Roblin," Lennox and Addington Historical Society, *Papers and Records*.

Alexander Campbell:
General Manager of the Conservative Party (Eastern Ontario)

1. For the pre-Kingston period of Campbell's life, see The Week, December 15, 1887, re-printed in *In Memoriam: Sir Alexander Campbell, 1822-1892* (Toronto, 1892), 3-4.
2. For Campbell's education, see *In Memoriam*, 4; and Mary Katherine Christie, *Sir Alexander Campbell*, M.A. thesis, University of Toronto, 1950, 2-7, passim.
3. His funeral was held at St. George's Cathedral, Kingston, *In Memoriam*, 15-17.
4. *In Memoriam*, 36.
5. Donald Creighton, *John A. Macdonald: The Young Politician* (Toronto, 1952), 351-52.
6. *The Week*, December 15, 1887.
7. *Canadian Parliamentary Companion*, 1873, 34.
8. For his business involvements, see *Canadian Parliamentary Companion*, 1873, 34; Christie, 82; In Memoriam, 37; Donald Swainson, "Richard Cartwright Joins the Liberal Party," *Queen's Quarterly*, No. 75 (1968), 129; and, for probable purchase of coal properties in 1872 from Tupper, *Campbell Papers*, P.A.O., Tupper to Campbell, March 28, 1872.
9. *Campbell Papers*, P.A.O., Ives Mining Company (Montreal) to Campbell, February 8, 1870.
10. *Campbell Papers*, Domville to Campbell, November 20, 1873.
11. For Domville's career see *Canadian Parliamentary Companion*, 1873, 163-64; A.S. Ferns and B. Ostry, *The Age of Mackenzie King* (Toronto, 1955), 295; W. Stewart Wallace, *The Macmillan Dictionary of Canadian Biography*, Third Edition (Toronto, 1963), 192.
12. *Campbell Papers*, P.A.O., Gildersleeve to Campbell, November 20, 1871, telegram.
13. *Campbell Papers*, Gildersleeve to Campbell, April 5, 1872.
14. Sarnia *Observer*, May 31, 1872.
15. *Campbell Papers*, Hamilton to Campbell, May 4, 1872.
16. Christie, 6.
17. *Morris Papers*, 1845-1911, P.A.M., No. 41, Campbell to Alexander Morris, August 14, 1873.
18. *Macdonald Papers*, P.A.C., 194, Campbell to Macdonald, June 24, 1872.
19. *Macdonald Papers*, Campbell to Macdonald, June 27, 1872.
20. *Campbell Papers*, P.A.O., Hamilton to Campbell, March 30, 1872.
21. *Campbell Papers*, G. McMicken to Campbell, November 20, 1872; *Macdonald Papers*, P.A.C., 194, Campbell to Macdonald, June 26, 1872; Morris Papers, 1872-77, Lieutenant-Governor Series, P.A.M., August 19, 1873 (draft telegram) and Campbell to Morris, August 21, 1873 (telegram).
22. *Macdonald Papers*, P.A.C., 194, Campbell to Macdonald, December 9, 1872.
23. Government of Canada, *Report of the Royal Commissioners* (Ottawa, 1873), 93.
24. *Campbell Papers*, P.A.O., Cleghorn to Campbell.
25. *Campbell Papers*, Charles to Alexander Campbell, August 28, 1872.
26. See Appendix.

27. For his contact with Toronto business, see *Campbell Papers*, P.A.O., Charles to Alexander Campbell, October 2, 5 and 23, 1872.
28. Christie, 77-79.
29. A.L. Burt, ed., "Peter Mitchell on John A. Macdonald," C.H.R., XLII (1961), 216-17.
30. *Campbell Papers*, P.A.O., F.M. Pearson to Campbell, July 3, 1871; John Carling to Campbell, July 27, 1871; George A. Drew to Campbell, September 7, 1871; T.R. Ferguson to Campbell, July 21, 1871; *Macdonald Papers*, P.A.C., 194, Campbell to Macdonald, November 14, 1872.
31. *Campbell Papers*, P.A.O., Kirkpatrick to Campbell, October 13, 1871.
32. *Macdonald Papers*, P.A.C., 194, Campbell to Macdonald, December 4, 1872.
33. *Campbell Papers*, P.A.O., F. Munro to Campbell, July 27, 1871.
34. *Campbell Papers*, Shannon to Campbell, December 5, 1871, January 10, September 21, 1872.
35. *Campbell Papers*, Eliza Barker to Campbell, October 16, 1871.
36. *Campbell Papers*, R.S.M. Bouchette to Campbell, October [?], 1872.
37. *Campbell Papers*, Moylan to Campbell, July 15, 1872.
38. Note on letter dated July 19, 1872, by Campbell: "Done & Mr. Moylan telegraphed."
39. *Campbell Papers*, Macdonald to Campbell, September 3, 1872.
40. Christie, 70.
41. *Macdonald Papers*, P.A.C., 194, Campbell to Macdonald, July 11, 1872.
42. *Campbell Papers*, 194, Campbell to Macdonald, July 11, 1872.
43. *Campbell Papers*, P.A.O., J.M. Taylor to Campbell, July 30, 1872; James Dakers to Campbell, July 30, 1872, telegram.
44. *Campbell Papers*, Henry Smith to Campbell, July 26, 1872; Edward Boyle to Campbell, July 29, 1872.
45. *Campbell Papers*, Thos. Newgate to Campbell, August 5, 1872; P. Cameron to Campbell, August 10, 1872.
46. *Macdonald Papers*, P.A.C., 194, Campbell to Macdonald, September 16, 1872.
47. This material is from studies of various members of the second Parliament, and especially of John White (East Hastings), Schuyler Shibley (Addington), Walter Ross (Prince Edward) and James O'Reilly (South Renfrew).
48. *Campbell Papers*, P.A.O., Hamilton to Campbell, August 2, 1872.
49. *Campbell Papers*, McCuaig to Campbell, December 3, 1871.
50. Sir Joseph Pope, *Sir John A. Macdonald Vindicated* (Toronto, 1912), 15.
51. Christie, VI.
52. *Macdonald Papers*, P.A.C., 194, Campbell to Macdonald, December 22, 1872.
53. Creighton, 326.

James O'Reilly and George Dormer: Catholic Politics
1. For O'Reilly's background and early life, see Nicholas Flood Davin, *The Irishman in Canada* (London and Toronto, 1877), 366ff; *Canadian Parliamentary Companion*, 1873, 226; J.K. Johnson, ed., *The Canadian Directory of Parliament, 1867-1967* (Ottawa, 1968), 451.

2. For an early indication see *Baldwin Papers*, Toronto Public Library, Mrs. W.H. Blake to Baldwin, August 8, 1848. I am indebted to Professor James Lovekin for this reference.

3. Robert Baldwin to W.W. Baldwin, August 4, 1843, cited in Violet Margaret Nelson, *The Orange Order in Canadian Politics*, M.A. thesis, Queen's, 1950, 83 and 83 note 12.

4. For O'Reilly's education and professional career, see *Canadian Parliamentary Companion*, 1873, 226-27; Davin, 367-69; Ottawa *Daily Citizen*, May 17, 1875; Ottawa *Daily Times*, May 17, 1875; *Trial of Patrick J. Whelan for the Murder of the Hon. Thos. D'Arcy McGee* (Ottawa, 1868), passim; J.O. Cote, *Political Appointments and Elections in the Province of Canada, 1841-65* (Ottawa, 1866), 126.

5. Davin, 367-68.

6. Cited in Davin, 369.

7. John Charles Dent, *The Last Forty Years* (Toronto, 1881), II, 486 note.

8. P.A.C., *James O'Reilly Papers*, Macdonald to O'Reilly, February 12, 1869.

9. Davin, 371.

10. Davin, 370.

11. P.A.C., *Macdonald Papers*, 204, telegram, January 23, 1871, R.J. Cartwright, Richd. Walkem, J. O'Reilly, C.F. Gildersleeve, G.A. Kirkpatrick, J. Bowden, to Macdonald.

12. For O'Reilly's local career see *Canadian Parliamentary Companion*, 1873, 227; Davin, 367-70; Ottawa *Daily Citizen*, May 17, 1875.

13. P.A.C., *Macdonald Papers*, 194, Campbell to Macdonald, July 16, 1872. See also P.A.O., *Campbell Papers*, O'Reilly to Campbell, October 5, 1872, and Macdonald's noted comment thereon for a successful intervention by O'Reilly on Shibley's behalf.

14. P.A.O., *Campbell Papers*, O'Reilly to Campbell, April 8, 1872.

15. For these incidents see *Campbell Papers*, Hamilton to Campbell, July 5, 1872 and Haggart to Campbell, July 23, 1872.

16. Davin, 370.

17. *Canadian Parliamentary Companion*, 1873, 227.

18. P.A.C., *Macdonald Papers*, 204, Cartwright to Macdonald, January 4, 1867.

19. Davin 370. See also Ottawa *Daily Citizen*, May 16, 1875.

20. P.A.C., Mackenzie Papers, Letterbooks, I, Mackenzie to Anglin, June 11, 1873.

21. P.A.C., *Macdonald Papers*, 228, Lynch to Smith, February 1, 1872.

22. *Macdonald Papers*, 228, Lynch to Macdonald, May 9, 1872.

23. W. Stewart Wallace, The Macmillan Dictionary of Canadian Biography, 3rd ed. (Toronto, 1963), 561.

24. P.A.O., *Campbell Papers*, Allan to Campbell, December 23, 1871.

25. *Campbell Papers*, Macdonald to Campbell, December 29, 1871.

26. On this point see also Donald Creighton, *John A. Macdonald: The Old Chieftain* (Toronto, 1955), 116.

27. *The Liberal Party and the Irish Roman Catholics, A Few Historical Extracts*, 1885, 11, in P.A.C., *Macdonald Papers*, 188.

28. *The History of the Roman Catholics in Canada by the Hon. George Brown*, in P.A.C., *Macdonald Papers*, 188. A Conservative broadsheet designed to embarrass Brown. It consists chiefly of anti-Catholic statements from the

Globe. Undated, it was almost certainly published in 1872.

29. P.A.C., *Macdonald Papers*, 194, Campbell to Macdonald, July 9, 1872.
30. *Macdonald Papers*, 194, Campbell to Macdonald, no date, but probably 18, 19 or 20 July, 1872. For the details of the campaign that follow, see P.A.O., *Campbell Papers*, Macdonald to Campbell, August ?, 1872; O'Reilly to Campbell, August 8, 1872; O'Reilly to Campbell, August 12, 1872 and O'Reilly to Campbell, August 16, 1872.
31. *Macdonald Papers*, O'Reilly to Campbell, August 6, 1872.
32. *Macdonald Papers*, O'Reilly to Campbell, August 12, 1872.
33. *Macdonald Papers*, O'Reilly to Campbell, August 14, 1872.
34. *Macdonald Papers*, O'Reilly to Campbell, August 14, 1872.
35. A.P. Cockburn, *Political Annals of Canada* (Toronto, 1905), 410.
36. P.A.C., *Macdonald Papers*, 194, Campbell to Macdonald, September 2, 1872.
37. See also J.M.S. Careless, *Brown of the Globe: Statesman of Confederation* (Toronto, 1963), 281-83.
38. *Canadian Parliamentary Companion*, 1873, 297.
39. For basic biographical material, see *The Liberal Party and the Irish Roman Catholics, A Few Historical Extracts*, 1885, 11, in P.A.C., *Macdonald Papers*, 188; *Canadian Parliamentary Companion*, 1873, 166-67; Ottawa *Daily Citizen,* June 25, 1875; Toronto *Globe,* June 25, 1875, and Johnson, 173.
40. *Canadian Parliamentary Companion*, 1873, 167.
41. Marie Salter, Research Assistant, Office of the Vice-President and Registrar, University of Toronto to D. Swainson, September 12, 1967, quoting Mr. A.B. Fennell.
42. *Canadian Parliamentary Companion*, 1873, 167.
43. P.A.O., *Campbell Papers*, Dormer to Campbell, October 14, 1871.
44. Quoted by Edward Blake in Address of Mr. Blake at Bowmanville, 1873, 6, in P.A.O., *Blake Papers*, II, 15(d).
45. Ottawa, *Daily Citizen,* June 25, 1875.

Schuyler Shibley: The Underside of Victorian Ontario

1. P.B. Waite, "Sir Oliver Mowat's Canada: Reflection on an Un-Victorian Society," in Donald Swainson, ed., *Oliver Mowat's Ontario* (Toronto, 1972).
2. Waite, 12.
3. Waite, 13.
4. *Canadian Parliamentary Companion*, 1875, 305-06.
5. Walter S. Herrington, *History of the County of Lennox and Addington* (Toronto, 1913), 408.
6. For this information, I am indebted to James Eadie of Napanee.
7. For Roblin's career, see James Eadie, "The Political Career of David Roblin," Lennox and Addington Historical Society, *Papers and Records*, vol. 14 (1972).
8. Herrington, 408.
9. *Macdonald Papers*, P.A.C., 339, Johnston to Macdonald, September 30, 1866.
10. Toronto *Globe*, October 13, 1866.
11. *Macdonald Papers*, P.A.C., 339, Johnston to Macdonald, September 30, 1866.

12. Kingston *Daily News*, September 6, 1866.

13. *Macdonald Papers*, P.A.C., 339, Johnston to Macdonald, September 30, 1866.

14. Kingston *Daily News*, September 13, 1866.

15. Toronto *Globe*, October 13, 1866.

16. Kingston *Daily News*, September 6, 1866

17. Toronto *Globe*, October 13, 1866.

18. Toronto *Globe*, October 13, 1866.

19. J.K. Johnson, "John A. Macdonald, The Young Non-Politician," C.H.A. Historical Papers, 1971, 143.

20. *Macdonald Papers*, P.A.C., 337-2, Johnston to Macdonald, December 14, 1866.

21. *Macdonald Papers*, 339, Johnston to Macdonald, October 4, 1866.

22. Herrington, 408.

23. Napanee *Standard*, June 27, 1867, letter from "An Elector," Portland. Typescript copy supplied by James Eadie.

24. The evidence was as follows: "Henry Courter was sworn, and said: – I know a man named James Deeks: he voted for Shibley. So did I. I had a conversation with him about the election; he seemed inclined to vote for Shibley, but said a neighbour wanted to vote for Waggoner, the other candidate. Albert Rousehorn told me that Deeks would vote for Shibley if I paid him for his day. I did pay him one dollar for his day. I got the money from Henry Shibley, a son of the respondent, aged about fifteen." Cited in Toronto *Globe*, September 22, 1874.

25. Toronto *Globe*, August 29, 1878.

26. Toronto *Globe*, June 17 and September 2, 1872.

27. Ottawa *Citizen*, August 14 and 29, 1872.

28. *Campbell Papers*, P.A.O., Rathbun to Campbell, January 19, 1872.

29. For Deroche's career, see *Canadian Parliamentary Companion*, 1872, 320; Roderick Lewis, *A Statistical History of all the Electoral Districts of the Province of Ontario Since 1867* (Toronto, n.d.), 3; *Canadian Biographical Dictionary and Portrait Gallery and Eminent and Self-Made Men*, Ontario Volume (Toronto, 1880), 502-03.

30. *Campbell Papers*, P.A.O., Lapum to Campbell, July 15, 1872.

31. James O'Reilly, a Kingstonian, was a powerful Roman Catholic lay leader. He was also an influential Conservative politician who aspired to the bench. See Donald Swainson, "James O'Reilly," *Dictionary of Canadian Biography*, vol. X.

32. *Macdonald Papers*, P.A.C., 194, Campbell to Macdonald, July 16, 1872.

33. *Macdonald Papers*, Campbell to Macdonald, July 18, 1872.

34. *Campbell Papers*, P.A.O., Lapum to Campbell, August 5, 1872.

35. *Campbell Papers*, Lahey to Campbell, August 5, 1872; Joyner to Campbell, August 12, 1872.

36. *Campbell Papers*, Lapum to Campbell, August 12, 1872.

37. *Campbell Papers*, Rathbun to Campbell, August 21, 1872.

38. *Campbell Papers*, Lapum to Campbell, August 30, 1872.

39. *Campbell Papers*, Lapum to Campbell, September 23, 1872.

40. *Macdonald Papers*, P.A.C., 194, Campbell to Macdonald, August 27, 1872.

41. *Macdonald Papers*, 194, Campbell to Macdonald, September 2, 1872.

42. *Canadian Parliamentary Companion*, 1873, 246.
43. *Macdonald Papers*, P.A.C., 194, Campbell to Macdonald, April 24, 1873. See also Letterbooks, 20, Drinkwater to Shibley, March 4, 1873.
44. *Macdonald Papers*, 342, Shibley to Macdonald, January 30, 1869 and October 7, 1869; and Letterbooks, 13, Macdonald to Shibley, October 13, 1869.
45. *Brown Papers*, P.A.C., 9, Mackenzie to Brown, March 7, 1873. See also letter of March 5, 1873.
46. *Brown Papers*, 8, Private memorandum, obviously prepared by or for Mackenzie early in the first session of the second Parliament.
47. *Macdonald Papers*, P.A.C., Letterbooks, 21, Macdonald to Shibley, September 24, 1873.
48. *Jones Papers*, reprinted in Report of the Board of Trustees of the Public Archives of Nova Scotia, 1952, Mackenzie to Jones, October 6, 1873.
49. *Cartwright Papers*, P.A.O., Cartwright to Blake, October 10, 1873, draft of letter.
50. *Cartwright Papers*, Blake to Cartwright, October 11, 1873.
51. *Mackenzie Papers*, P.A.C., Letterbooks, 1, Mackenzie to Deroche, October 15, 1873.
52. *Morris Papers*, 1845-1911, P.A.M., No. 81, Campbell to Morris, November 29, 1873.
53. Toronto *Globe*, January 10, 1874.
54. Toronto *Globe*, January 16, 1874.
55. It is necessary to search the *Parliamentary Debates* with care to find any record of contribution from Shibley. His recorded utterances are brief comments or questions concerning dams in Frontenac county. See Canadian Library Association, *Canadian Parliamentary Debates*, 8173-74, microfilm, 1873, 125 (April 30, 1873); and *House of Commons Debates*, 1877, 623-24, 626-27 (March 12, 1877).
56. *Canadian Parliamentary Companion*, 1879, 234, 201.
57. Information supplied by S.J. Robson, Secretary, Cataraqui Cemetery Company, July 25, 1967. Herrington, 408, is inaccurate when he gives the date as 1886.
58. This group included A. Hagar, S. Shibley, D. Glass, and J.B. Lewis. Richard Cartwright was an Independent Conservative before the Pacific Scandal.
59. Donald Swainson, *The Personnel of Politics: A Study of the Ontario Members of the Second Federal Parliament*, Ph.D. thesis, University of Toronto, 1968, chapter III and 504-05.
60. *Brown Papers*, P.A.C., 9, Mackenzie to Brown, November 5, 1873. Italics in original.

Richard Cartwright's Tory Phase
1. W.R. Graham, *Sir Richard Cartwright and the Liberal Party, 1863-96*, Ph.D. thesis, University of Toronto, 1950, abstract.
2. Donald C. Macdonald, *Honourable Richard Cartwright, 1759-1815*, M.A. thesis, Queen's University, published by the Ontario Department of Public Records and Archives, 1961, passim.
3. W. Stewart Wallace, *The Macmillan Dictionary of Canadian Biography*, 3rd ed. (Toronto, 1963), 120.

4. For various personal items see Wallace, 120; Henry James Morgan, *The Canadian Men and Women of the Time*, 1st ed. (Toronto, 1898), 165; *Canadian Parliamentary Companion*, 1873, 145.
5. Richard Cartwright, *Reminiscences* (Toronto, 1912), 39.
6. Graham, 11.
7. *Reminiscences*, 39.
8. *Reminiscences*, 16.
9. *Reminiscences*, 12.
10. *Reminiscences*, 11.
11. *Reminiscences*, 14; see also Morgan, 164.
12. Graham, 15; Merril Denison, *Canada's First Bank*, vol. II (Toronto and Montreal, 1967), 150-52; Oscar Douglas Skelton, *Life and Times of Sir Alexander Tilloch Galt*, Carleton Library Edition, (Toronto, 1966), 200-07.
13. Donald Creighton, *John A. Macdonald: The Old Chieftain* (Toronto, 1955), 34.
14. *Cartwright Papers*, P.A.O., C.J. Brydges, Managing Director of the Grand Trunk Railway, to Cartwright, August 29, 1864.
15. *Cartwright Papers*, Campbell to Cartwright, March 2, 1866.
16. *Cartwright Papers*, Campbell to Cartwright, February 24, 1866.
17. Ross G. Babion, *Alexander Morris: His Place in Canadian History*, M.A. thesis, Queen's University, 1945, 55-57, 153.
18. Graham, 16; *Cartwright Papers*, P.A.O., Frontenac Loan and Investment Society, Kingston, Notice of Monthly Meeting of Board of Directors, November 9, 1869, Certificate of Stock, Bank of Montreal, in the name of R.J. Cartwright, 40 shares, for $8,000, September 16, 1872, Certificate of Stock, No. 664, Bank of Montreal to R.J. Cartwright, for 20 shares, worth $4,000, December 6, 1872; Morgan, 164-65.
19. *Macdonald Papers*, P.A.C., 204, Telegram, R.J. Cartwright, Richd. Walkem, J. O'Reilly, C.F. Gildersleeve, G.A. Kirkpatrick, and J. Bowden to J.A. Macdonald, January 23, 1871.
20. *Cartwright Papers*, P.A.O. Bowden to Cartwright, April 18, 1871, Kingston & Pembroke Railway Company to Cartwright, July 14, 1871, Kingston & Pembroke Railway Company Receipt, August 28, 1871.
21. *Cartwright Papers*, Macdonald to Cartwright, February 12, 1872.
22. *Cartwright Papers*, Campbell to Cartwright, February 12, 1872.
23. *Macdonald Papers*, P.A.C., 204, Cartwright to Macdonald, February 13, 1872.
24. Geo. Maclean Rose, ed., *A Cyclopaedia of Canadian Biography being Chiefly Men of the Time*, First Edition (Toronto, 1886), 587.
25. *Cartwright Papers*, P.A.O., Receipt of R.J. Cartwright, May 15, 1868, for 10,000 shares of the Kingston and Sherbrooke Gold Mining Company (Nova Scotia), issued by Alfred M. Patton; Stock Certificate, Canada Gold Mining Company of Nova Scotia, February 24, 1869. Report of Professor F.B. Nicholas, Professor of Chemistry and Geology, Halifax, to R. Cartwright, September 5, 1872, on Cornwallis Magnetic Iron Mine: "The deposite (sic) of ore is very extensive ...;" Mary Katherine Christie, *Sir Alexander Campbell*, M.A. thesis, University of Toronto, 1950, 82.
26. *Cartwright Papers*, P.A.O., Campbell to Cartwright, October 16, 1873; see also Campbell to Cartwright, October 20, 1873.

27. For these day-to-day operations, see *Sir Richard Cartwright Papers*, Q.U., boxes 5 and 6: "Correspondence – Business, 1872-73."
28. *Cartwright Papers*, P.A.O., Simpson to Cartwright, July 8, 1873.
29. Graham, 16; G.H. Armstrong, *The Origin and Meaning of Place Names in Canada* (Toronto, 1930), 58.
30. Graham, 11.
31. Cartwright, 2.
32. Graham, 13.
33. James Albert Eadie, *Politics In Lennox and Addington County in the Pre-Confederation Period, 1854-1867*, M.A. thesis, Queen's University, 1967, 129-30.
34. *Cartwright Papers*, P.A.O., T.S. Carman, *The Weekly Express*, to Cartwright, March 19, 1872; see also Carman to Cartwright, March 25, 1872.
35. *Cartwright Papers*, A.M. Morden, Mayor's Office, Napanee, to Cartwright, July 25, 1872.
36. Paul G. Cornell, *The Alignment of Political Groups in Canada, 1841-1867* (Toronto, 1962), 11, 110 notes s, 111.
37. Morgan, 165; Graham, abstract.
38. Donald Swainson, "Richard Cartwright Joins the Liberal Party," *Queen's Quarterly*, No. 75 (1968), 124-34.
39. Skelton, 213.
40. R.O. MacFarlane, "The Appointment of Sir Francis Hincks as Minister of Finance in 1869," *Canadian Historical Review*, XX (1939), 288; see also W.R. Graham, 29, 47; Sister Teresa Avila Burke, *Canadian Cabinets in the Making: A Study in the Problems of a Pluralistic Society, 1867-1896*, Ph.D. thesis, Columbia University, 1958, 66; Wallace, 120; and Ronald Stewart Longley, Sir Francis Hincks, *Railways, and Finance in the Nineteenth Century* (Toronto, 1943), 357-360, 370.
41. An abundance of material in the *Macdonald Papers*, P.A.C., 204 illustrates Cartwright's place in the party and his relationship with Macdonald. Some of these letters are copies; Cartwright to Macdonald, August 24, 1861, September 6, 1864, September 21, 1864, February 9, 1865, May 8, 1866, October 11, 1866, January 4, 1867, April 20, 1867, December 14, 1867, September 24, 1868, November 14, 1868, January 11, 1869; and Macdonald to Cartwright August 22, 1865, October 12, 1866, June 24, 1868, September 26 (or 28), 1868, December 11, 1868, January 6, 1869. For additional evidence, see *Cartwright Papers*, P.A.O., Macdonald to Cartwright, March 27, 1866 and September 26, 1868; and McDougall to Cartwright, May 29, 1866. See also Eadie, Chapters 7-8, passim.
42. *Macdonald Papers*, P.A.C., 204, Cartwright to Macdonald, September 23, 1869.
43. *Macdonald Papers*, 204, Cartwright to Macdonald, October 12, 1869.
44. *Macdonald Papers*, 204, Cartwright to Macdonald, November 23, 1869.
45. Joseph Pope, *Sir John A. Macdonald Vindicated* (Toronto, 1912), 17-18.
46. *Cartwright Papers*, P.A.O., Galt to Cartwright, October 29, 1869 and Bowell to Cartwright, October 9, 1869.
47. *Cartwright Papers*, Galt to Cartwright, November 1, 1869 and Cartwright to Galt, November 6, 1869, draft of letter.
48. Joseph Pope, *Memoirs of the Right Honourable Sir John Alexander Macdonald*

(London, 1894) 11, 70.

49. *Cartwright Papers*, P.A.O., Cartwright to Galt, November 6, 1869, draft of letter.

50. *Cartwright Papers*, Cockburn to Cartwright, December 7, 1869.

51. *Cartwright Papers*, Cartwright to Galt, October 29, 1869, copy.

52. Cartwright, 70.

53. *Cartwright Papers*, P.A.O., Macpherson to Cartwright, December 12, 1870.

54. *Canadian Parliamentary Companion*, 1873, 286.

55. Cited in *Mail* clipping, 1876, on Cartwright as a Reformer, in *Macdonald Papers*, P.A.C., 204. See also Toronto *Globe*, August 19, 1872, which lists him under "opposition."

56. Cartwright, 102-03.

57. C.L.A. *Debates, March 14, 1873*.

58. *Canadian Parliamentary Companion*, 1875, 187.

59. *Cartwright Papers*, P.A.O., Cartwright to Mackenzie, February 4, 1873.

60. *Cartwright Papers*, Mackenzie to Cartwright, February 21, 1873.

61. *Cartwright Papers*, Blake to Cartwright, October 11, 1873.

62. *Brown Papers*, P.A.C., 9, Mackenzie to Brown, November 13, 1873.

63. Graham, 61-67. For the bitter and personal nature of the campaign, see *Cartwright Papers*, P.A.O., Galt to Cartwright, November 27, 1873; Cartwright, 135-36; Pope, *Sir John A. Macdonald Vindicated*, 5-9; and, Lorne A. Brown, "The Macdonald-Cartwright Struggle in Lennox, November, 1873," *Ontario History*, LXI (1969), 33-50.

64. R.O. MacFarlane, "The Appointment of Sir Francis Hincks as Minister of Finance in 1869," *Canadian Historical Review*, XX (1939), 288.

65. See evidence referred to in citation 59 above.

Richard Cartwright Joins the Liberal Party

1. Oscar Douglas *Skelton, Life and Times of Sir Alexander Tilloch Galt*, Carleton Library Edition (Toronto, 1966), 213; R.O. MacFarlane, "The Appointment of Sir Francis Hincks as Minister of Finance in 1869," *Canadian Historical Review*, Vol. 20 (1939), 228; W.R. Graham, Sir Richard Cartwright and the Liberal Party, Ph.D. thesis, University of Toronto, 1950, 47, and 29: "There appears to be no important reason why Cartwright could not have remained a Conservative to the end of his days had it not been for his personal quarrel with Macdonald in 1869." For similar views, see Sister Teresa Avila Burke, *Canadian Cabinets in the Making: A Study in the Problems of a Pluralistic Society: 1867-1896*, Ph.D. thesis, Columbia University, 1958, 66; W.S. Wallace, *The Macmillan Dictionary of Canadian Biography*, 3rd ed. (Toronto, 1963), 120; Ronald Stewart Longley, *Sir Francis Hincks: A Study of Canadian Politics, Railways, and Finance in the Nineteenth Century* (Toronto, 1943), 357-60, 370.

2. *Macdonald Papers*, Public Archives of Canada, vol. 204, passim; *Cartwright Papers*, Public Archives of Ontario, Macdonald to Cartwright, March 27, 1866 and September 26, 1868, William McDougall to Cartwright, May 29, 1866.

3. *Macdonald Papers*, P.A.C., vol. 204, Cartwright to Macdonald, September 23, 1869.

4. Unless otherwise indicated, quotations are from the *Macdonald Papers*,

P.A.C. or the *Cartwright Papers*, P.A.O., two very rich collections of source material. Cartwright kept copies of many letters to political colleagues.

5. Sir Joseph Pope, *Sir John A. Macdonald Vindicated* (Toronto, 1912), 17-18.
6. *Cartwright Papers*, P.A.O., Galt to Cartwright, October 29, 1869, and Bowell to Cartwright, October 9, 1869.
7. Sir Joseph Pope, *Memoirs of the Right Honourable Sir John Alexander Macdonald* (London, 1894), II, 70.
8. *Macdonald Papers*, P.A.C., 204, *Mail* clipping, 1876, on Cartwright as a Liberal; and based on an analysis of voting in the second Parliament.
9. *Campbell Papers*, P.A.O., John Hamilton to Alexander Campbell, August 2, 1872.
10. *Cartwright Papers*, P.A.O., E.W. Rathbun to Cartwright, December 5, 1872. Having the enclosed material would be most useful. It seems that only part is extant and it is not comprehensible.
11. *Macdonald Papers*, P.A.C., vol. 194, Campbell to Macdonald, n.d., but almost certainly July, 1872; *Campbell Papers*, P.A.O., Rathbun to Campbell, March 21, 1872, July 19, 1872, May 8, 1872, July 15, 1872, July 11, 1872, Robert Jellett to John A. Macdonald, July 18, 1872, and Bowell to Campbell, August 6, 1872.
12. Cited in *Macdonald Papers*, P.A.C., vol. 204, *Mail* clipping, 1876.
13. Sir Richard Cartwright, *Reminiscences* (Toronto, 1912), 102-3.
14. *Canadian Parliamentary Companion*, 1875, 187.
15. In addition to *Cartwright Papers*, P.A.O., see *Blake Papers*, P.A.O., II, 4., Cartwright to Blake, July 19, 1873, July 22, 1873.
16. Donald Creighton, *John A. Macdonald: The Old Chieftain* (Toronto, 1955), 167.
17. *Brown Papers*, P.A.C., vol. 9, Mackenzie to Brown, November 13, 1873.
18. *Brown Papers*, vol. 9, Mackenzie to Brown, November 12, 1873.
20. Graham, 61-7; for bitter and personal nature of the campaign see *Cartwright Papers*, P.A.O., Galt to Cartwright, November 27, 1873; Cartwright, *Reminiscences*, 135-6; Pope, *Sir John A. Macdonald Vindicated*, 5-9.

George Airey Kirkpatrick: Political Patrician
1. Inscription on fountain in front of the County Courthouse, Kingston:

KIRKPATRICK
Sir george airey Kirkpatrick, k.c.m.g.
Member for Frontenac
Speaker house of commons
Lieutenant-governor of Ontario
1841-1899

2. Kingston *Daily News*, August 29, 1872.
3. *House of Commons Debates*, 1891, II, 4190 (August 20, 1891).
4. Henry James Morgan, *The Canadian Men and Women of the Time*, 1st ed. (Toronto, 1898), 543; *Canadian Parliamentary Companion*, 1873, 196; Geo. Maclean Rose, ed., *A Cyclopaedia of Canadian Biography being Chiefly Men of the Time*, 1st ed. (Toronto, 1886), 127.
5. Rose, 127.

6. *Canadian Biographical Dictionary and Portrait Gallery of Eminent and Self-Made Men*, Ontario Volume (Toronto, Chicago and New York, 1880), 662.
7. Nicholas Flood Davin, *The Irishman in Canada* (London and Toronto, 1877), 593.
8. Edwin E. Horsey, *Kingston A Century Ago* (Kingston, 1938), 18; James A. Roy, *Kingston: The King's Town* (Toronto, 1952), 183-84.
9. Roy, 239.
10. Toronto *Globe*, December 14, 1899.
11. *Macdonald Papers*, P.A.C., 224, Kirkpatrick to Macdonald, May 24, 1873.
12. *Canadian Parliamentary Companion*, 1879, 182; W. Stewart Wallace, *The Macmillan Dictionary of Canadian Biography*, 3rd ed. (Toronto, 1963), 372, 428.
13. Morgan, 543; Wallace, 372, 486.
14. W.R. Graham, *Sir Richard Cartwright and the Liberal Party, 1863-1896*, Ph.D. thesis, University of Toronto, 1950, 251-55.
15. *Canadian Parliamentary Companion*, 1873, 196; Rose, 128.
16. *Canadian Parliamentary Companion*, 1873, 196; Morgan, 542-43.
17. Wallace, 62.
18. Graham, 11.
19. *Canadian Parliamentary Companion*, 1873, 196 and 1891, 142; D.B. Read, *The Lieutenant-Governors of Upper Canada and Ontario 1792-1899* (Toronto, 1900), 237; Morgan, 543; G. Mercer Adam, *Prominent Men of Canada* (Toronto, 1892), 155.
20. Read, 237.
21. Roy, 280; *Encyclopaedia Canadiana*, V (1958), 417-18.
22. *Encyclopaedia Canadiana*, V (1958), 417-18.
23. *Macdonald Papers*, P.A.C., 204, *Telegram*, January 23, 1871, R.J. Cartwright, Richd. Walkem, J. O'Reilly, C.F. Gildersleeve, G.A. Kirkpatrick, J. Bowden to Macdonald.
24. Morgan, 378-79.
25. *Campbell Papers*, P.A.O., Kirkpatrick to Campbell, February 14, 1872.
26. Adam, 156.
27. *House of Commons Debates*, 1889, I, 300 (February 25, 1889).
28. R.A. Preston, *Canada's RMC* (Toronto, 1969), passim.
29. Preston, 79, 183 note.
30. Read, 236.
31. *Campbell Papers*, P.A.O., James A. Shannon (Office of The *Daily News* and Chronicle) to Campbell, May 30, 1872.
32. Cited in P.B. Waite, "The Political Ideas of John A. Macdonald," in Marcel Hamelin, ed., *The Political Ideas of the Prime Ministers of Canada* (Ottawa, 1969), 58. See also W.F. Dawson, *Procedure in the Canadian House of Commons* (Toronto, 1962), 69.
33. John Willison, *Sir Wilfrid Laurier and the Liberal Party* (London and Toronto, 1926), II, 222; Sister Teresa Avila Burke, *Canadian Cabinets in the Making: A Study in the Problems of a Pluralistic Society: 1867-1896*, Ph.D. thesis, Columbia University, 1958, 285 [Sister Burke's source is Oscar Douglas Skelton, *Life and Letters of Sir Wilfrid Laurier* (Toronto, 1921), I, 481.]
34. *House of Commons Debates*, 1891, I, 1071-73 (June 19, 1891).
35. *House of Commons Debates*, 1880-81, I, 534 (January 19, 1881).

36. *House of Commons Debates*, 1883, 1449 (May 11, 1882).
37. *House of Commons Debates*, 1875, 592 (March 9, 1875).
38. *House of Commons Debates*, 1876, 639 March 14, 1876).
39. *House of Commons Debates*, 1879, I, 383-84 (March 13, 1879).
40. *House of Commons Debates*, 1882, 1449 (May 11, 1882).
41. *House of Commons Debates*, 1882, 1449 (May 11, 1882).
42. *House of Commons Debates*, 1890, I, 2051 (March 17, 1890).
43. *House of Commons Debates*, 1880-81, I, 534 (January 19, 1881).
44. *House of Commons Debates*, 1880-81, II, 1127-29 (February 24, 1881).
45. *Macdonald Papers*, P.A.C., 224, Kirkpatrick to Macdonald, May 24, 1873.
46. *Cartwright Papers*, P.A.O., Cartwright to Mackenzie, August 23, 1873, draft of letter.
47. *Cartwright Papers*, Cartwright to Blake, August 18, 1873, draft of letter.
48. *Cartwright Papers*, Blake to Cartwright, August 19, 1873.
49. *Cartwright Papers*, Cartwright to Mackenzie, August 23, 1873, draft of letter.
50. *Cartwright Papers*, Mackenzie to Cartwright, September 4, 1873.
51. *Cartwright Papers*, Cartwright to Mackenzie, September 8, 1873, draft of letter.
52. *Jones Papers*, reprinted in *Report of the Board of Trustees of the Public Archives of Nova Scotia*, 1952, Mackenzie to Jones, October 6, 1873.
53. *Cartwright Papers*, P.A.O., Cartwright to Mackenzie, September 8, 1873.
54. *Cartwright Papers*, Cartwright to Blake, October 10, 1873.
55. *Cartwright Papers*, Blake to Cartwright, August 19, 1873.
56. *Cartwright Papers*, Blake to Cartwright, October 11, 1873.
57. Preston, 129, 112. See also pp. 79 and 91.
58. Preston, 92. For another example of Kirkpatrick's patronage activities, see J.K. Johnson, ed., *Affectionately Yours: The Letters of Sir John A. Macdonald and his Family* (Toronto, 1969), Number 162.
59. Preston, 129.
60. *House of Commons Debates*, 1890, I, 1047 (February 24, 1890).
61. John Porter, *The Vertical Mosaic* (Toronto, 1965), 391.

Delano Dexter Calvin: Garden Island Patriarch

1. Cited D.D. Calvin, *A Saga of the St. Lawrence: Timber and Shipping Through Three Generations* (Toronto, 1945), 145; hereafter cited as Saga.
2. See for example Saga; Marion Calvin Boyd, *The Story of Garden Island*, ed. By Margaret A. Boyd (Kingston, 1973); T.R. Glover and D.D. Calvin, *A Corner of Empire; The Old Ontario Strand* (Cambridge, 1937); D.D. Calvin, "Rafting on the St. Lawrence," in W.J. Megill, ed., *Patterns of Canada* (Toronto, 1967). [Reprinted from *Canadian Geographical Journal*, October, 1931.]; D.D. Calvin, "A Lake-Built Ocean Vessel," *Queen's Quarterly*, XL (1933); D.D. Calvin, "The Sail Loft," *Queen's Quarterly*, XLIX (1942); J.D. Calvin, "Operation Garden Island," *Historic Kingston*, 12 (1964); A.A. Calvin, *Timber Trading in Canada, 1812-1849*; special emphasis on Forwarding, B.A. Honours thesis, Queen's University, 1930.
3. Beverley Doherty, *Real Wage Changes as Revealed in the Manuscripts of the Shipyard of the Calvin Company, Selected Years: 1848-1884*, B.A. Honours thesis, Queen's University, 1973; Chris Norman, "Garden Island: A Social

Study at Mid-Century, An Introductory Survey of an Early Company Community," unpublished paper, Department of History, Queen's University, 1977; Sarah Edinborough, "Garden Island: A Unique Community Seen Through its Social Institutions," unpublished paper, Department of History, Queen's University, 1978.

4. The first map shows Garden Island in context. It was prepared by Mr. Ross Hough, Cartographic Laboratory, Department of Geography, Queen's University. Mr. Hough also prepared the two additional maps that appear with this paper.

5. Mary Quayle Innis, ed., *Mrs. Simcoe's Diary* (Toronto, 1965), 73.

6. Kingston *Chronicle*, July 14, 1826.

7. Kingston *Chronicle and Gazette*, September 20, 1834.

8. Kingston *British Whig*, September 8, 1835.

9. Kingston *Chronicle and Gazette*, June 3, 1835 and twice weekly to October 17, 1835.

10. For early family history, see my article on D.D. Calvin in *Dictionary of Canadian Biography*, XI.

11. See *Calvin Papers*, Q.U.A., Mayflower ancestry of Sandford Jenks Calvin and his Descendents, 1949; Calvin, Saga, 9.

12. *Saga*, 9.

13. For this early aspect of his career, see *Calvin Family Scrapbooks* [in possession of Meg and John d'Esterre, Kingston], Blue, undated and unidentified clipping. It was, however, written within a couple of days of Calvin's death. This information is confirmed in Saga, 9.

14. A.R.M. Lower, *Settlement and the Forest Frontier in Eastern Canada* (Toronto, 1936), 44-45.

15. *Calvin Family Scrapbooks*, Blue, undated and unidentified clipping reporting on Elder Meeks' oration at Calvin's funeral at Clayton.

16. Calvin's gravemarker; *Calvin Family Scrapbooks*, Blue, undated and unidentified clipping.

17. For details of D.D. Calvin's marriages and children, see *Calvin Papers*, Q.U.A., some notes including "extract from a letter from Claude Calvin to Jonathan Calvin." See also *Canadian Parliamentary Companion*, 1874, 326.

18. *Calvin Papers*, Q.U.A., Box 8, Breck to Storey, June 25, 1868.

19. *Saga*, 20; for tariff system, see Orville John McDiarmid, *Commercial Policy in the Canadian Economy* (Harvard, 1946). The map of Garden Island in the later nineteenth century is based on the map of the island in *Illustrated Historical Atlas of the Counties of Frontenac, Lennox and Addington, Ontario* (Toronto, 1878).

20. Brian S. Osborne, "Kingston in the Nineteenth Century: A Study in Urban Decline," in J. David Wood, ed., *Perspectives on Landscape and Settlement in Nineteenth- Century Ontario* (Toronto, 1975); for a discussion of the timber raft see Calvin, *Saga*, 25.

21. Doherty, 21.

22. *Saga*, 16. The date is given as 1835 in an extended and extremely useful obituary in *Calvin Family Scrapbooks*, Blue, undated and unidentified clipping that was published within a couple of days of Calvin's death.

23. *Saga*, 16, 17, 19; for a summary of Calvin's partnerships see Anthony

Malone, *Reminiscences* (in *Calvin Papers*, Q.U.A.; this manuscript is unpaginated.).

24. For excellent descriptions of raft making and St. Lawrence rafting, see *Saga* 63ff; and George S. Thompson, *Up to Date, or the Life of a Lumberman* (Peterborough, 1895), 57-63.

25. *Saga*, 160.

26. Cited in *Dictionary of Canadianisms*, 865.

27. *Saga*, 160.

28. See for example, Adam Shortt, "Down the St. Lawrence on a Timber Raft," *Queen's Quarterly*, X (1902).

29. *Calvin Papers*, Q.U.A., Box 6, Britton to Calvin Co., December 18, 1843; for a typical list of owners of timber so delivered see Box 76: "Specifications of Stave Cribs in Raft No. 14 left Garden Island, 6th Sept. 1866."

30. Doherty, 18; for a good general description of this business activity, see W.T. Easterbrook and Hugh G.J. Aitken, *Canadian Economic History* (Toronto, 1961), 197-98.

31. The Input-Output map illustrates the Calvin Company's collecting area, and shows where the timber went after it left Garden Island.

32. For an introduction to the details of the operations of this vast enterprise, see *Saga*, 17, 25-28; Doherty, 16-17; [Rose Mary Gibson], *Preliminary Inventory, The Calvin Company Papers*, Q.U.A.; *Calvin Family Scrapbooks*, Blue, undated and unidentified clipping.

33. Doherty, 27; *Calvin Family Scrapbooks*, Blue, letter of Capt. Joseph Dix to editor of unidentified newspaper, September 1, 1914; Malone, *Reminiscences*.

34. See *Saga*, 18, 22-23, 127; memorandum regarding the Government tug line on the St. Lawrence, in the possession of Meg and John d'Esterre.

35. For assets and wage rates see *Saga*, 28 and Doherty, 46-49, 85; for towing and wrecking investment see *Macdonald Papers*, P.A.C. Calvin and Son to Macdonald, December 25, 1880.

36. *Calvin Family Scrapbooks*, Blue, undated and unidentified clipping; *Canadian Parliamentary Companion*, 1874, 326; Walter Lewis, "The Promotion of the Kingston & Pembroke Railway, 1870-72," unpublished paper, Department of History, Queen's University, 1979.

37. Evidence before a select committee of the Assembly; cited in *Saga*, 98; Michael Sean Cross, *The Dark Druidical Groves: The Lumber Community and the Commercial Frontier in British North America to 1854*, Ph.D. thesis, university of Toronto, 1968, 205.

38. *Calvin Legal Papers*, Q.U.A., Box 6, "Inventory and Valuation in the Surrogate Court of the County of Frontenac in the Goods of Dileno Dexter Calvin."

39. For ownership of Garden Island, see Malone, *Reminiscences*.

40. *Saga*, 12, 19 and passim; Doherty, 52.

41. *Kingston City Directory*, 1885-86, C-68 to C-69; *Calvin Family Scrapbooks*, Blue, letter of Capt. Joseph Dix to editor of unidentified newspaper, September 1, 1914.

42. Doherty, 19.

43. These bills are in the possession of Meg and John d'Esterre, Kingston.

44. Susan Edinborough, *Catalogue of Books Contained in the Library of the Garden Island Mechanics' Institute* (Kingston, 1883).

45. Edinborough.

46. *By-Laws of Elysian Lodge, No. 212, A.F.A.M., Garden Island Ontario* (Hamilton, 1872); Boyd, 27; Edinborough,.

47. Charles Addington, "Garden Island – The Postal Connection," unpublished paper, 1976.

48. Malone, *Reminiscences*; *Saga*, 79.

49. See for example, *Calvin Papers*, Q.U.A., Box 6, passim; Glover and Calvin.

50. Michael Sean Cross, "The Lumber Community of Upper Canada, 1815-1867," *Ontario History*, 1960, 213, 233.

51. Doherty, 80; Norman, Edinborough.

52. Given the fact that Garden Island was a functioning society led by a religious man dedicated to the welfare and unity of his community, it is logical to ask why there was no church on the island. Sarah Edinborough explains this apparent anomaly: "Faced with a company town which comprised French and English, Catholic and Protestant alike, Calvin obviously saw no point in building a church for one faith when it would do little but antagonize the others. The compromise which Garden Island learned to live with was very open minded for the nineteenth century. It appears that Calvin considered a church necessary for installing Christian values into the community; at the same time he was not didactic about the faith which had to profess those values. Again we see the image of a man who was primarily concerned with the development of a community. Unlike the Wrights of Hull who helped to build an Anglican church for the sake of status for the community, Calvin's religious commitment led him to attempt to instill sound values through a variety of different faiths."

53. Doherty, 20.

54. *Calvin Family Scrapbooks*, Brown, undated and unidentified clipping – clearly written in 1881.

55. Malone, *Reminiscences*; *Saga*, 57.

56. *Calvin Family Scrapbooks*, Brown, undated and unidentified clipping – clearly written in 1881.

57. For the incident concerning the Seamen's Union, see a series of undated and unidentified clippings in *Calvin Family Scrapbooks*, Blue and Brown. See also Ottawa *Daily Citizen*, May 19, 1881. I am indebted to Dr. Bryan Palmer and Mr. Walter Lewis for drawing my attention to some specific newspaper articles concerning the Seamen's Union and the Calvin Company. This assistance enabled me to date the material in the Scrapbooks. For some general comment on nineteenth-century seamen as labourers, see Judith Fingard, "The Decline of the Sailor as a Ship Labourer in 19th Century Timber Ports," *Labour/Le Travailleur*, 2 (1977).

58. It must be noted that some social historians will disagree with the very concept that a nineteenth- century business leader was in any real way "benevolent" or "paternalistic." Professor Michael Bliss, in his generally pro-business *A Living Profit: Studies in the Social History of Canadian Business, 1883-1911* (Toronto, 1974), deals with the concept of paternalism in a fair and responsible manner. Bliss is concerned with the motivation of paternalistic businessmen. Why were such men paternalistic or benevolent if the overriding motivation of a capitalist is to maximize profit? "It was ... often realized," says Bliss, "that high wages and good working conditions produced

contented workers." (69) "It was commonly argued that welfare work would be both humanitarian and profitable because happy workers produced more." (71) Bliss notes that there "were also, of course, the anti-union implications of some forms of paternalism …" (71) These points are *all* valid, but we have no pressing reason to conclude that all nineteenth-century businessmen were greedy capitalistic theorists who sought to maximize profits and suppress the omnipresent class struggle. The average businessman was no doubt much like most citizens. He grew up within a system that was not of his design; he functioned within that system and more or less followed the conventions and practices of society. It is highly unlikely that he ever thought about economic or social organization in any systematic or theoretical way: if D.D. Calvin did, no evidence has survived. Nineteenth-century Ontario's business sector produced crooks, reformers, schemers, innovators, men of great competence and men of genuine compassion. It is surely unreasonable to assume that union leaders and reformers were motivated by ideals, while capitalists were grasping men who thought only of profit. The evidence indicated that D.D. Calvin was a benevolent and paternalistic man. Why not accept him for what he was? It is noted that he broke a maritime union; maybe he was right. Even a cursory glance at the history of maritime unions on the great lakes indicates that the workers were far better off with capitalists like D.D. Calvin than they ever were with powerful labour leaders like Hal Banks.

59. *Calvin Family Scrapbooks*, Blue, undated and unidentified clipping.
60. Malone, *Reminiscences.*
61. For early municipal and other local activities, see *Calvin Family Scrapbooks*, Blue, undated and unidentified clipping; Malone, *Reminiscences, Kingston City Directory*, 1865, 219; R.M. Spankie, "Wolfe Island, Past and Present," *Proceedings of the New York State Historical Association, XIII* (1914), 231.
62. Glover and Calvin, 96-7.
63. Malone, *Reminiscences; Canadian Parliamentary Companion*, 1872, 312 and 1874, 326.
64. *Calvin Family Scrapbooks*, Blue, undated and unidentified clipping; George Fletcher Henderson, *Federal Royal Commissions in Canada 1867-1966: A Checklist* (Toronto, 1967), 4-5.
65. *Macdonald Papers*, P.A.C., Cartwright to Macdonald, September 24, 1868; *Cartwright Papers*, P.A.O., Macdonald to Cartwright, September 26, 1868.
66. Donald Swainson, "Richard Cartwright Joins the Liberal party," *Queen's Quarterly*, LXXV (1968).
67. Roderick Lewis, *Centennial Edition of a History of the Electoral Districts, Legislatures and Ministries of the Province of Ontario, 1867-1968* (Toronto, n.d.), 90; Calvin Company: Odds and Ends, Q.U.A., Kirkpatrick to Calvin, 1875.
68. See *Macdonald Papers*, P.A.C., Calvin to Macdonald, November 29, 1880, December 8, 1880, September 21, 1881.
69. *Legislative Debates*, Ontario, microfilm, January 23, 1873.
70. *Calvin Family Scrapbooks*, Brown, undated and unidentified clipping. For his views on agriculture see also other similar clippings in the same volume. Toronto *Globe*, November 5, 1868.
71. H.V. Nelles, *The Politics of Development: Forests, Mines and Hydro-Electric Power in Ontario, 1849-1941* (Toronto, 1974), 195; see also Thompson, 11, 45.

72. Cited in C.F. Coons, *The John R. Booth Story*, 16 [originally published as an article in Your Forests, Vol. II, No. 2 (Summer, 1978)].

73. Toronto *Leader*, November 5, 1868; *Legislative Debates*, Ontario, microfilm, February 25, 1873, February 25, 1874, February 25, 1880. Why he regularly spoke on the subject on February 25 is unknown.

74. Charles Clarke, *Sixty Years in Upper Canada* (Toronto, 1908), 147.

75. *Calvin Family Scrapbooks*, Blue, undated and unidentified clipping; Calvin's gravemarker.

76. Anna G. Young, *Great Lakes' Saga: The Influence of One Family on the Development of Canadian Shipping on the Great Lakes, 1816-1931* (Owen Sound, Toronto, Montreal, 1965), 66.

77. Calvin's funeral is described in *Calvin Family Scrapbooks*, Blue and Brown.

78. Thompson, 58.

James Richardson: Founder of Firms

1. The circumstances involved in the research for this paper were somewhat unusual, and the result has been the accumulation of several major debts. First, the paper grew out of *Kingston: Building on the Past*, which I researched and wrote jointly with Brian S. Osborne. Later, we jointly wrote an article on James Richardson for the *Dictionary of Canadian Biography*, Volume XII. So, while I have completed considerable Richardson research since the DCB article was completed, it is obvious that I am heavily in debt to Brian Osborne. I, of course, am responsible for the views contained in the paper. Second, I was fortunate in obtaining the research assistance of Laurie Stanley-Blackwell, who combed a number of local collections and provided material assistance. Third, two historians of Kingston assisted. Peg Angus gave a copy of her family file on the Richardsons. Neil Patterson let me see some of his valuable material on the nineteenth-century mining activity to the north of Kingston. Fourth, James Richardson and Sons, Ltd. gave me generous access to the company's private archives in Winnipeg. Fifth, because this research was expensive, financial assistance was required. That assistance was generously provided by the Faculty of Arts and Science, Queen's University and by the Principal of Queen's.

2. Ian Brown, "Richardson: Shy, Shrewd Gentry of Grain," *The Financial Post*, December 4, 1976.

3. Brown.

4. Toronto *Globe and Mail*, November 30, 1988.

5. Toronto *Globe and Mail*, November 30, 1988.

6. Kingston *Daily British Whig*, November 16, 1892; James Richardson and Sons Limited, Manuscript, Richardson Company Archives, 1 – hereafter cited as Manuscript. For concise overviews of Richardson's life, see Brian S. Osborne and Donald Swainson, "James Richardson," *Dictionary of Canadian Biography*, Volume XII. For his Kingston context, see, by the same authors, *Kingston: Building on the Past* (Westport, 1988).

7. See *The Parliamentary Gazetteer of Ireland' 1844-45*, Volume I, A-C (Dublin, London and Edinburgh, 1846).

8. Cataraqui Cemetery, Kingston, *Tombstone Inscription* for James Richardson et al.

9. *Register of Burials, Cataraqui Cemetery*, Volume I, Kingston Public Library,

microfilm.
10. *Manuscript*, 4.
11. Kingston *Daily British Whig*, November 16, 1892.
12. *Family Files* of Margaret Angus.
13. Toronto *Globe*, November 25, 1845.
14. Kingston *Argus*, May 15, 1846, cited in *Manuscript*, 5.
15. *Family Files* of Margaret Angus.
16. When Richardson's will was probated, the surrogate court referred to this son as George Algernon Richardson. See Will of James Richardson, Kingston Registry Office, GR 1128.
17. Kingston *Daily British Whig*, November 16, 1892; Manuscript, 1.
18. Kingston *Daily British Whig*, November 16, 1892.
19. Kingston *Daily British Whig*, November 16, 1892.
20. [Patrick Burrage], *125 Years of Progress* (Winnipeg, James Richardson and Sons, Ltd., 1982). This pamphlet is unpaginated and will hereafter be referred to as *125 Years of Progress*.
21. Manuscript, 4.
22. Kingston *Chronicle and Gazette*, November 21, 1841.
23. Kingston *Chronicle and Gazette*, September 16, 1844.
24. Kingston *Argus*, November 3, 1846, cited in *Manuscript* (1955), 5.
25. Kingston *Argus*, November 3, 1846, cited in *Manuscript* (1955), 5.
26. Kingston *Argus*, November 3, 1846, cited in *Manuscript* (1955), 5-7.
27. For a comprehensive overview of the construction of the Custom House, see John H. Aylen, *Custom House Kingston 1800-1859*, typescript, August 1972, QUA, Coll. 2285.
28. *Kingston Custom House*, typescript memorandum, 1972, QUA, COII.
29. *Kingston Custom House*, typescript memorandum, 1972, QUA, COII.
30. See Donald Swainson, "James O'Reilly and Catholic Politics," *Historic Kingston*, 75 (1973).
31. *Kingston Custom House*.
32. Kingston *Daily British Whig*, November 16, 1892.
33. Reprinted in Brown.
34. *Buildings of Architectural and Historical Significance*, Volume I (Kingston, 1971), 25.
35. Richardson left Eliza $1,000 in his will.
36. *Manuscript*, 8.
37. *125 Years of Progress*.
38. The directories cited are *Kingston City Directories*, 1855, 1857, 1858, 1862, 1863, 1865, 1873, 1874, 1875, 1881.
39. *Kingston Custom House*.
40. Kingston *Daily British Whig*, December 1, 1897.
41. Kingston *Daily British Whig*, March 7, 1864.
42. For the barley broom and trade, see Robert Leslie Jones, *History of Agriculture in Ontario 1613-1880* (Toronto, 1946); and Richard and Janet Lunn, *The County: The First Hundred Years in Loyalist Prince Edward* (Picton, 1967).
43. Edwin Ernest Horsey, *Cataraqui-Fort Frontenac-Kingston*, typescript, 1937, QUA, 300.
44. Kingston *Daily British Whig*, April 10, 1869.
45. *125 Years of Progress*; Horsey, 300.

46. Kingston *Daily British Whig*, December 1, 1897.

47. *Manuscript*, 17.

48. Kingston *Daily British Whig*, December 1, 1897.

49. For related developments see R.A. Preston, "The History of the Port of Kingston," *Historic Kingston* (1954).

50. Kingston *Daily British Whig*, September 22, 1904.

51. Kingston *Daily British Whig*, September 22, 1904.

52. Kingston *Daily British Whig*, September 22, 1904.

53. *Manuscript*, 38.

54. James A. Richardson to A.R. Bingham, 1923, reprinted in *Manuscript*, 20.

55. Kingston *Daily British Whig*, November 16, 1892; *Manuscript*, 10, 16, 25.

56. Much of the diversification data is from Kingston *Daily British Whig*, November 16, 1892; *Manuscript*, 16-34; Brown; *Mining Records*, Private Papers of Neil Patterson, Kingston.

57. E.S. Moore, *The Mineral Resources of Canada* (Toronto, 1933), cited in M.E. Miller, *Report on Small Scale Mining*, Ontario Ministry of Natural Resources (1972) Typescript, p.79.

58. *Ontario Bureau of Mines Report* (hereafter cited as *OBMR*), 1905; W.D. Harding, "1947: Geology of the Olden-Bedford Area," Ontario Department of Mines, Volume LVI (1951), 6.

59. *OBMR*, 1907.

60. H.S. de Schmid, "Feldspar in Canada," Department of Mines, Ottawa, 1916.

61. Moore, 248-251; Neil Patterson, "Feldspar Mining: Once a Major Industry in Kingston Area", Kingston *Whig-Standard*, November 14, 1981.

62. *Report of the Royal Commission on the Mineral Resources of Ontario and Measures for their Development* (Toronto, 1890).

63. D.F. Hewitt, "Pegmatite Mineral Resources of Ontario," Ontario Department of Mines, Industrial Report No. 21 (Toronto, 1967).

64. *OBMR*, 1902.

65. *OBMR*, 1913.

66. *OBMR*, 1914.

67. *Registry Records*, Lanark County.

68. *Canadian Department of Mines Report*, 1916.

69. *OBMR*, 1903, 1915, 1916.

70. Brown.

71. See Will.

72. *Minute book of Board of Trade*, 1851-1904, Kingston, QUA.

73-80. *Minute book of Board of Trade*, 1851-1904, Kingston, QUA.

81. *Proceedings of City Council*, City of Kingston Papers, QUA.

82-85. *Proceedings of City Council*, City of Kingston Papers, QUA.

86. To the intense disappointment of Kingstonians, the Prince refused to land at Kingston and no visit took place. See Osborne and Swainson, *Kingston*, 135-136.

87. *Proceedings of City Council*.

88. *Proceedings of City Council*.

89. *Macdonald Papers*, QUA (MF 1246), James Richardson and Sons to George Taylor, 5 August 1889. Given Macdonald's obviously warm view, it is a mystery why the Richardsons did not write directly to the Prime Minister.

90. *Macdonald Papers*. (MF 1247), George Richardson to George Taylor, 19 October 1889.
91. *Macdonald Papers*. (MF 1240), James Richardson to Macdonald, 18 May 1888.
92. Macdonald Paper. (MF 1252), James Richardson and Sons to Macdonald, 15 December 1890.
93. *Macdonald Papers*. (MF 1228), E.H. Smythe to Macdonald, 1 November 1886.